MICHAELLA McCOLLUM

YOU'LL NEVER SEE DAYLIGHT AGAIN

MY PRISON JOURNEY AS ONE OF THE INFAMOUS PERU TWO

JOHN BLAKE

Published by John Blake Publishing,
The Plaza,
535 Kings Road,
Chelsea Harbour,
London SW10 0SZ

www.facebook.com/johnblakebooks
twitter.com/jblakebooks

First published in Trade Paperback in 2019

Trade Paperback ISBN: 978 1 78606 880 4
eBook ISBN: 978 1 78946 014 8

British Library Cataloguing-in-Publication Data:

A catalogue record for this book is available from the British Library.

Design by www.envydesign.co.uk

Printed and bound in Great Britain by Clays Ltd, Elcograf S.p.A.

3 5 7 9 10 8 6 4 2

John Blake Publishing is an imprint of Bonnier Books UK
www.bonnierbooks.co.uk

For my mother

CONTENTS

THE WOLF OF WALL STREET

'**M**ichaella, look out!'

The voice belongs to Lyra. A Spanish girl. A friend. I turn just in time to see the blade. It's a kitchen knife, unmistakably sharp, unmistakably gleaming. And unmistakably aimed at my head.

I freeze. In a film everything would slow down and I'd see my life flash before my eyes. There would be a powerful soundtrack and the whole thing would take minutes. But this isn't the movies. This is real life. My life. And I don't have minutes. I know for sure that in two seconds I'll be dead.

I feel myself twist, and raise my arm, as if that's going to stop the piercing steel from reaching my heart. I close my eyes. It's stupid, it's the wrong move, but it's instinct. I'm terrified. What else can I do? There's a scream – blood-curdling – but it's not mine. I open my eyes just in time to see Lyra flying in front of me, rugby-tackling my assailant to the floor. I know my attacker all too well – it's Danielle, a Brazilian, and a psycho by any other name.

I'm not her first target and I won't be her last. She has serious mental health issues, and she doesn't mess about when her blood's up. Both women stagger to their feet and Lyra grabs Danielle around the waist from behind. Lyra's tall, big built. The Brazilian is tiny, small and skinny, but she has a dozen different drugs in her bloodstream and, for that moment, the strength of someone twice her size. Maybe three times. And she still has a knife.

'Get out of the fucking way!' Lyra yells. She cannot believe I'm still standing there. She has lifted Danielle off the floor but the Brazilian's a wildcat. She's screaming all manner of curses in Portuguese, her arms and legs flailing. In truth, the way she's windmilling her limbs, she's as likely to cut herself as she is me, but I'm still a target.

I snap to my senses and get out of the way in time to see the blade swish through the space I've just vacated. What now? I literally have no idea how to help Lyra. I've never hit anyone in my life. What am I supposed to do?

'For God's sake,' Lyra says, 'get Vanessa.'

Of course! *Vanessa*. She's the boss. She'll sort it out. I tear out of the room and into the corridor. A group of women are running towards me. Luckily, one of them is the Colombian I'm looking for.

'Thank God, Vanessa, you've gotta come. Danielle tried to stab me.'

'Keep your voice down,' she hisses, and grabs my arm to lead me back to the room. Danielle is stable and disarmed when we arrive but flares up again the second she sets eyes on me.

'Look, Vanessa,' I say, 'you need to sort her out. She's crazy.'

'I'll be sorting out nothing till I've heard both sides,' Vanessa says.

'Are you not listening? She tried to kill me.'

'And I suppose you did nothing to her?'

What? 'No, nothing.'

'Really? *Nothing?* Nothing at all?'

'All I did was change the channel on the TV. That's all, okay?'

Vanessa nods. She's judge, jury and executioner. She's heard the evidence and she's going to deliver her verdict. Even psychotic Danielle quietens down for this.

'So, it's simple then,' Vanessa says. 'You two are going to have to sort this out by yourselves.'

'And what the hell is that supposed to mean?' I can't believe what I'm hearing.

'It means, my child, that you and Danielle are going to be locked in a room and the winner will be the one who walks out of it.'

It takes a few moments for the words to sink in. But Danielle has already worked it out. She's smiling, gesticulating at me like some cage-fighter winding up her opponent. In a flash, she breaks out of Lyra's grasp and spits an inch from my feet.

What if she'd still had the knife?

I feel sick. I'm going to be put into a locked room with a madwoman who has already tried to kill me once. I'm not a fighter. There's no way I'm coming out of there alive.

'Come on, Vanessa,' I beg. 'Don't make me do this. I've done nothing wrong!'

The crowd of women laughs. Vanessa most of all.

'Look where we are, girl,' she says, gesturing her arms around her. 'Everyone's done something wrong – whether they admit it or not.'

*

There are many things a girl would do for a couple of hours with Leonardo DiCaprio. I never figured getting myself killed to be one of them.

The DVD of *The Wolf of Wall Street* had been burning in my hand. I'd had it a couple of weeks. Never had the chance to see it. Not that I didn't want to. Not that I didn't have the time. Time was all I *did* have.

It just wasn't my turn.

There was always someone ahead of me in the line for the TV who wanted to watch their own movie. I'm not talking about my family or a housemate. The people I'd been queuing behind were strangers. But then I wasn't at home. I wasn't even in my own country. I was in a maximum-security prison.

In Peru.

Ancón Prison isn't on any TripAdvisor 'must see' lists. You'd be hard pushed to find it on a map. Even if you knew exactly where to head, you'd struggle to find it first time. Trust me, I know. Ancón Prison is in a desert in the middle of nowhere, outside Lima, the capital of Peru. It's not easy to find because you shouldn't want to go there, simple as that. It's like anyone who visits needs to be punished as much as the people they know on the inside. And if you do find yourself living in that hellhole, you're just getting what you deserve. And that includes all the other people in there with you.

People like Danielle, who get so irate when it's your turn to choose the movie that they'd kill you rather than let you watch your film. What's it matter to her if she kills me? She's in for life. What are they going to do? Keep her alive longer so she serves another sentence?

In Ancón, life has no value. No meaning. Not to her, not to many of the others like her. But it did to me. Every day was a battle to stay alive. Every day brought me one step closer to being reunited with my family.

So how did I wind up in one of South America's toughest maximum-security penitentiaries? The answer lies in the dozen kilos of cocaine I was caught trying to smuggle out of the country.

Was I guilty? Yes.

Did I know what I was doing? Sort of.

Was I hung out to dry by a bunch of gangsters and the Peruvian justice system? Absolutely!

So why did I do it? Why did I jeopardise everything and bring untold stress and heartache on my family – getting myself locked up with terrorists and murderers – for a few easy quid?

It's a long story. And it begins in Northern Ireland . . .

CHAPTER ONE

I KEEP FORGETTING YOU'RE A KID

The explosion lit up the whole house.

'Mum, what's going on? What was that?'

'Get in your room,' she yelled. 'Don't come out till I say it's safe.'

I didn't budge. 'I'm going nowhere. I'm staying with you.'

She edged over to the bedroom wall and peered gingerly through the window. 'It's not good, Michaella,' she said. 'Please hide.'

I couldn't, not with her so obviously scared. I was probably only about thirteen at this time, as reckless as I was terrified. I crept next to her and stole a glance outside. It was like a vampire film. The villagers were storming Dracula's castle. We were surrounded by sixty angry men with alcohol in their blood, hatred in their veins and Molotov cocktails in their hands. What I could do to help the situation was unclear. All I knew for sure was that I couldn't let her handle it alone.

Of course, she wasn't alone. My brothers were there. We were a big family but at the end of the day it was only five of them and a few mates against five-dozen attackers.

'Mum,' I said, 'are we going to die?'

'Michaella, love,' she said. 'I'm not going to lie to you. I honestly don't know.'

*

If I said I grew up in Syria or Iraq, you'd maybe have a picture in your head of what it was like. But this wasn't the Middle East, it wasn't a town out of a Hollywood horror movie populated by pitchfork-wielding vampire hunters, it was the United Kingdom. Northern Ireland, to be precise. Home of so many cultural icons – Seamus Heaney, Alex Higgins, George Best, Van Morrison – but also, I swear, the biggest religious stupidity outside of Islamic State.

According to the papers and the government, the so-called 'troubles' in Northern Ireland had ended in 1998 with the Good Friday Agreement. Hiding from an angry mob out for our blood in 2006, I wasn't so sure. I'd like to say that night was a one off – that we never saw that kind of hatred every day. The truth is, as a Catholic family living in a Protestant area, we were fish in a toxic barrel.

I was born in 1993 to Robert and Norah McCollum, the youngest of ten. You can tell we were Catholics from that alone. There was pretty much a two-year gap between each of us. Stephanie, my mum's eldest, was already making her own way in the world when I came along. Within a couple of years, Aisling and Tina had moved out too. By the time my parents separated in 1998, it was just me at home with Samantha and the boys: Keith, Gavin, Glenn, Ryan and David.

Mum was from the north and Dad was from the south, so while they were together we lived in his part of the world, in County Monaghan, just south of the border. When the marriage collapsed, Mum took us north. Things had got really bad with his gambling and treatment of us that we did what Mum called a 'moonlit flit' to get away from him. My sister Aisling was living in Auchnacloy, a tiny village in County Tyrone, about twenty kilometres south-west of Dungannon, and we needed somewhere to live, so Mum thought, why not there? Aisling had just given birth, so she would now have a lot of unexpected family help nearby.

We lived in a big old townhouse on Main Street. My sister Samantha and I shared one room and the boys spread themselves out among the others. When Samantha moved out years later I'd get the run of the place. Until then, I was content to share. We were close, all of us.

But then we needed to be.

Auchnacloy was barely a stone's throw from Monaghan, but in terms of enlightenment they were light years apart. I'd never considered the religion I was born into as having any hold over me. We were baptised, we went to church on Sunday, we said the odd 'hail Mary', but that was the extent of our attachment. Other people, I soon realised, liked to get a little more involved.

There was a lane behind our house, and beyond that some form of military structure. I think it was a prison of sorts. The soldiers patrolling the grounds were armed to the teeth and there were regular incidents where these gun-toting, fully grown men seemed to regard my seven- and nine-year-old brothers as some kind of threat. If they played football too near to them, or were cheeky, their response always seemed completely over the top. One day I saw them pointing their guns at my brothers and I screamed. Of course I did. I thought they were going to be shot for playing football.

My mum heard me yelling, so she came out to see what was going on. When she saw the scale of the predicament she went silent. She grabbed both boys and shooed them into the house.

'Don't say a word,' Mum said. 'Just get inside.'

When my older brothers found out what had happened they made straight for the back door, ready to defend us. But our mother wouldn't let them out. She was shaking and the colour had drained totally from her face. She remembered the days when the tensions were even more strained. When Catholics were dragged from their homes and beaten. Or worse.

After the football incident, it was days before she allowed us out into the garden again. When she did it was under strict instruction not to venture near the wall. Nothing else happened that day but it wasn't long before there was a repeat performance. Once again we were minding our business when suddenly there was the distinctive crack of a weapon being engaged.

This sort of thing happened time after time, but at least we only saw about a year of troops on the streets. After the Good Friday Agreement they gradually pulled out and things calmed down, at least on an official level. The armed soldiers may have gone, but the cowardly behaviour of the paramilitaries stayed the same. It took me years to understand what was going on, and even then I didn't comprehend it. I still don't. We were Catholics living in a loyalist area, but so what? That shouldn't matter to sensible human beings. There's no other way to explain it – religion in Ireland drains the sense you were born with.

This was the twenty-first century and yet people were carrying on like they were back in the Middle Ages. I had no life experience to back me up, but I knew I couldn't be around this sort of mentality for the rest of my life. I didn't know how and I didn't know when, but I was certain of one thing: *I needed to escape.* That is, if I survived.

*

We suspected something was going to happen on the night of the firebombs because the police had told us it would. It was marching season and the police had received a coded message from loyalist paramilitaries that our house would be attacked. They had sent death threats! It was 12 July. I know because our favourite team had won the Gaelic football league. We had a team flag flying outside our house in celebration. Gaelic football's a Catholic game, and there were problems just supporting the sport, let alone a team.

12 July is also the big date for the Ulster loyalist groups commemorating the anniversary of the Battle of the Boyne. This year it just so happened to coincide with the championship final. Their route took them through our street. Usually we stayed indoors and battened down the hatches. This time we planned to do the same. The police came and handed over a steel cube. 'You fasten it behind your letterbox. It stops them posting grenades through your door.'

My mum told me to leave the room but she knew I'd seen enough to last most adults a lifetime. What was the point in protecting me now? This was the world we lived in.

Counting down the hours until the end of the school holidays is one thing. Counting down the hours until you're going to be attacked with bombs is another. Even with the warning it was hellish. On the one hand, we anticipated what was coming. On the other hand, no one had a clue if it really would. Not even the police. The same police who were nowhere to be seen when the shit hit the fan.

As the evening drew in we got phone calls and whispers that the march was over and the crowds had dispersed. Then later, when it was dark, new messages came in. The pubs round the way were full of loyalists, all hammered after a day's bigotry and a night's intoxication.

'They're coming, Norah, I suggest you get ready,' a neighbour warned us.

Every single detail about that night only strengthened my resolve: the sooner I got out the better. But there was something more than that at play. As we all huddled upstairs, I remember thinking, *Why are we going through this? We wouldn't even be here if we could've stayed in Monaghan. If my dad hadn't made life impossible for us.*

*

I wish I could say that the sectarian nonsense was the worst thing that happened to us. Sometimes, though, it's the people closest to you that can cause the most heartache.

My dad was in security. He was ex-army, big built, balding and kind – to me, anyway. My sisters told a different story, one backed up by my hazy memories. Apparently, he wasn't always loving towards our mum. The shouting I heard as a kid every other week wasn't the limit of their fallings out. If Dad couldn't win a fight with words he'd resort to other means. In a weird way, I think I witnessed some of these occasions without taking it in. The visions came back to me later. In a weirder way, as horrific as they were, I couldn't honestly say I knew he was doing anything wrong. Yes, my mother was battered and bruised, crying and broken. It made me sad, but at three, four, five years old, how do you know that isn't normal family behaviour up and down the land?

My mum never spoke of it. It was only later when my sister brought up the subject that I got to accept the truth. Dad was an unpleasant man, plain and simple – a compulsive gambler who didn't like losing. I'd been a bit of a daddy's girl as a small child, coming along after sons, and I'd convinced myself he was this gentle giant. The more I learned of the truth, the harder I found it to comprehend.

After we left him, I'd see him once or twice a month for eight or nine years. He had a new partner for a while, so we'd stay with them. It was generally fun, although the older I got the less comfortable I was blocking out the past. When I heard he'd never contributed to our upkeep after the separation that was the end of it. We always had the essentials, but money was tight. My mum worked all hours, three jobs at a time sometimes, just to keep the roof over our heads. Hotel cleaning, waitressing in restaurants here and there, she was always on the go. With me and Glenn being so young, we were often dragged along with her. During school holidays I spent as much time in her hotel as she did.

I never formally broke off contact with my dad, but when our meetings began to fizzle out I didn't fight it. Tellingly, neither did he. Maybe I'd have been more upset if I hadn't had a built-in replacement.

Mum's oldest brother Eugene lived about twenty minutes from us. His kids were all boys, so once again I was the apple of his eye. He was a lorry driver, he had a massive ten-wheeler, and he used to let me climb up into his cab. It was so cool looking down on the world like a bird in a tree.

After everything I learned about my dad, it was good to have such a positive male influence in my life. The less I saw my own father the more I saw Gene. I'd hold his hand walking down the street as if he were my dad. I felt in my heart that Uncle Gene was on my side.

We were together one day when he said, 'I've got something to tell you, love.'

'What is it?'

'I've been in for tests. I have cancer.'

I didn't know whether to bombard him with questions or give him his space. But what I did know was that I was going to be there for him. Every hospital appointment he had, I went along with him, school be damned. All the scans, all the visits, all the chemo treatments, I held his hand as often as I could throughout the entire process. I couldn't bear it if anything happened to him. But, I have to be honest, it didn't look good.

*

What with Gene, my dad and loyalist marchers, I knew I had to find a way to get out. But at thirteen what were my options? I started wondering how my brothers coped. They had the same stuff to deal with as me. If anything, it affected them less. They didn't cower behind our mother's skirt when the trouble came. They faced it. Embraced it even. And then they went out and partied.

I'd been sheltered from the more reckless side of teenage life because I'd been attending a Catholic school in the country, and when I wasn't working I already had two jobs that kept me busy, whereas my older brothers went to a town school. They knew all these people around Dungannon – older brothers of school friends and their mates. From about the age of fifteen I started coming into town after school with my girlfriends and I quickly realised how much cooler everyone was compared to us. They were a lot more clued-up and streetwise.

At the start of my GCSE year I decided to chuck in my local school and move to a college in Belfast. The commute was a drag, but it freed up a lot of space in my brain. I did well. Thrived, in fact. The work was hard, the hours harder still, but the realisation dawned on me: my escape, my safe haven, wasn't a place; it was a state of mind.

One day I asked Glenn if I could tag along. He thought about it and said, 'Why not? But you stay with us and you don't talk to anyone, okay?'

Of course, I agreed. Who was I going to talk to anyway?

I've since been to much better clubs. But that club was my first, and that night was like heaven on earth. From the moment I stepped in I was transported to a new world – one where religious bigotry didn't get a look in. The only thing that mattered was if you had a drink in your hand. My brothers were very protective but, since they were all on the booze, they didn't see why I shouldn't join in, as long as I stayed next to them, which, after the first shot of vodka, I was more than happy to do.

I was struck by the realisation that I felt properly happy and relaxed for the first time in my life. There were still sectarian morons around town, and Uncle Gene still had cancer, but somehow it all seemed less overwhelming if I could get dressed up, go out and have fun now and then.

That night was totally transformative, and I couldn't wait to do it again. Yet again I fell into the paradise of self-discovery – and, more crucially, escape. Half an hour in that bar and I couldn't believe I was in the same postcode as all the crap and violence that had plagued my life.

It wasn't just clubs and bars that provided the shelter from reality. Drink was just one form of escape. Around this time loads of teenagers were taking mephedrone – also known as M-Cat or Miaow-Miaow – a chemical stimulant similar to MDMA, which was yet to be made illegal. Kids at school and college were doing it, even the 'good kids', and it was everywhere. It made everything that bit more sparkly.

There was one guy I met around this time. The lad in question was older than me by some six or seven years. To my young eyes he was a man, not a boy. He had money, he had a body-builder's physique, and he had eyes for me. I admit I was flattered. No one had ever taken an interest in me like that before – my watchdog brothers saw to that. But they weren't here and he – Michael – was. I could see that people looked up to him. Like so many girls at an impressionable age, I fell for the bad boy. But I didn't realise at the time just how bad he was. No one did.

When he offered me weed I didn't want to appear immature, so I took it. When he and everyone else in the place moved onto the harder stuff later in the evening, I merrily joined in. I'd barely turned sixteen and I'd enjoyed my first experience of cocaine. Suddenly, the booze bubble I'd been in for six months seemed tame. The drugs didn't just make me forget my problems. They showed me an alternative reality.

Michael played his part as well. He was quite the force of nature. Flash, you'd call him. But that appealed to me. He seemed to have the answers to questions I hadn't even thought to ask. He was so mature, so worldly.

We bumped into each other a few times and he always made a beeline for me, more often than not bearing gifts. One day I was at a party drinking vodka and cranberry juice, the healthy option, when he appeared.

'You look like you need perking up,' he said. He wasn't wrong. I'd had a hard day at college.

We went into the lounge and he shooed some people off the sofa so we could sit down. Then he unwrapped a clump of foil.

'Is it cocaine?' I asked.

'No, better. Watch.'

He tipped a line of white powder onto the back of his hand and snorted. Then he repeated the action and offered it to me.

'I don't think so, Michael. I'm okay with my drink.'

'Come on, no one's here to drink. That's not why people come here.'

'Well, that's why I come here.'

He sat up. 'Okay, don't worry about it,' he mumbled. 'I keep forgetting you're a kid.'

Bastard.

'I am not!' I said, indignant. 'Show me that stuff right now.'

I don't know if he was clever enough for such mind games, but it certainly worked. I was sick of being treated like a child. If I needed to take harder drugs to prove otherwise then so be it.

The powder hit my brain instantly. My whole mind burst into colourful flames flickering one wonderful idea after another.

'Incredible, right?' Michael said.

'Yeah,' I said. '*Yeah*!'

Two words, all I could muster, because as quickly as it arrived the inferno in my brain dampened to a kaleidoscopic wash. It was mesmerising, totally overwhelming, like someone had pulled the plug on my body.

'Ketamine, babe,' Michael said. 'Horse tranquilliser – nothing better.'

I went to pick up my drink but had to watch as my arm stayed where it was. It didn't budge, didn't leave my lap. I thought about standing up and realised my legs weren't talking to my brain. Nothing was.

'Tranquilliser,' I giggled. I should have panicked. I was one of the few girls in a house full of men, but I wasn't worried. I just had this feeling that everything was all right. More than all right. The best feeling ever.

I looked around the room and realised everyone was on the stuff. What drinks there were stood untouched. We all shared the same goofy expression. Everyone was in their own happy place.

As people got control of their limbs they gradually began to pair up and peel off to different nooks of the house. When Michael made his move on me, it seemed the most natural thing in the world.

After that, Michael and I were a couple – not that anyone knew about it. Our partying circle was so small that you saw the same faces every time you went out. Everyone was too wasted to see who was spending time with whom.

Dungannon still had it's drawbacks. The only difference was, it no longer bothered me. I remember the next time I was verbally abused by loyalists. They'd been so used to me freaking out for years they just looked shocked when I coolly said, 'Get a life,' and walked on.

I'd done it. I'd escaped their powers of intimidation. And I would do anything to keep that distance – which meant one thing.

The partying had to continue.

CHAPTER TWO

IS THIS WHAT YOU WANT?

Aged sixteen I was on top of the world. Most nights would find me out with Michael. My brothers were in the dark as far as Michael was concerned but, because of the circles they all moved in, he was an ever-present figure at every club or house party, so we got to spend time together even under their noses.

We were pretty serious by then, but I never felt ready to share the news of my new relationship with my family. Something told me they wouldn't be exactly thrilled.

The highlight in my life at this point was going with Uncle Gene to the hospital and learning his cancer had been beaten into remission.

'What does that mean exactly?' I asked the doctor.

'It means your uncle should see out his days as nature intended.'

He was still frail from the chemo and all the stress but we celebrated as best we could.

My GCSEs came and went and, I don't know how with all the partying and the lack of sleep, but I passed every one with decent grades. I had the summer holidays to look forward to, then I planned further education in photography.

Michael couldn't have been happier for me about my qualifications but I got the sense he felt a wee bit left out. He had his moods, no question. We were at a party one time when a woman told me he was taking steroids – that was why he was so built. It hadn't crossed my mind. I just thought he worked out a lot. I started to notice how aggressive he could be to other people, but it was always to men.

Then I heard a rumour that he'd had children with another woman and had been abusive to her many times. I was really shocked. I'd never seen him behave aggressively to a woman. When I confronted him, he said it was lies. And as he treated me like a princess, I gave him the benefit of the doubt. When I look back now, I can see how manipulative he was.

One night, he invited me to a party just around the corner from our house. I managed to evade the watchdogs back home and walked the 300 yards to the address he'd given me. When I arrived at this nice little end-of-terrace, about five minutes' walk from my family, I was a bit confused because I couldn't hear any music, or the familiar sound of partygoers. I double-checked the address. No, this was definitely the place.

Maybe I've got the wrong night?

I gave Michael a call.

'Just checking this party's tonight,' I said. 'Because I'm at the house and there's no sign of life.'

'Are you outside?' he said.

'I am.'

A second later the front door opened and there he was.

'Come on in,' he said. 'Welcome to your new home.'

It was a little two-up, two-down – very sweet and completely empty other than us two.

'I can't move in here,' I said. 'My family doesn't even know I'm seeing you.'

'Then let's tell them.'

I'm not sure I ever saw Michael 100 per cent clean, but I knew this much: he'd never been more serious.

Two minutes later we were making the short walk round to my

mum's. Luckily, she was still up. Unluckily, so were my brothers. When I announced I was leaving home to live with my boyfriend the place erupted. It turned out none of them rated Michael that much.

But the fact he had come round with me and bit his tongue the entire time he was being criticised just made me want to be with him even more.

'I'm going to live with him either with your blessing or not,' I said. 'End of discussion.'

My mum was heartbroken and pleaded with me not to go.

'I know what I'm doing,' I shouted. 'I'm old enough to make up my mind.'

I thought I knew everything but I was just a silly little girl. I collected a few things and that was it, off we went to start our new life together.

*

I'd like to say it was paradise but what, honestly, did I know about living on my own? Young people moving in together is very romantic until you realise someone has to wash up. To be fair, there wasn't that much to clean up. I'd never cooked anything, I'd never cleaned anything, I barely knew how to shop. I remember wandering around Sainsbury's looking at the shelves, not having a clue what to buy. I knew nothing about the world and even less about ingredients. I suppose we must have eaten something but there was so much else going on that neither of us ever cooked a thing.

However badly we were doing it, I liked being my own girl, and part of a couple. It felt grown up. I didn't even mind that he had children from an ex – and had her name tattooed on his arm. We were together and we were in our own place, that's all that mattered. I was partying every day and my boyfriend was a pretty big deal in the community. Even my brothers were friendly towards him in public.

It helped that I had my own income. I found a job working part-time in a boutique in Belfast. It was only a sales job, selling hair extensions, beauty accessories and the like, but at least it was something I knew about. I could picture myself running my own business later when my education was over. Women will always want to make themselves look nice, and I was no exception. Which Michael loved.

It was a while coming but I eventually realised he liked being seen with me. I was that bit younger, I looked after myself, and he normally only socialised with men, so I really did stand out. Which he loved – up to a point. We had parties at the house three or four nights a week and it was only ever his mates. He never let me invite my friends. It gave his ego a bit of a boost if he knew I was the only girl his mates could look at. But woe betide anyone if it went further. We'd been together maybe a month when one night he got really aggressive with me, accusing me of flirting with one of the fellas.

'We were only talking,' I said. Which was true.

'Why do you have to talk to men?'

'Because you don't let me have any female friends over!'

I cringe now to admit it, but I was as much flattered by his jealousy as annoyed. But it wasn't just his own friends he didn't trust me around. We were in a shop, he was going to buy me something to wear for a party, and the shop assistant made the terrible mistake of being male. Michael watched him like a hawk. It was fine until the moment the guy held a dress up against me. That was it. We were out of there and the assistant was left with a load of expletives ringing in his ear.

Another time, we were walking and the traffic was slow and a lorry driver honked his horn at me, like Neanderthal men do. It wasn't the first time it had happened, and I was daft enough to perk up at the attention, but Michael wasn't having it. He flew across the road and started banging on the driver's door. Luckily, it was too high for him to reach the handle otherwise God knows what he would have done. He was still trying to get a foot up on the wheel when the traffic cleared and the driver put the pedal down.

It wasn't so long ago I was dodging petrol bombs from sectarian dickheads, so anything seemed better than that, but still . . . Michael's temper was getting worse. Looking back, that kind of intensity could only be sustainable for so long. Even within my bubble of happiness I knew that when it tipped over into full-scale jealousy, it was going to be catastrophic.

*

Six months of parties and good times and I wasn't looking back. When I got back from college one day and Michael announced another big night I didn't complain. Things got off to a slow start but by midnight the place was packed. There were people in the kitchen, the living room, and a load upstairs in the bedrooms and bathroom. With the drug crowd it's all about territory. People are very protective of their stash. If you've got cocaine, it's expensive and you don't want to share it with every Tom, Dick and Harry, so that's why you get these splinter groups. They had meth, coke, ketamine . . . you name it, it was on the table.

The guys I was tight with, about five or six of them, were upstairs in our room. A few bodies were on the floor, giggling against the wall. There were three of us lying on the bed, me, another girl and a guy, all stoked with ketamine. No one was talking. We were all wasted, staring at the ceiling, lost in our own worlds.

And then Michael came upstairs.

He burst into the room and just started shouting. It took a while for it to sink in, we were all that gone. I was one of the last to snap out of the trance because by the time I did everyone else in the room had made their exit. It was just me and Michael perched on the edge of the bed shouting rubbish.

'Why were you encouraging him?' he said. It didn't matter that I was too blissed out to answer.

'Dave,' he continued, 'he was trying it on.'

Dave was the guy on the bed with me. He wasn't capable of trying it on with anyone. No one was. In any case, his girlfriend had been lying between us. But Michael wasn't interested in the facts. In his rage he accused me of cheating on him with every man in the house.

'I know why you do it,' he said. 'You're jealous of my ex.'

Still I said nothing, which wound him up even more. He ran over to the dressing table, smashed a mirror and started cutting at the tattoo of his ex-girlfriend's name with a shard of glass.

'Is this what you want?' he screamed. 'Is it? Is this what you want me to do?'

I should have been petrified. He was going full-on mega meltdown for my benefit. The problem was, I was still in my happy place. Watching him going crazy was like doing the ironing with the TV on in the background. I was aware of it being on but not paying any real attention. For the longest time it was just this muffled noise. But that couldn't last for ever. I became aware of the shouting and the screaming getting louder and louder like someone was turning the volume up on the TV. In truth, I was starting to come round. When I did, I really wished I hadn't.

There was blood everywhere. His forearm was in tatters.

That snapped me right out of it.

'What are you fucking doing?' I shouted. Still he carried on hacking away at himself. I threw myself out of bed and ran downstairs where the others were huddled in their little groups, oblivious to the carnage upstairs.

'Michael's gone crazy, you've got to help him.' These were his friends, after all.

Barely half of them looked up. One bloke said, 'Don't you worry, he'll be fine.'

'For fuck's sake, he's cutting his own arm off. Go and help him!'

God, I hate druggies sometimes. Not one of these arseholes budged. In fact, another lad said, 'It's getting a bit heavy here, let's go.' They started funnelling out like comatose lemmings.

I wish I could have left with them. But that idiot upstairs cutting himself to ribbons was my boyfriend. Someone needed to calm him down and that someone, by the look of it, was going to be me.

Back in the room I found Michael curled up on the bed in the foetal position. I sat down next to him. He was rocking, clutching his arm, going on and on about someone making him do something.

I couldn't quite make it out with the howling and the swearing. I touched his hair and that's when he looked at me with new eyes.

'It's your fault,' he said, the shakiness in his voice replaced by a chilly calm.

'What's my fault? What's my fault? What are you going on about?'

'This!' he screamed, and twisted his lacerated arm into my face. 'You and your jealousy, you made me do it.'

'I don't care about your tattoos. Or your ex.'

He pulled himself up. 'God, I'm so stupid,' he said.

Finally, I thought, *I'm getting through to him*. But he hadn't finished.

'I'm so stupid for believing you, you cheating slut!'

I never saw the fist coming. The next thing I knew I was by the door. My head was against the skirting board. My arms were pinned by my own body to the wall. It was ages until I even worked out what had happened. When I did, I knew one thing.

I have to get out.

I started scrambling to my feet, my head fuzzy with a cocktail of Class As. I managed to get myself upright but as I turned to the door it slammed shut. My head wrenched back as Michael took a fistful of my hair.

'You're not going anywhere.'

'Please. Please. Don't hurt me.'

'You should have thought of that before you slept with all my mates. Did you think I wouldn't find out? Do you think I'm that stupid?'

'God, no, Michael, listen to me, I've not touched anyone else. You've got it all wrong.' I was part crying, part begging, totally scared.

I felt my neck fall forwards as my hair was released. Keeping as close to the door as I dared I turned slowly to face him. He looked like he'd come from an abattoir. His face, his clothes, his hands were top to bottom soaked in blood. It was still streaming from his arm. He looked like the walking dead.

At that moment I didn't know who I was most scared for, me or him. I honestly thought he was going to bleed out.

'Listen to me, Michael, this isn't you, it's the drugs.'

'It isn't me, you're right.' He paused. 'It's you.'

He leant over to the bed and grabbed another shard of mirror. It was the size of a dinner knife but twice as sharp. Even as he clutched it I could see it slicing open his palm. Not that he felt it. Not that he could feel anything right then.

'This is all your fault,' he said, and swung the blade at me. I screamed and dropped to the floor. Big mistake. He got hold of my hair again and slashed down with his makeshift machete. How close it came to finding my brain as it scythed through my hair I don't know. But at least now I could escape.

The steroids made Michael mental and strong, but the fear made me quicker. I was over the other side of the bedroom before he could even turn. When he lunged again, I was ready. I got out the way with seconds to spare. Again and again he tried. Again and again I dodged as best I could. But the room was small. There were only so many pockets of space I could find. After a dozen successful feints, he caught me. The back of my wrist exploded in blood. I wanted to fall to the floor and cry, but I knew if I did it would be over. One more slip up and it wouldn't just be my wrist he was cutting.

It's no exaggeration to say this torture went on for more than an hour. There were periods where Michael would just look at me, staring, not saying a word for what felt like ten or twenty minutes at a time. There were occasions when he threw the shard down and just charged at me like a bull. Once he caught me, grabbed my wrists in one of his giant hands and started punching me against the wall. I don't know why he stopped. But he did. I saw my chance and ran to the door. I was at the top of the stairs when he caught up with me. A second later I was flying through the air. My next memory is coming to in a crumpled heap at the bottom. Four of Michael's friends – the only ones who hadn't left – were kneeling over me. Asking me if I was all right. Did I need an ambulance?

That set him off again.

'She doesn't need no fucking ambulance. Get out of my house!'

I remember the guys not wanting to leave me, but even though there were four of them and only one of him, ketamine in heavy doses is no match for steroids mixed with meth.

To their credit, the guys didn't give up and eventually the drugs must have started to wear off. Michael was kneeling over me, yelling into my face, when I was aware of the sound of a window smashing. Suddenly, the guys were back in the hallway, dragging that monster off me.

They did it a dozen times, I swear. Even together they couldn't beat him physically. The best they could do, in their drug-addled logic, was to just stop him hurting me any more. Each time he managed to shake them off and straddled me again with fury in his eyes.

Finally, one of them took a run up and knocked him off me hard enough to put enough distance between me and Michael so I could get outside. I couldn't believe it but there was a taxi pulling into the close.

'It's for you,' one of the guys said. 'Now run!'

I didn't need telling twice. I bolted while they dealt with Michael as best they could. I knew they couldn't stop him, but they could slow him down. As I was running up the garden a shining object flew past my head. It was a knife. I didn't dare turn round. Michael was running after me, throwing the entire contents of the cutlery drawer. I felt the next one hit my back, another got my legs, luckily both handle first. I managed to climb in the cab and we pulled away with Michael tearing at the door, his mates in pursuit.

I thought it was over. But suddenly the taxi screeched to a halt. We weren't even out of the estate.

'I can't do this,' the driver said. 'I know who that is. I've got a wife and family. I can't get involved in this shit.'

'Oh my God, what are you talking about?'

'I'm sorry,' he said, and started reaching over to open my door, the coward. Obviously, he wasn't budging. Maybe if I just stayed put I'd be all right. But then I looked out the rear window and saw Michael coming back out of the house waving a samurai sword. Where the hell he got that from I have no idea. But I could see what he wanted to do with it.

I kicked open the door and ran. For the first time I was glad my mum's house was just round the corner. I fell against the door, hammering and hammering. It was so late she was already up and getting ready for her morning work.

'What on earth's the matter?' she said as I fell into the house, but I couldn't answer. I just slammed the door and started bolting every lock.

My brothers were down in an instant and as soon as they worked out what was going on they went crazy outside with Michael. The police were called, more for his safety at that stage. When you've faced down sectarian machine guns, I guess a Japanese blade is nothing.

And that's all I remember. I must have collapsed because my next memory is waking up in hospital a day later, with a cracked jaw, four broken ribs and bruises and cuts everywhere else.

The police visited me in hospital and saw the extent of my injuries. I gave them a statement. Michael was arrested and served eight months in prison. I really didn't want to be around when he got out, but my mum and brothers were insistent I stayed with them. At first I was grateful. After five days in hospital I didn't have the strength to go outside and when I did I was scared of my own shadow. Even though I knew Michael couldn't reach me, the memories of that night would not stop playing in my head. It didn't help that his friends blamed me for him being put away. Cars would slow down and girls I'd never seen before would swear at me. Guys threatened me with violence. Strangers, all of them.

I desperately wanted to forget everything but the only way I could think of was getting back on the drugs. Which obviously wasn't going to happen in my mother's house.

This was October 2010, I was seventeen years old, and I swear I was going crazy. The more I wasn't allowed any of my old habits the more it became all I could think about. I just wanted to lie down and not have a care in the world. I didn't expect my mother to understand but surely my brothers could?

Whether they did or they didn't, I wasn't getting my way.

'My God,' I said one day, 'you're making me like a prisoner in my own home.'

'Don't be soft,' Glenn said. 'What do you know about prison?'

He was right. I was exaggerating. I wasn't in prison at all. Because I was free to leave any minute I chose.

Which is how, in March 2011, I ended up moving to Belfast.

*

It could have been anywhere, I just needed a fresh start away from people spitting at me in supermarkets and mollycoddling me in my own home. But it was Belfast because my sister Stephanie was living there, and she said I could stay with her and enrol at college for my foundation degree.

It was exactly the clean break I needed. The eighteen-year age gap between us meant we'd never shared the same roof before, but she was studying as well and we both got jobs in the same restaurant, so we had a lot in common. Her house was just outside the city, on the coast, which was beautiful, so we'd drive in together, do our studies, do our work, then drive back. It was idyllic. Hard work but blissful.

And I didn't think about drugs once.

After the shitstorm of the past couple of years I couldn't believe how happy I was just being 'normal'. The time flew by and, before I knew it, my course was over and I'd done the exams. It would be a few months before I got my results, so my career as a photographer would have to wait. In the meantime, I got a job as a hostess in a club called Rain. I basically had to make the VIP guests feel like kings for the night. The better I did, the more champagne they bought and the bigger my earnings. It wasn't particularly challenging, especially for someone sober for the last year or more.

I guess it's a small world, so I began receiving offers from other clubs to run their PR and get punters in. Soon I was working seven days and nights a week all over the city. By the time my results came in – and I passed! – suddenly photography didn't seem such a great career move.

The way I saw it, I'd been wanting to escape the world I'd been born into my whole adult life. At nineteen years old I discovered the true secret of how I could do that: money. I'd had to stay with my family because I couldn't afford my own place. I'd stayed with Michael as his kept house pet. And now I was staying with my sister as her guest. The only way I'd truly be 'free' was if I was financially independent. And if working every hour under the sun could get me that freedom, I wasn't going to throw it away.

Because of my working hours I decided it made sense to move into the city. I got a place with a couple of girls from one of the other clubs but that didn't last long. I was no saint but those girls loved to party at home and it just brought back memories of being with Michael. Having strangers sprawled all over your inner sanctum no longer made me feel comfortable. Another girl I knew, Katie, worked in club PR. She was looking for a flatmate so I moved in with her. Her family were always around, which was nice, but more importantly, like me, she liked to keep a clean house. If there was partying to be done it had to be done at work after hours or in another club. I have to admit, dipping my toe back into my old world after so long staring in from the outside was nicer than I imagined. I never got as messy as I had before but a couple of tabs a couple of times a month seemed to hit the spot.

I started imagining building a life in the city. My bank account was looking okay, I had some good jobs, some good friends and some good qualifications, should I need them. Without stupid men or religious bigots around me for the first time in my life, the future was looking rosy. I'd done it. I'd actually escaped.

And then I clicked 'like'.

*

Murder is murder, whichever way you look at it. At least that's what I thought. When someone I knew posted an article on Facebook about one of the old Long Kesh murders from during the Troubles, I was appalled and I did what everyone does with articles of interest: click: 'like', 'share', done.

Obviously, I thought nothing of it. Then about a fortnight later Katie and I were at home watching TV when there was a hammering on the flat door. Her face turned white. She leapt up, killed the TV, turned off all the lights then dragged me into the bathroom and locked the door.

'What the hell?' I said, but her expression told me to keep quiet.

'Michaella McCollum!' a woman's voice roared from outside the flat. 'Scum like you are not welcome here. Get out of my daughter's home or you'll pay for it.'

Now it was my turn to go pale as a sheet. That was Katie's mother yelling at me. What the fuck had I ever done to her?

I looked at my flatmate. She just mouthed 'sorry' and handed me her phone. On it was the link to the article I'd shared.

'My family saw it,' she whispered. 'They think you're IRA.'

'Oh, shit. More idiots.'

She couldn't disagree. But a minute later I was including her in the description. She was Protestant, I was Catholic, and we were both okay with that. Of course, though, the second her family saw anything even vaguely inflammatory on my Facebook page they were going to explode.

And, based on past experience, that could actually be literal.

To be fair, I was in a fairly murderous mood myself. Obviously, Katie knew all about this and she hadn't bothered to warn me.

She was trying to make amends. 'They won't do anything while I'm inside with you,' she said. 'But for God's sake do not open the door.'

All evening the mob hounded us, shouting death threats at me. From the noise there must have been more than a dozen of them, mostly angry men. What a surprise. What they actually planned to do to me didn't bear thinking about. Finally, about three in the morning, we heard them leave. Katie still didn't let me open the door but she did let me put the bedroom light on so I could see what I was packing.

'I'm so sorry,' she said, over and over. 'There's nothing I can do.'

'You couldn't even warn me?'

Five hours later I called a cab and took my belongings to another friend's flat. But I had no intention of staying. I was done with Belfast and its religious crap. What was I thinking even trying to build a life there? It wasn't my escape – it was where I needed to escape *from*.

Still without sleep I applied for a passport. The British passport office said there was a three-week wait, minimum. This was June 2013, and the summer rush was in full swing. My next stop was the Irish office. They said I could have one within seven days. I filled in the forms, handed over my photo then went straight online but not, this time, to Facebook. Ten minutes later I was the proud owner of a Ryanair ticket.

Ibiza, here I come.

CHAPTER THREE

THAT'S WHAT FRIENDS ARE FOR

The signs were there. On the way to the airport on 24 June 2013 I realised I'd left my passport at Stephanie's, so back we went. That was fate's first attempt to stop me. We got nearly there again and she asked if I'd printed out my boarding pass. I hadn't. 'That's a fine right there.' She was spot on, although the fine was nothing compared to the surcharge I got for an overweight suitcase.

Every inch of the way the omens were saying, 'Don't go! Don't go!' but I was that determined to get away I would have boarded the plane if its wings were on fire. I had to escape, even if it was just for a week.

At least that's what I told my family.

The truth was, I didn't have a long-term plan. I just knew I had to escape the confines of the place I was born into. Whatever challenges the rest of the world might hold, they couldn't be worse for me than the sectarianism back home. I didn't know where I was going to end up, but I did know I was never coming back.

*

On the flight over I sat next to an Italian girl. Like me she had a ticket to paradise and no plan. At least I had a hotel booked for a week. I offered her my room for the night but in fact we didn't use it. We shared a cab to San Antonio, dumped our cases then hit the clubs and bars in the West End of the town. My new friend just wanted to let her hair down. I was on the hunt for work. I'd given myself a week to get a job and an apartment sorted. It had to happen. There was no Plan B.

I met a Scottish girl called Carly who did PR outside a club. She put me in touch with a couple of bar owners. The next day I got a hit off a Facebook group looking for bar workers. By the time I came to vacate the hotel I had jobs in three clubs and a room share with Carly. Mission accomplished.

The work varied. I started hostessing at a place on the same strip as Ocean Beach. That was a nice job, and I began to really like the workers' life. In another place I performed a fire-dancing act. That craze came over from Goa and Thailand, where carefree travellers would watch fire-breathing and juggling at full moon beach parties.

At first I just wanted to earn money to secure my apartment, but I soon realised that everybody was always off their heads – workers and holidaymakers alike – and I soon got swept up in the party lifestyle. It's hard to do your own thing and live a normal life when the majority of people you're in contact with are throwing themselves into the hedonistic scene. You're young, it's sunny and you go along with the crowd.

I very quickly became a part of it all. I started partying hard with Carly and some of the other workers, mixing cocaine and ketamine. That sounds really hardcore but it's actually quite controllable. You can still function pretty well.

Another bar job had me waitressing. But it wasn't just drinks. Customers would order a round of gin and tonics along with a side of coke or MDMA or anything else that took their fancy, and we'd put the order into the bar like it was the most normal thing in the world. Of course, in Ibiza, it was.

The waiting staff were on commission, so the more powders and pills we shifted the bigger our wage packet. It was thirty-five euros for a gram of MDMA and forty for a gram of cocaine. About 50 per cent of that money went straight in my pocket.

One night I put in a full 11 p.m.–7 a.m. shift at the bar, the second half of which had me ingesting as much as I was selling. When I got back to our place Carly still hadn't returned with the keys, so I did the obvious thing and hit another bar where I met a bunch of English lads getting ready for a big day-trip cruise. I was too tired but there was a darts competition going on in the bar over breakfast and I won a bottle of bubbly. Obviously that got opened immediately and then lo and behold I was ready for the high seas.

All the lads were fun, but I got on best with one called Jake and we had a holiday fling. I was letting my hair down and having a laugh in the sun, a long way from the grey streets of Dungannon.

Most tourists were a laugh, but they were only ever passing through. I had more time for people like Paul, who ran another bar and lived in the same apartment block as us. He was older than me, sober most of the time, and wealthy. He seemed to know everything and everyone worth knowing.

One night we were chatting at his bar when a cockney guy pulled up on a motorbike and took a shine to me. His name was Davey and he lived up in the hills, he said, hence the need for the bike. I wasn't actually sure what it was he was doing out there. It crossed my mind that it might be something dodgy, but I didn't really care.

Paul was due to fly back to the UK for a visit the following day but, on this rare occasion, he was in a mood to party. When he suggested we go back to his I said yes.

He never caught that flight.

It's not like we slept. The familiar ketamine paralysis that I remembered from back home kept us where we were for a good while. A full forty-eight hours, I reckon. That's how late Paul was for his plane anyway.

Regardless of how wasted I got, I always remembered to call my sister every couple of days and text my mother once in the morning and once at night. That was our deal. If I missed one I'd get it in the ear the next time. If I missed two – which I never did – she promised she'd be onto Interpol to find me. Obviously, I didn't tell her a fraction of what was going on. She just needed to hear I was happy and safe.

This particular day, thanks to Paul, I wasn't up to anything more than a text. Once it was sent I tried to get my thoughts in some sort of order. At some point I remember Paul warning me about Davey.

'That's someone you wanna steer clear of,' he said.

'Why? He seems nice enough.'

'He's a drug dealer. Let's leave it at that.'

Those words carry a different meaning for different people. The fact we'd spent two or three days unable to walk because of our enjoyment of various substances meant I was okay with the idea of someone supplying it. Where else were we going to get the stuff? Put it down to the Ibiza bubble, but I didn't see the problem. Davey wasn't some sleazy, backstreet pusher. He was nicely turned out. Clean. Groomed. Fun.

Paul had also mentioned something about spending time in the jungle in South America with Davey but I didn't give it much thought. People went all over the world on adventure holidays, didn't they?

A few days later I was walking along the main street and I saw Davey with a mutual friend. They said they were going on a road trip to Bora Bora Beach Club – did I want to come? Bora Bora was located in one of the best spots on the island. There would be fun, up-for-it people, great dance music and cool vibes. Paul was a good pal but I wasn't listening to any of his warnings about Davey. I was in his car like a shot.

It was a great day, full of laughs, some coke-fuelled, some not. A bunch of Davey's friends showed up. They were all fine but one guy, a Brummie by the sound of him, stood out as the alpha of the group. He radiated confidence with his surfer looks, but he was no beach bum. When I asked Davey who he was, he said, 'My business partner.'

'Oh,' I said, all innocent, 'and what exactly is your business?'

I think for a second he considered the possibility that I really didn't know. Then he twigged and laughed. We were sizing each other up, I guess, but we both knew we were part of the 'night-time economy'. There's the life people lead in the normal world and the life people lead on the island. Everyone was on something, everyone was happy and everyone was having a good time. Although Davey didn't say it by name, he knew I got what he was about.

The rest of the day was brilliant fun and it wasn't long before I bumped into Davey again on the main strip in San Antonio. He was often around – one of the 'faces' on the scene. We chatted about clubs and pills and he gradually let me into his confidence about what it was he did and how he made his money. He liked the lifestyle and the comforts it brought him. He'd say, 'You'll never make anything more than peanuts working in a bar.' He had the attitude that an honest day's work was for mugs.

At some point he asked me if I fancied doing a 'run' – nipping over to the mainland and bringing back a package for him. I refused, almost insulted he would ask me such a thing, but he dangled the fact he'd pay me really well and it must've lodged somewhere in my mind as easy money. Certainly money was the priority for people like Paul and Davey. They weren't getting off their heads all the time like the rest of us. And they weren't grafting all hours for a basic wage either. Bar wages were fine for people on a working holiday but I needed more than that. I was determined not to be returning to Dungannon once the season was over. I needed a boost in my earnings to help me secure my path to the next thing – even though I wasn't sure what that'd be.

*

About a week later, Carly and I went to a barbecue at Davey's new place in San Antonio. We'd been on it for several days straight, so neither of us felt tip-top. But no sooner did the burgers go on than the powders came out. We were soon having a great time when Davey came up to me and quietly said, 'How would you like to go to Barcelona?'

'Wow,' I said, 'sure.'

'Not with me, though,' he said.

'Then what for?' I was too chilled to care about the answer.

'I've got a package there that needs lifting.'

'Oh,' I said, remembering his previous offer. 'Is it urgent?'

'Fairly.'

I didn't think too much about my reply, which people may think odd, considering it was such a huge thing he was asking me to do. But then, I was in a mindset that barely registered importing party drugs as illegal.

'Go on then, Davey, why not. I'll do it.'

I told Carly everything when I found her at the other side of the party. She was slightly more sober than me. She said, 'You know what it is, don't you?'

'What?'

'Drugs. Coke, meth, Es, whatever. You're gonna be a smuggler.'

I'd taken so much of all of them during the five weeks I'd been there that I honestly didn't see the problem. As I said, we were in that Ibizan bubble. In my addled logic, everyone I knew took drugs, and they had to get them from somewhere. I saw lifting this package no differently to how I would see some kind of cash-in-hand payment. Not legal, as such, but a minor crime at worst, like a traffic offence.

'I'll come with you,' said Carly. 'It'll be a blast.'

'Don't be silly, you have to work. I'll tell Davey you'll go next time if you like.'

'Cool.'

'I don't know how much he's paying me, but he seems to be pretty well off.'

'Go for it.'

'I will!'

I'm sure I meant every word but, as the party wore on, I got more and more drawn into the hedonistic mood of the day. Everyone was high and, just to make things even more animated, I was persuaded by a group of friends to drop some acid. At one point I could have sworn one of the club staff was a train conductor trying to show me to my seat. Another time, I was seeing Disney characters everywhere. Basically, of all the drugs, acid is not the one to be on when there are decisions to be made. By the time Davey caught up with me later, I might as well have been in outer space.

'It's on for later,' he said.

'What is?' I asked.

'Your trip.'

Interesting . . . 'What trip?'

'To Barcelona, remember. We discussed it. You were going to collect something for me.'

I stared at him for a couple of seconds. *Barcelona? Collect something?* I didn't even know what time of day it was – just before dawn, I think. But in the back of my mind a bell was ringing. A little bell, but it was ringing nonetheless.

'Oh yeah,' I said. 'I remember. Sure, whatever. That's cool.'

I'd promised something and I wouldn't have done it if I didn't think it was okay, would I? The fact I'd been wasted for a few days didn't come into it. But Davey was an okay guy. I didn't think he'd do me any harm.

'Tell me what you need me to do,' I said.

'We're gonna leave here soon. We have to get an early start. Don't worry, you won't be alone. My friend will take you to the airport. You'll be back in Ibiza before you know it.'

*

On 1 August 2013, as the sun was coming up over San Antonio, my fate was sealed. Davey escorted me back to my apartment and helped me pack my bag. I was still wobbly from the acid. I grabbed my passport and some tiny bits of clothing – bikinis and some shorts and a T-shirt.

At 6 a.m. we hailed a cab to Ibiza Town and headed off. *Next stop Barcelona.* Actually, there was a stop before that. When Davey said we were meeting someone at McDonald's I thought he was a mind reader. I desperately needed coffee and breakfast. I ordered the full works and was just about to tuck in when a familiar face bowled in. It was Davey's business partner – the Brummie.

Some things don't change. Our breakfasts were on two trays in front of us. The first thing the Brummie did was swat them aside then lay down lines of K and coke.

He laughed. 'Bon appétit, my friends.'

I looked at Davey. He looked at me. We both looked at the guy and his smile didn't look like it would be there all day. The last thing I wanted – or needed – was any more drugs, but when even teetotal Davey took a line I knew it wasn't a choice. *Ah well,* I thought, *rude not to.*

Of everything I've done, everything that I regret, sniffing Class A drugs off a table in McDonald's is up there. But that's hindsight for you. Within a minute the table was clean and the Brummie was standing up. 'Come on, darling,' he said, 'I've got a friend I want you to meet.'

I looked at Davey. He said, 'You're gonna have so much fun.' After my McDonald's breakfast, I believed him.

I didn't get my food. The Brummie took my arm and my case and led me into the street. Around the corner a Spanish guy was waiting for us. The Brummie didn't speak Spanish but that didn't seem to matter. He gave me a hug then pushed me over to his mate and said, 'I'll see you next week, yeah?' Then he sauntered off, not a care in the world.

The Spaniard trotted out a stream of the local language, all of which went completely over my head. I'd been in Ibiza five weeks and, because everyone was speaking English all the time, my Spanish extended no further than '*Hola*' and '*Dos cervezas por favor*'. He wasn't fazed. For the second time that morning I felt my arm being grabbed and I was led along a side street. We stopped outside what looked like an old Thomas Cook travel agent. There were faded pictures of holiday resorts in the window alongside out-of-date prices on boards. As far as I could tell, the guy was ordering plane tickets for me. I know this because he gave the travel agent my passport. It was weird but not a problem. That came a few minutes later when I realised that not once had I heard the word 'Barcelona'.

I saw the ticket as it was handed over. It was stamped 'Palma'. I knew that was in Majorca. Why was I going there?

The coke and ketamine cocktail was really kicking in, so I didn't question anything. Not even when we didn't head straight to the airport. Instead I was taken to a street full of terraced apartment blocks and led again by the arm up to the second floor. I was expecting to be taken into some kind of office. But the moment he opened the door we were hit with the rich smell of cooking and the sound of small children playing. It was clearly a family home. But whose? And why was I there?

What the hell was going on?

The Spanish guy could tell I was agitated. He made the shush sign with his fingers and led me quietly along a corridor into a bedroom at the back of the apartment. If the children heard us they didn't come out.

Standing in the doorway, he gestured for me to make myself at home. I genuinely think he was as uncomfortable as I was. He tried to talk to me, again and again, but it was gibberish to my ears. I sat down on the bed and he relaxed a little then left, closing the door behind him. It gave me time to realise how exhausted my body was, even though I was being kept awake artificially.

He returned a few minutes later with a cold drink. He was just about to leave again when there was a ferocious hammering on the flat door. He bolted down the corridor like he was on fire. When he returned it was with another guy, talking nineteen to the dozen in Spanish. The newcomer was tall, skinny, pale, wearing a hat, baggy shorts and an oversized jacket despite the temperature. When he saw me, he calmed down and smiled. He came in and turned on the TV, which of course just added more of the language I didn't understand.

With the volume blaring he came over to me and said, 'I'm Mateo, it is nice to meet you.' I was so relieved to understand him.

'Wow, you speak good English for a Spanish person,' I said.

'I lived in London for a long time. What makes you think I'm from Spain?'

'Well, it sounds like you're speaking the language all right.'

'Ah,' he said, 'it's not just this country that speaks that language. It's how we speak back home as well.'

'Oh,' I said. 'So where is it you're from?'

He smiled. 'A beautiful place,' he said. 'You might have heard of it.' He paused. 'It's called Colombia.'

Oh shit.

I had an instant picture in my mind of what Colombia was about. Probably the same thing everyone else thinks – cocaine and violence and drug cartels. Even with my McDonald's breakfast still painting a nice gloss on everything, I knew I'd be a fool to get involved with anything over that side of the world. Luckily for me, I was only going to Barcelona.

Or so I thought.

'About that,' the Colombian said, 'there's been a change of plan. You're not going to Barcelona any more.'

'Then where am I going?'

'You're going to Peru.'

CHAPTER FOUR

ARE YOU THE GIRL?

I should have been shocked. I should have said, 'That's not what Davey said'. I should have done a lot of things, and I would have done – if I'd known where Peru was.

People will have their own opinions of me for everything that's happened, and this is only going to give some of them more fuel. But the sorry truth is I had no idea where Peru was. No clue. *I thought it was another Spanish town.*

Barcelona, Madrid, Seville, Peru – what did it matter where I went? I'd only be gone a couple of days. That was the deal. In and out, Davey had said. And now Mateo was saying the same thing. At least I think he was. It's fair to say I was there in body, but I was watching his lips more than watching what he was saying. I hadn't slept in thirty or forty hours. I was coming down off acid and being held up by other drugs. I'm not complaining, but it doesn't make you the most attentive listener.

'I don't want you to worry about anything,' Mateo was saying. 'One of my guys will be with you all the way. Planes, buses, hotels, you'll have a pair of friendly eyes on you. You won't know who it is or where they are, but trust me, they're there for you.'

'In fact,' he continued, 'because this is your first time, you won't be travelling alone. Another girl will be travelling with you, to help. You will meet her soon, in Majorca.'

'Oh, so that's why Paulo bought tickets for Palma?' My memory was working even if my brain wasn't particularly interested.

Mateo smiled. 'Indeed. Now, here is the important thing. When you pick up the package you will put it in your case, and you will go to the airport in Peru. You will go through customs as normal and, I swear, nothing will happen to you.'

I believed him. But then I'd have believed in flying space-monkeys at that point. Still, I had to ask.

'How can you be so sure?'

'Trust me, Michaella, I have friends everywhere.' It felt strange to hear this guy using my name, as if he'd known me ages. 'The security in Peru have a photo of the other girl, so they know who to look for and wave through. They know what she'll be wearing and everything. As soon as you enter the airport they'll make sure you don't get hassled. Your suitcase will be searched by one of my people and they will find nothing out of the ordinary. So you'll just get on your plane, fly here, hand over the package and I pay you.'

The mention of money reminded me why I was doing this. Davey had mentioned there would be money but I had no idea how much.

'Everyone who works with me earns,' Mateo went on. 'It's only fair. You drop off the package and I give you five thousand pounds.'

Holy Christ.

For the first time in twenty-four hours my brain flickered into activity. That was a lot of money. Was I even hearing straight? The things I could do with that. The freedom it could buy me. I'd be set up and what did I have to do in exchange? Catch a couple of flights with another girl? I was definitely waking up now. Mateo's next instruction speeded it up.

'So now I need to give you this,' he said, and handed over a BlackBerry.

'It's okay, I have my own phone,' I said.

'No, you need to give me that.'

'What?'

I'd just turned twenty years old. There's not a girl that age on the planet who gives up her mobile.

'Just for a couple of days,' he said. 'It's for your own safety.'

'Why do I need to be worrying about my safety?' I said, a bit more alert by the second. 'You said there'd be no problems.'

For a second the smiling guy in front of me disappeared and I saw a glimmer of something else on his face – anger maybe, frustration definitely. Then suddenly the smile and the calm British accent were back.

'Nothing will happen to you or my package, that I promise. But people can listen in on normal cellphones.'

'I didn't know that.'

'It's true. Whereas messages on the BlackBerry are invisible to everyone. Even the police.'

'I thought this was going to be straightforward.'

He sighed. 'If you listen to me, and do exactly as I say, it will be straightforward.' He was no longer even trying to smile.

'So please, Michaella, give me your cellphone now.'

'Okay, okay,' I said. 'I just need to send one text.'

'Out of the question! Have you not listened to a word I've said? No one must know where you are.'

'I know, I know, but if I don't tell my family I'm going away for a few days they'll bring the house down looking for me.'

'Okay,' he said. 'But do not mention Peru.'

I texted my sister and said I was going to Barcelona for a few days and so might be out of contact due to the 'partying' – she'd know what that meant. I left it to her to translate into words my mother would understand. I'd be in touch when I got back, I told them. I showed Mateo the text and he was fine with it. Then I handed over my phone and watched as he dismantled it before my eyes, took out the SIM card and battery and threw it all in a drawer. It was like handing over a kidney. Could I survive without it?

Mateo left and the other guy, who I now knew as Paulo, came back into the room. He looked as sad as ever. We sat together on the edge of the bed and watched TV for an hour or so. Any moments of clarity or lucidity I'd had speaking with Mateo were in the past. If I'd closed my eyes I could probably have flown to Majorca without a plane.

I never got the chance to put it to the test. A couple of hours later I was being shepherded through Ibiza airport by an anxious-looking Paulo. I kept telling him to 'chill'. He didn't know what I was saying but wrangling a high, sleep-deprived party girl through an international airport clearly wasn't something that filled him with joy.

I managed to get onboard okay and it was only a short flight, about forty minutes, to the other Balearic island of Majorca. I spent plenty of them trying to work out who had 'eyes' on me. Mateo had promised I'd have protection everywhere. Which fellow passenger was it?

It was when I was landing that an idea occurred to me: what if he's not looking out for me? What if he's making sure I do as I'm told? But a second later Captain Ketamine and his friend Colonel Coke kicked back in and I was more interested in imagining my shoes were ice skates. That is, until we landed and got a text from Mateo telling me to head outside the building right away.

Once outside, I heard a woman's voice speaking English, addressing me.

'Hey, are you the girl?'

I stopped. Looked around, looked at my shoes. Where were my skates? Had this woman taken them?

The woman was actually a girl, really, about my age. She was wearing short shorts and a bikini top, her hair was pinned back, and she had a great tan – impressive for someone with a Scottish accent. Her look said 'beach' but her manner said 'office'.

'Are you Mateo's girl?'

'Yes.'

'I'm Melissa,' she said, straight and to the point. 'Come with me.'

We walked over to a taxi and she introduced me to a short chubby guy called Julio. He was Peruvian, she pointed out. We drove in silence. I was still in an altered state, so the lack of conversation barely registered. We pulled up outside a bar-type place in Palma and Melissa led us in. Julio followed with my near-empty case. I only had enough clothes for two days and they barely filled the bottom of the case. It must have been so light that I can't imagine what the customs people at Ibiza must have thought.

My heart sank when I realised we were there to eat. I had no appetite, and my stomach was like a tumble dryer. A couple of people from the restaurant joined us but since no one spoke English it was just another load of noise in my busy head. I had tons of questions, but Melissa was nodding away with the others like a native. When she finally looked over, I pounced.

'Have you done this before?'

She pulled a dismissive face. 'You'll get used to it.'

'Yeah, but have you done it before? The lifting, I mean.'

It was the first time I'd used that word, but Davey had used it and I didn't want to seem totally naive. I guess I'd known that's what I'd signed up for but saying it out loud made it more real. It made me nervous.

'I was meant to be doing this with someone else,' she said, 'but she pulled out. So Mateo's guy found you.'

'What do you mean "found me"?'

'They needed someone to come with me. Mateo thinks pairs of girls are safer than single ones. Anyway, I was in Madrid with the guys and I was sent here to pick you up.'

'But you've never done this before?'

She paused. Looked around at all the Spanish speakers. Then back at me. 'No,' she said, 'I've never done this before. But,' she added quickly, 'there's nothing to it. Just do everything I say and you'll be fine.'

I knew I had a head full of chemicals and confused thoughts, but I wasn't sure I liked this woman. She was a first-timer like me. So why was she coming over all hoity-toity about everything?

I decided I'd heard enough from her and she'd obviously tired of me. She went back to the other conversation and I drifted off again. After a while Melissa started looking over at me translating what the others were saying: so and so was doing this, so and so was doing that. It was fairly humdrum, but I appreciated the effort.

'How long did it take you to learn the language?' I asked.

She shrugged. 'You pick it up.'

Suddenly, the group began laughing. 'What's going on?' I said.

From the look on her face she clearly didn't know. She'd been winging it.

'Do you actually speak Spanish?' I asked.

'It's time to go,' she said.

We got another cab to a nice-enough house. Our minders plus the restaurant owners came in as well. My stuff was dumped in a large room. As buzzing as I still was, the sight of the freshly made double bed seemed suddenly really appealing. To be frank, I felt like shit. I perched on the edge and tried to summon the motivation to get undressed. Suddenly, the restaurant owner's wife appeared and began to undress me.

I jumped away from her and backed myself towards the wall. That had to be comprehensible in any language. Melissa, the know-it-all, appeared in the doorway.

'We have to clean your clothes,' she said. 'It's a long trip.'

'It was only forty minutes to get here. I'm sure my top can survive another hour or two in the air.'

'Whatever,' she said, and left the room.

The next time I saw Melissa she was hovering over me. For some reason we were sharing the same bed. And, because of the drugs, I wasn't sleeping soundly.

'Stop moving, for Christ's sake!' she snapped.

'I'm *not* moving,' I said.

'You are.'

Obviously I had no idea what I'd been doing but her high-and-mighty attitude would wind up a saint. It made sense that I was twitchy in my sleep. That's standard comedown behaviour. The fact I kept waking up in sweats pretty much underlined it. Not that I was backing down for her. I just needed to be left alone.

And when I woke up the next morning, I *was* alone.

And I was sober. I felt sick to my stomach. My chest felt like there was an anvil on it. I could barely breathe. I thought, *I'm in this house, I don't know where the fuck I am. I'm with some random girl and people I can't understand and I am going to some Spanish town to smuggle drugs.*

This wasn't the freedom I'd been searching for.

I found Melissa having breakfast in the kitchen with Julio. He got up and gave me a plate. It was as if nothing was out of the ordinary. And maybe it wasn't – for them. For me, I was chilled enough to realise I was getting cold feet. But I was clear enough in my own mind to appreciate that I was beyond the point of no return. From Davey to the Brummie to the Colombian to Paulo and Julio, and now this girl and the restaurant guys, there seemed to be a lot of people involved in simply lifting a package to Ibiza. I could only imagine the consequences if I were to pull out. As if to prove he was always there, always watching, my BlackBerry buzzed with a message from Mateo.

'Michaella, you must keep this phone on you at all times,' it read. 'When I call, I need you to answer within two rings. This is very important. Do not disappoint me.'

There was activity downstairs as people started hunting around for their beach stuff. I'd packed a bikini but it was a prop more than anything. I never expected to use it. I never expected to have time. Why weren't we heading to Spain? What time was the flight?

With a mixture of Spanish and hand signals, Julio got everyone outside. Our first stop wasn't the beach but another travel agent. Melissa's ticket had already been booked. Julio tried to get me on the same flight, but it was full, so she would fly out on Monday and I'd follow the day after. I didn't mind. The idea of spending an hour in the air next to this controlling Scottish girl didn't exactly get me dreaming. As long as it didn't delay the return journey, I was cool.

We still had an afternoon to kill so we went to the beach. We'd been there twenty minutes when Melissa's BlackBerry rang. She didn't look too happy. When she hung up, she came straight over.

'That was Mateo. Why didn't you answer his call?'

'My phone's in our room.'

'Why? He told us to carry them everywhere.'

'Yeah, well, I've been told a lot of things.'

Melissa went quiet for a second. Then she said, 'You can't joke around with these guys. You'll only get so many chances.'

'Okay,' I said. 'I won't forget again.' Anything to shut her up. In truth, I was in complete denial about the kind of people I'd been thrown in with.

Clearly the conversation with Mateo was weighing on Melissa's mind. Even with my eyes closed in the sun I was aware that she was angsty about something. She made such a fuss of having my ticket on her that I eventually took the bait and asked about our itinerary.

'Okay,' she said. 'I'll be in Peru a day earlier, so I'll get everything in place. You won't have to worry about anything.'

Yeah, whatever . . .

'Then we've got a couple of days doing all the tourist sites. Machu Picchu and all that.'

'We're not going there to be tourists,' I said, confused. 'Anyway, Davey said I'd be back in Ibiza in two days.'

Melissa laughed. 'You can't get to Peru and back in two days.'

Jesus, I thought. Spain's not that big. But I didn't think to argue. I just let her babble on with her itinerary. She obviously got a kick out of being the one in charge and I was happy to leave her to it.

I sat back and stared at the clear blue ocean. But after a while a sense of nagging dread came over me.

What have I got myself into?

CHAPTER FIVE

BE CAREFUL

What indeed.

Julio watched over us like a hawk, but he was obviously a nice guy. I didn't need to be able to speak his language to appreciate that. Whenever it was just us together, he'd get this sad look in his eyes and say, 'You know . . .'

I didn't know what he was getting at but it seemed important. After a couple of days of babysitting he went out one day, just for an hour, but it gave me and Melissa the run of the house. Having now been sober for a couple of days, I started getting ideas. My first instinct was to search the place from top to bottom. I figured Melissa would be too uptight to join in but I was wrong. She started scouring the rooms the second the front door closed. I don't know what we expected to find. It certainly wasn't a drawer full of passports and phones . . .

. . . *And guns.*

'Oh shit. Shit. Shit.'

I didn't know what else to say. Melissa didn't either. Whatever we'd ingested, whatever stuff we'd done in our lives, whatever decisions we'd made, neither of us envisioned ending up here – in a domestic house, a family home – where people kept weapons in their wardrobes.

I felt sick. Ruined. I could see Melissa responding the same but for once I needed her know-it-all personality to take control.

'We have to stop this,' she said suddenly. 'If they discover we've been in here . . .' The fact she left the sentence unfinished spoke volumes.

I could barely look at Julio when he returned. If we'd had any language in common he'd have broken me in a flash. What actually happened is that Melissa dropped her 'I'm in charge' persona and she and I actually started to bond. We spoke about our backgrounds and it turned out we'd both been living within 200 yards of each other in San Antonio. From the list of acquaintances we had in common, we'd obviously been at the same parties sometimes. We'd just never actually met. The second the locals returned Melissa reverted to type. She was cocky, she was confident, she was bossing me around.

Later I went with Julio as he drove Melissa to the airport. We exchanged good lucks and off she went. Then Julio and I hit McDonald's. It was nice to go there with an appetite – and not get loaded on coke. Before we finished, Julio ducked into a local shop to use their phone. He was always doing that. He preferred landlines because calls were harder to trace. It was another clue to the seriousness of my situation. Sadly, it wasn't one I picked up on until it was too late.

The next day Julio drove me to the Spanish clothes chain Zara to buy some new gear. I got a pair of trousers, a jacket and some shoes. I had the feeling this was coming out of Julio's pocket because when it was time to head to the airport he kept shaking his head when he looked at the ticket. I couldn't help noticing it was first class. Clearly that's all they had.

A couple of hours before my flight was due Julio took me and the rest of the household to the same restaurant we'd visited on our first night. I couldn't follow the conversations but at one point everyone started to hold hands.

Well, this is weird, I thought. But I still didn't know what was going on. Then I realised they were praying. And even though they had their eyes closed, it was my name they kept repeating.

Oh my God. They're praying for me. Why?

*

Melissa flew out on Monday 5 August. My flight was booked for Tuesday 6. I was already three or four days beyond the time I'd informed my sister I'd be back in Ibiza. Without my phone, I had no idea of her number to update her. I hoped she'd put the absence down to me having a great time.

Before we left for the airport, Julio called me into the house owner's bedroom. The woman was sitting there holding a baby. She gestured at me to take him. The pair of them were asking me questions but I didn't understand a word. I didn't understand why they would entrust the baby to a stranger – especially one who was about to become a drug smuggler. Or was that the message in itself?

I'd ignored the omens on the way out to Ibiza and look where I'd ended up. Was Julio trying to tell me something? And should I be listening? Then I remembered the guns. No one was to be trusted, including the young mother. Even killers had babies.

Via a series of mimes and bad English, they managed to convey that Peru, wherever it was, wouldn't be as warm as Majorca. It was hard to imagine anywhere in Spain being anything but boiling but I packed a jacket in my hand luggage.

At the airport, Julio hoiked my suitcase through the terminal and escorted me right up to passport control, where the armed guards marked the end of the road. I was just going to nod at him as a sort of international symbol of 'thank you' but he grabbed my shoulders, stared into my eyes and said, 'Be careful.'

'What?'

'Be careful. Be careful.'

I continued alone, my head spinning. Julio's job as far as Melissa explained was to keep us chilled until we set off. If we got cold feet we might not go. So why, after doing so well – taking us to the beach, to restaurants, just being calm – would he jeopardise it all by telling me to 'be careful'. The fact they were the only two words of English I'd ever heard from him was significant as well. He could have learned 'hello' and 'goodbye' but he went instead for this warning.

But what was he warning me about?

I flew into Madrid, where there was a five-hour wait for the connecting flight. That gave Mateo plenty of time to message me that everything was going to plan. He told me I was doing well. It creeped me out that he even knew. Or was it a bluff? A minute later this guy came up to me, Italian by the sound of it. I thought it was odd, but he seemed keen to let me know he was a policeman.

I just stared at him. *My God, are you for real?* Are Interpol onto me? Was this another warning? Or was he on Mateo's payroll? I was sick with anxiety. I seriously thought about not getting on the plane. Even as I was debating with myself, I felt the BlackBerry ping again.

'Get on the plane. You're doing fine.'

An hour later I was boarding the plane but I still didn't know where Lima or Peru were. Then, when I was in the air, I guessed it was the opposite side of the country from Barcelona by the time it was taking. As the flight entered hour number three, I expected the landing signs to light up. Nothing happened. Two hours after that I got super twitchy. I knew Spain wasn't that big. Unless we were flying on the world's slowest airline something was up.

I was in a tricky position. I desperately wanted to know where I was travelling to but to come out and ask someone directly would paint me as a madwoman, if not desperately suspicious. By hour six I had no choice. I leant over to the guy next to me and asked what he knew of our airport.

'Jorge Chávez?' he said. 'Not bad. Fairly modern like these countries try to be.'

That was good information. 'Have you been there before?' I asked.

'What, Lima? A couple of times.'

'What's it like?'

'It's like the rest of South America. There's poverty and riches right next door to each other. Hard to get used to, if I'm honest.' We chatted a bit longer. I didn't hear anything else though. There were only two words stuck in my head.

South America? Shit. How the hell had I got roped into that? My family would go mental if they knew I'd left Europe. *I* was starting to go mental. I kept looking at my BlackBerry and wishing it worked on planes. I wanted to call Samantha and ask her to pick me up. I knew she'd be worrying about me. And with good cause, because I was worried about me too.

Six hours of torment and self-analysis later, I stepped into Lima's Jorge Chávez Airport. A world map in the arrivals area showed me that Peru was about five thousand miles from where I'd imagined. I couldn't believe I was on South American soil. It felt as shitty as every other airport I'd ever stepped foot in. And then I realised it was nothing like anywhere I'd ever been in my life.

Heathrow in London has airport police carrying machine guns these days but in Lima it wasn't just the police. It was military personnel in full camouflage outfits; it was security guards. I wouldn't have been surprised if the cleaners were armed to the teeth. Guns were everywhere and not one person I saw looked the type to ask questions before he fired. Only a mug with a death wish would even attempt to cross these guys.

Casual artillery wasn't the only difference from home. The stench of poverty hit me the second I was outside the gate. You couldn't move for beggars and homeless-looking people, but that wasn't the length of it. Every city, Belfast, London, Barcelona, they all have those. But in Lima the men and women going about their business may as well have been wearing rags. No one looked threatening, they just looked so, so poor – and so downtrodden. You can't read everything into someone's looks but I knew this much: this was not the sort of city you'd want to get stuck in for any period of time.

I was starting to panic with the unpleasantness of it all when I heard a shout and looked to see Melissa marching over. As annoying as she was back in Majorca, I was mightily relieved to see her here. Tellingly, for all her badass bravado, she didn't look too unhappy to see me either.

She immediately took charge, which, on this occasion, was just fine by me. I think having someone to boss gave her confidence, and right then we needed some of that. We got another flight straight away, to the south-eastern city of Cusco, but the second we sat down all the air sapped out of us and we travelled in silence. My brain was whirring. I'd seen so much since Melissa had left, and none of it good. I just needed to find the words – and the balls – to tell her.

After nearly twenty-four hours of travelling, when we finally checked into our hotel, I just wanted to collapse. Melissa wasn't having it.

'Come on, get up,' she said, 'we need to go.'

'What? Go where?'

'Machu Picchu, remember? We discussed this. Mateo says if we don't act like tourists we're going to stand out.'

It was ridiculous.

The thing that really got me about the people there on holiday, on their gap year or ticking off their bucket list, was how they stood out from the locals. If Lima was down at heel, Cusco was its poor relation. The locals had bare feet, they carried their naked babies around in their arms, and they wore rags rather than actual shirts or skirts. I'd seen nothing of the world at that stage, but I knew this was bad. I had no idea people lived that way in 2013.

Mateo had given Melissa a camera to get as many legit tourist snaps as possible, so we looked as gormless as everyone else. I had no idea how deep the cover went till this family got chatting to her and asked about our backgrounds. Melissa trotted out this whole story where we had different names, different backgrounds, different lives. She was a nurse, apparently, and I was a photography student – which I actually had been, but she didn't know that. I was stunned by how comfortable she was with the charade. We were just killing time before we committed a crime that could have serious consequences.

How could she be so normal?

Day two was another pointless exercise in staring at things we couldn't enjoy. I couldn't even pretend to be happy. I was so desperate to pull out of the whole plan that it made everything else seem like a waste of time.

I must have looked really miserable and sullen. We were on a bus packed like sardines en route to some archaeological site when Melissa said, 'Why have you got a face like a slapped arse?' I tried to ignore her. I didn't fancy wasting my energy on the row.

'Cheer up and try to blend in, for God's sake. That's all Mateo wants us to do.'

That got me. 'That's *all he wants us to do*? Are you crazy?'

Now it was time for her expression to change. 'Keep it down, Michaella. We'll talk later.' She was looking anxiously around her, but I didn't care how many pairs of Colombian eyes were on the bus with us.

'He's taken me away from my family. They've no clue where in the world I am and he won't let me tell them.' Melissa was pulling all manner of faces to get me to shut up. But I hadn't finished.

'Do you even know what we're doing tomorrow? I'm telling you now, I want out. I don't care about the money. I don't even need it. I was only told I was going to Barcelona.'

So much for blending in.

There was no respite from the feeling I was under constant surveillance. Even halfway up Mount Ainu, where there were only four other people, I knew one of them had to be working for the Colombian. Not knowing exactly who was a horrible feeling. My paranoia wasn't helped by Melissa being on her phone all the time. I knew exactly who she was speaking to, and while each call from Mateo seemed to fill her with confidence, I couldn't shake the feeling that we were already in trouble. It didn't sit well with me that he was micromanaging our every move. He'd played the 'Big I Am' card so convincingly back in Ibiza but all the checking and fussing made me suspect he wasn't as confident as he made out.

On the tourist trail there were other Europeans but we still stood out like sore thumbs – me with my pale Irish skin and jet-black hair and Melissa the blondest person in town. Which is how one day the policemen spotted us.

'Oh shit,' I said.

Melissa stopped marching for a second. 'What's wrong?'

'Don't look behind you, but there are two policemen following us.' I started losing it. 'I told you this was a set-up. We're going to get done.'

'Get a grip. We're only tourists. We haven't done anything. Yet.'

'So, what do they want, then?' They were right next to us by now.

'Keep quiet,' Melissa hissed. 'Let me do the talking.'

As if I ever had any choice.

Lying to a family with nothing more threatening than oversized rucksacks is one thing; being able to spin a yarn of bullshit to two heavily-armed officers was something else. I couldn't take my eyes off the massive guns these cops had in their holsters. How to escape was all I could think about.

When Melissa said, all smiles, '*Hola*,' to one of the cops, I was ready to sprint, I swear.

'Are you English?' he replied.

'Yes!' Melissa lied. It was close enough.

The police looked at each other. *Here it comes,* I thought. *They've obviously been looking for us.*

The other man reached for his belt and, instead of running, I froze. A fat lot of good my plan was if my legs were too scared to work. I flinched. *Don't shoot me, don't shoot me, don't shoot me.* But he didn't grab his gun. Instead, he unclipped his phone and said in broken English, 'I'm sorry, do you mind if we have a photograph?'

'Really?'

'Such beautiful ladies. Just one photograph, please.'

I don't remember if I managed to force a smile or not. I do recall still being rooted to the spot five minutes after they'd passed. My nerves were shot. That much was clear. How on earth was I going to make it through an airport carrying a case full of narcotics? You wouldn't need a body language expert to see I had something to hide. I hadn't even done anything yet and I was acting guilty.

We were so fucked.

*

I swear Melissa must have been on something to keep so calm. I kept processing the whole scenario and I couldn't see any way we were going to get away with this stupid plan. Mateo's assurances were worthless, I was convinced of that. The following day we were going to walk directly into the jaws of hell – that's if we didn't get shot first.

We flew back to Lima with barely a word shared and checked into another hotel, both sulking. We had separate rooms and I was just unpacking when she wandered in, ear glued to her phone.

'What does he want now?' I asked.

'He said we should put our passports in the hotel safe overnight.'

I handed mine over but that wasn't the end of the horror: we had a bus tour of the city lined up. I couldn't be arsed, but of course somehow Mateo knew that, and I got a message reminding me to go. On the plus side we met some Brazilian boys who spoke decent enough English to ask us out for a beer. I was suddenly reminded about the 'rules'.

'No mixing with locals, remember?' she said.

'They're no more local than we are.' But she'd made her point.

'Okay, okay, I'll get a beer at the hotel. On my own.'

The lounge was nice and had air con. In any case, I had nothing better to do for the next forty minutes. That's when, according to the plan, our lives would change forever. That's when we were being given the drugs.

I felt so claustrophobic and impotent. Something massive was going on around me and I couldn't do anything about it. All I could think of was blocking it out any way possible. I just wanted it out of my head for a few minutes.

I was vaguely aware of other people around us. They could all have been spies for all I cared. Let them watch. I knew I was screwed whether they saw me or not. I don't know what was going through Melissa's mind. Frankly I didn't care. And then her phone buzzed and all the beers in Lima couldn't have kept me calm.

'Is it?' I asked.

'Yeah,' she mouthed. 'It's time.'

Fuck, I thought. *Shit just got real.*

CHAPTER SIX

WHERE'S MY PASSPORT?

Melissa was nodding and saying, 'Okay, okay.'

When she hung up, she finally looked as concerned as me.

'What did he say?' I asked.

'I'm to go outside. I have to take a bag and meet a guy.'

My phone rang. It was Mateo again. 'I want you to stay in the hotel,' he instructed. 'Do not leave until I tell you.'

The whole situation was extremely unnerving. It was like being in someone else's reality. We went up to Melissa's room, where she retrieved a large handbag and disappeared outside. A few minutes later she returned, flushed, and hoisted the now heavy bag onto the bed.

'Is that what I think it is?'

'It's not even half,' she said.

'What?'

She didn't reply, just picked up another large handbag, more like a holdall, and went back outside. When she returned, the bag was bulging. She dumped it down and caught her breath.

'There was a guy in a car around the corner. His boot was stuffed with this shit. I didn't think I'd be able to carry it.'

'No wonder they needed two people,' I said. I was dumbfounded by what was unfolding in front of me.

'Go and get your case, then,' said Melissa, jolting me out of my trance. It was like I'd temporarily forgotten I was a part of this. I went across the landing to my room and wheeled my own case in. The holdalls seemed even more stuffed when I came back.

'This is a lot of drugs,' I said. 'This isn't ounces, this is *kilos*.'

Now I could see the scale of the operation I was more convinced than ever we were about to get screwed. The Colombian might have paid a few guards to turn a blind eye, but you'd need to bribe the whole airport to get this amount through. It must have weighed a couple of stone. Melissa was as shocked as me. When we calmed down a bit we unzipped the bags and discovered loads of little bundles of newspaper.

'Well, that doesn't look dodgy at all,' I said.

Obviously we had to check what was inside the newspaper. I don't know what I was expecting. It wasn't bags of cereal but that's what was staring back. I looked at Melissa.

'Are they having us on?'

We counted thirty-one sachets of porridge oats and various local soya brands, all bright colours. Green Villa Rica bags, red and orange Kewicha Avenas, red and blue Quakers 'avena tradicional' – all these words I'd never heard of yet somehow looking very familiar. The idea that they didn't contain what they purported to was surreal.

'Are you sure you haven't just popped round the supermarket?'

Nerves make terrible comedians. I picked a bag up, expecting to see amateurish resealing where they'd shoved the stuff in. There was nothing of the sort. You'd never suspect someone had emptied out the original contents and refilled each pack with cocaine. Each one was immaculate. And very, very professional, I had to give them that. And the attention to detail didn't stop there. Mateo rang me to explain the next step. We weren't going to lug these huge holdalls through the airport. He instructed us to divide the packets between us and store them in the bottom left-hand corner of our cases.

'Bottom left?'

'If you sit the case upright, the bottom left as you look at it. Anywhere else and it's going to be detected.'

I looked at the mound of sachets on the bed and then at Melissa's case. It wasn't one that would fit in the overhead luggage bins, but it wasn't designed for heavy lifting either. Mine was even smaller.

'Look,' I said, 'have you seen what we've got here? If I put sixteen packets in my case it'll fill the bottom left *and* the bottom right *and* the top left as well.'

He thought for a second.

'Tell you what,' he said, 'I want you to wrap every packet in an item of clothing. Can you do that?'

I was still staring at the cereal packs on the bed. 'I don't think I've got enough clothes.'

'You'll think of something.' He paused. 'Won't you?'

There was something about the way he said those last words that stopped me arguing. The second he rang off I flung the phone at the bed.

'Come on, Melissa, this is never going to work. Look how much we're expected to carry. It's suicide. I'm not doing it.'

She looked at me like she was sizing up a problem. I'd seen her lose her temper a couple of times in the last few days, so I waited for the eruption. It didn't come.

'Fine,' she said, 'I'll take it all. And I'll take all the money.'

I stood there immobile. Nothing in my life so far had prepared me for such a situation. I felt that I was hurtling towards an inevitable disaster but what could I do to save myself?

'Look,' I said. 'You take everything, you keep everything. I'll get my family to buy my ticket home.'

Then Melissa's phone rang. I didn't hear what Matec said but her reply made it obvious.

'Ask her yourself,' she said, sullenly handing me the phone.

'Are you all right, Michaella?' Mateo said. 'You're not going to disappoint me, are you?'

'I just don't see how it can work,' I said. 'They've got an X-ray machine and dogs.'

'I've told you, it's sorted. My contacts have Melissa's photo. They've all been paid. No one's going to stop you.' I wasn't convinced but gradually he wore me down.

'Okay,' I said finally, 'I'll do it.' I ended the call and tossed the phone to Melissa, who just scowled. Then I walked out without another word.

*

Lying on my bed I had a dozen separate thoughts whirling around my head. They all had different voices but the loudest seemed the most sensible.

There's no way this caper is going to work. Bail out now. Just leave the hotel. In the end it wasn't Mateo's words that calmed me but simple maths. There must have been ten or more kilos in Melissa's room. On the face of it, attempting to take that amount of pure cocaine through an international airport seemed ridiculous. However, it obviously wasn't Mateo's first gig. I didn't know what that amount of coke was worth on the open market, but it had to be around a million. There's no way he'd risk that amount of money being confiscated if he wasn't sure of his numbers.

Maybe it was going to be all right; maybe I needed to think positively. If we pulled it off, I would walk back into Ibiza with five grand in my pocket. I needed something to get me on my feet. I'd be set up for a year at least.

And then there were the practicalities. I was checked into the hotel under my real name. If I left, the drugs would still be there; there was nowhere for me to go. To get home I'd need a passport. Under Mateo's orders, mine was either in a safe in the hotel or somewhere else. It was nine o'clock in the evening. Wherever it was at the moment, I'd be seeing my passport again in nine hours' time when we checked in. Either that or I'd die of nerves during the night.

We were flying at 6 a.m. We set the alarms for about 1.30 a.m. – the middle of the night. When I woke up my stomach was in knots. I threw my hair into a messy top-bun and dressed in jeans, a thin black leather jacket and a black T-shirt with the words '*la vie est belle*' – I didn't know at the time it's French for 'life is good'. How ironic.

In the taxi, Melissa and I didn't speak a word to each other. For once it wasn't because we were fighting. We both had the weight of what we were about to do on our shoulders. By the time we reached the airport, though, the old antagonisms resurfaced.

'We need to wrap the cases in cellophane, so they don't open them,' Melissa said. 'You wait here, I'll go and check out the luggage-wrapping service.'

'You're joking,' I said. 'What sort of security guard is going to be put off by that?'

'Do you have a better idea?'

'Yeah, I do. I'm going to the bathroom.'

On my way to the toilet I saw three heavily-armed men stop what they were doing and stare at me. I'd experienced a lot of that in the few days I had been in the country. I knew we stood out. But this felt different. Were they waiting for me? Did they know who I was? Suddenly, I was glad I'd left my case with Melissa.

I didn't even need to pee. I just wanted my own space. I sat on the toilet lid for twenty minutes contemplating how my life had come to this. When I finally forced myself to go back Melissa was already queueing to check in behind a few families and a crowd of lads in Hawaiian shirts.

The hairs on my neck were standing up. I was aware of where every guard was standing. I didn't dare look, but I knew they were all staring at us. As the queue edged forwards, I noticed new security personnel beyond the check-in counter. After the cases were weighed and tagged they were being put on the conveyor belt that ferried them out the back to be loaded onto the plane. Standing between the check-in woman and the hole where the luggage would disappear, was a man with a machine gun. By his side was a sniffer dog.

Enough is enough, I thought. *How many omens do we need?* Mateo might have told the staff what we looked like but when that dog started singing and dancing anyone who wasn't in on the deal was going to come running.

My heart rate was through the roof but Melissa seemed as cool as a cucumber. How was that possible when things were getting so desperate?

The people in front of us shuffled away from the check-in desk and it was our turn. Calmly, Melissa did the talking for both of us. She was told to put her case on one set of scales, and I was asked to do the same on another. I couldn't breathe. I didn't blink. I did not take my eyes off that case for one second. The check-in woman tagged the case with our destination and barcode. Then she took another look at my papers and hit the button to send the case on its journey.

So far so good. But it still had to get past the dog. I watched as the conveyor belt began to move towards the animal whose sole job was to sniff out drugs. This was it. Make or break time. If those cereal packets weren't airtight then I was done for. My pulse was racing. Which is the last thing you want in that situation. Apparently, dogs can read that too. It didn't matter. I wouldn't rest until the case passed safely through the hole at the back.

Ten feet. That's how far away the case was from the dog. Then nine feet, eight feet, seven feet. I had to take a breath, but my heart was still coming out of my chest.

Six feet to go. Five feet. Four feet.

Oh my God, I just want to run. But I had to stand still. For both of us.

Three feet until make or break. Then two feet. Then . . .

My case was next to the dog and a man with a machine gun. Neither of them flinched. It passed them both and headed towards the gap in the wall. Somehow, miraculously, we had got away with it.

Then I realised Melissa was no longer standing next to me. She was being led by the arm into a room behind the check-in desk. Her bags were being carried there as well. Behind her were six men wielding semi-automatic weapons. Three dogs strained anxiously on their leashes. We'd got away with fuck all.

The game was up.

CHAPTER SEVEN

POSITIVO!

*J*ust breathe, just breathe. No one's looking at you. Maybe Melissa said the wrong thing. Maybe it's unrelated to what's in the case. Just be cool. Act normal. No one's watching you.

Except they were.

Security uniforms were swarming all over the place and every other one had a dog. All around me I could hear a rise in voices and the clatter of urgent footsteps. People were getting agitated. And the voices were getting closer.

I sensed the man standing at my shoulder before I saw him. When I turned, I was looking at his neck. He was massive. And so was the gun pointed at me.

'Come,' he said.

So many things went through my head but the only answer that made any sense at gunpoint was, 'Okay.' I watched as the conveyor stopped and another guard dragged my luggage off. I was marched over to the office where Melissa was standing.

She didn't look at me. She couldn't. Her eyes never left her case for a second. It was lifted onto a metal trestle table and one of the guards put on gloves and opened it. All the polythene wrapping in the world wouldn't have stopped him getting in. Even though I knew what was in there I was appalled at how easily they found it. Like me, Melissa had travelled light. She had sixteen packages in her case but only about half a dozen items of clothing. As soon as the guard picked up the first bundle, all the sealed packets were exposed underneath.

Just like I'd warned Mateo.

For a multi-million-dollar operation this was a major oversight on his part. But not as big as the cock-up where he said we wouldn't be caught. Or was this all part of the plan? I was scared and tired and maybe delusional. Even as the guard lifted the package out and opened it with a knife, I found myself holding onto the belief that this was all part of Mateo's grand design. It made sense that he would take us aside, away from the main body of security personnel. Best-case scenario: they were going through the motions just to ensure no one else stopped us. I couldn't bear to think about the worst-case scenario.

The room was so silent I could hear my own heartbeat. Without a word another guard delivered a tray of equipment onto the table. It looked like a kid's science kit. The one with the packet dipped a cotton bud from the tray into a beaker of clear liquid, then lowered it into the package. The contents clung to the bud as he dipped it into the liquid. I had no idea what was supposed to happen. But I did know that Quaker oats should not turn any liquid blue.

Suddenly, the whole room exploded in noise.

'*Positivo! Positivo!*'

They were shouting it to each other, into radios and out the door to colleagues. There couldn't have been a soul at check-in who didn't hear. I heard running footsteps and within a minute the room went from having six of us in it to twenty-seven. Only half the men were in uniform. The rest were dressed as holidaymakers, like us. We'd obviously been watched from the moment we'd set foot inside the airport.

So much for Melissa's photo keeping us safe.

There was such a lot of shouting in the tiny office that no one stopped me calling over to Melissa.

'What are we going to do? What are you going to say?'

She didn't reply. She was in total shock. Unlike me she'd actually believed the plan would work. Her brain couldn't cope with the reality in front of her. Even as a guard slapped handcuffs on her wrists she didn't respond. She was in a trance.

And I was on my own.

There were too many people in the room and more were trying to squeeze in to witness my suitcase undergo the same forensic test. It was chaos. I felt like a contestant on a reality TV programme. Ant and Dec could have popped out any second and it wouldn't have shocked me.

They opened my case and, surprise surprise, discovered seventeen packages identical to the ones Melissa was carrying. The guard leading the search was a lot more confident now and played to the gallery.

He gestured theatrically to the packages. 'What is this?' he asked.

I shrugged. 'I don't know. It's not mine.'

'Yes, yes!' he said, anxious to regain control in his broken English. 'It's yours. It's yours.'

Then he tested one of the packages as he'd done with Melissa's case, and the place descended into a circus of whooping and high-fiving when the inevitable positive result came back.

I wanted the earth to swallow me up, but the torment was just beginning. I felt the pinch as handcuffs bit into my wrists, but the physical pain was nothing compared to the shame of being led out of the room and across the main hall in front of everyone waiting to board their flights. It didn't matter that it was six o'clock in the morning. The place was heaving with people. And every single one of them was staring and pointing and scrabbling for their cameras and phones as our procession filed by. Some were even taking selfies with me in the background. I was mortified. My hands were cuffed. I couldn't even hide my face. All I could think was, *What if my mum sees this?*

As if that was all I had to worry about.

I was aware enough to notice we were being led towards Departures but at the top of a staircase we took a turn into a smaller off-limits corridor where there were interview rooms. Behind the door was a hive of activity. People were running around, squeezing past us down the narrow hallway, gabbling away at top volume. We passed a room containing beds, I guessed for the shift workers, then entered another room opposite. This one didn't look as comfortable. Along one wall was a metal table. Across from it was a desk full of computers. In the middle were three metal chairs screwed into the floor. To one side was a door to a smaller anteroom, on the other was a hole in the ground – what passed for a toilet, in other words. That was pretty common for Peru, but I'd never seen one in a working office before. This was backwards by anybody's standards.

We were hustled over to the metal chairs and our handcuffs were adjusted to lock our wrists to the arm of the chairs. A metal bar attached my feet to the chair legs. It was beyond degrading. I felt like some dangerous dog they needed to contain. They could have done anything to me and I wouldn't have been able to put up a fight.

I suppose that was the idea.

The only good thing about the room was the fact that the crowd hadn't followed us in. We had two guards standing unnervingly close behind us but the rest of the baying mob hadn't made the journey at least.

It didn't take long before a sickening thought entered my head: what would my family think when they found out what had happened to me? The stress of this was overwhelming. Various scenarios played through my mind. Maybe if we were cautioned or let out on bail, there was still a slim chance they might not find out. We had no idea what was going to happen to us or what the official procedure was in such circumstances.

'What do you think they're going to do?' I asked Melissa, who wasn't looking so confident now.

'I have no idea,' she said. 'I can't believe this happened.'

Since I'd awoken at 1.30 a.m. that morning, adrenalin had been pumping through my bloodstream. I was exhausted but also sick with fear. My whole body ached.

'Look,' whispered Melissa after a long silence. 'We'll tell them we were forced to do it – that we didn't have a choice as we'd been threatened with guns. They can't keep us if we stick to that.'

'I'm not sure,' I whispered back. 'How d'you think that's going to work? You thought this would be all right and look where we are now.'

'It's all we've got. Can you think of anything better?'

We were interrupted by a uniformed woman coming in followed by two men carrying our suitcases and hand luggage. The first thing they did was take photos and a video of us standing beside our cases. Then she ordered everything to be put on the long metal bench, uncuffed us and gestured for us to walk over to the table.

I think she was brought in because she had some basic English. Unfortunately, it was nothing we could understand. It took five goes for us to realise she was asking Melissa's name.

'Melissa Reid. Are these your drugs?' Again, it took a while to interpret but we got there.

'No.'

'They are in your case.'

'They are not my drugs. I was kidnapped and forced to carry them by a man with a gun. He would have killed me if I didn't do it.'

There. Our amended version of the truth was out. Neither of us considered the consequences. The woman wrote a few notes then asked me the same questions. Against my better judgement I decided to follow Melissa's lead.

We sat down again, and two men started carving up our belongings. Every inch was gone over with a fine-toothed comb. They took everything out and laid it on the table. I had two pairs of pants, some spare shorts, a top and a bikini. That was it. Oh, and seventeen bags of high-grade narcotics.

The process was very thorough. After about an hour, the woman was satisfied they'd discovered everything, so she went to the other room and beckoned me to follow. As soon as I was through the door, she began unbuttoning my jeans.

'What are you doing?' I shrieked.

She looked annoyed and barked something in Spanish. Two other women came running in. My leather jacket wasn't exactly Dolce & Gabbana but it was mine. When they tried to wrestle that off me, I protested but I was never going to win. My jeans and underwear proved trickier to peel off, but I was outnumbered three to one. There were also two armed men barely three feet away on the other side of the open door. Resistance was futile.

I thought the walk of shame through the departure hall was as low as I could go. Standing there butt naked with an open door to another office took the humiliation to new depths. I couldn't look anyone in the eye. Luckily, only Melissa was actually facing me. The computer operators had their sides to me, but they only had to turn ninety degrees and I was exposed. There was no privacy.

Which again was intentional.

While the boss lady stood back, her two henchwomen walked around me like I was a museum exhibit. They studied every inch, really, really closely. I hated it. I closed my eyes. Maybe if I couldn't see them they wouldn't be able to see me. That's how desperate my thinking was.

The constant Spanish continued then one of them tapped my arm. I opened my eyes and saw one of the women demonstrating touching her toes. Without a word of English, she made it clear that's what I had to do.

Naked.

I said, 'There is no way I'm doing that.'

The woman mimed it again. This time she made it clear I had to cough at the same time as touching my toes. There was no use fighting. I took a deep breath and tipped reluctantly forwards. When they'd finished their search I scrambled into my clothes as quickly as possible.

The leader came over. 'Friend, friend,' was all I could understand but the way she was pointing towards Melissa I guessed she wanted her to do the same. While Melissa was being told to bend over, I had to watch while my jacket and shoes were torn off, cut open and searched like all my other possessions. I was left handcuffed top to toe, barefoot and cold.

No one in the room, at the computers or guarding us seemed to speak English. Or they weren't prepared to. I kept asking, 'What's going on?' but nothing came back. I didn't even know the time. We'd been caught around 5.10 a.m. So many traumatic things were going on I had no idea how long any of it had taken. And no one was willing to tell me.

When Melissa was thrown back in, I thought we'd get answers. Actually, we got the opposite. Everyone apart from one guard left the room. And that's how it stayed for ages. It was horrible. I was so restless. You can get twitchy enough sitting on a comfy sofa watching TV. Tied by your hands and feet to a steel chair for hour after hour was another level of suffering, mentally as much as anything.

Knowing I couldn't move got me all angsty and panicky. My breathing became shallow. We'd had no food, no water, nothing. At one point a bunch of guards came into the room and ate their lunches. We sat there drooling. We had headaches from hunger. My shoes were so cut up they were good for nothing and my precious jacket was in tatters. Whichever way you looked at it, there was no way out.

We spoke quietly about the kidnap story and agreed we'd tell it exactly as it happened but add that we were forced to do it by guys with guns. It wasn't such a stretch of reality. We'd found guns in the house in Palma . . . who's to say we wouldn't have really been threatened if we'd backed out? Right now, all I could think about was my family discovering what had gone on. The news would break them.

I don't know how much time passed but I became aware of Melissa crying. There's something about tears that triggers a reaction in you. If she'd listened to me we wouldn't have gone through with the whole stupid plan. But tears were tears.

'Come on,' I said. 'We need to get through this.'

'How?' she sobbed. 'We're going to prison. We're going to rot in this fucking country.'

I tried to prevent that thought from taking root in my sleep-deprived brain. I knew in my gut we were in deep trouble. We wouldn't get a slap on the wrist as though we'd got caught in possession at a beach party. We were drug smugglers. *International* drug smugglers. And not very good ones at that.

'Well, the British Embassy has to get involved, doesn't it?' I ventured. 'Isn't that their job? When was the last time you heard of girls going to prison over here?'

That was desperation talking. A week earlier I didn't even know the country existed. What did I know about their prison history?

'And we haven't been charged yet,' I continued, feebly clinging onto the hope that all was not lost.

'We haven't even seen any police,' said Melissa. 'All these idiots are just security.'

Now it was my turn to cry.

*

It must have been one or two o'clock in the afternoon when there was some movement in the corridor at last. I wasn't sure whether I preferred being ignored over being charged, but in the end I got neither. We'd been there so long other suspects were being wheeled through. There was some kind of fiesta going on that day as well, just to add to the surreal horror of everything, but the two of us sat in shocked silence.

A pretty dark-haired girl was the next one in. She was local-looking, certainly Hispanic. She was shoved into the chair next to Melissa and, because of the lack of handcuffs, they were tied together. The girl's suitcase was up on the table, just where ours had been, and the same mob of security officers came in to cut it apart while dozens of others squeezed round to watch the results.

After catching me and Melissa, they thought they were on a roll.

But they tore back the lid and just stared. Inside were clothes, shoes, toiletries – but no drugs. There was shouting – there was always shouting, happy or sad – then after ages of them turfing everything out, one of them produced a knife and slit the fabric around the inside of the case.

Bingo.

Dozens of packets fell out. The officers started celebrating then one of them turned towards us and nodded for the girl to go into the room to be searched.

I had no interest in seeing this poor woman be manhandled but I couldn't help but have half an eye on the room, just to see everything was above board. When she resisted undressing, I felt for her. We'd all been there. Except when her clothes fell to the floor, I could see her reason was different.

'Christ, Melissa, it's a guy!'

I never saw that coming. Neither did the guards. Two of the women shot out and started yelling for male officers to come down. The person was dressed like a woman, had jeans and boots on in female styles, ladies' lingerie and full-on make-up. There was only one obvious giveaway.

The distraction was quite welcome but soon enough my thoughts were only on myself. It was about four o'clock, some eleven hours after we'd arrived, and I felt that unmistakable sensation of my period coming on. Enduring it chained to a metal seat was going to be hell. It would be even worse if I didn't get some sanitary products.

I tried to get the attention of one of the women who'd done the searches. Eventually one came in but no manner of pronunciation was going to help her comprehend the word 'tampon'. I was getting really stressed, worried I was going be in a mess. I tried doing some hand signals to show I needed the bathroom but they fell on blind eyes. In the end, I basically had to mime inserting the thing in myself. Oh, she understood then all right. She called out to the corridor and a bunch of guys came laughing hysterically, pointing at me and even taking selfies with me while they mimicked my actions.

'Why is this funny to you? You're all despicable!' I was crying my eyes out.

The laughter only subsided when a new guy came in. I guessed he was their superior the way everyone drifted back to their jobs. He had a smattering of English, so I told him what I needed and he said he'd buy them for me if I had any money. There was a €50 note that had been in my case. In local money it equated to around 250 Peruvian soles, there being about five soles to the euro. A box of Tampax should have been around fifteen soles – but when he returned an hour later there was no change. He shrugged and wouldn't hand over the box until I agreed to shut up.

'Okay,' I said, 'now let me go to the toilet.'

He uncuffed me and summoned two women. I expected to have to squat over the hole in the same room, but they took me to a cubicle with a Western toilet and even a door – not that I was allowed to close it. One of the women came into the cubicle with me. I tried to shove her out, but she was stronger than any man I'd met, Michael included. She stood her ground, shook her head and called for her mate. Now I had two of them in there, one wedged between my knees and the wall and the other directly in front.

After everything I'd been through, I was tired of the fighting. I just closed my eyes and went about my business pretending they weren't there. But I didn't even get any peace when it was over. I went to flush the toilet and the strong woman grabbed my arms and dragged me out of the stall so her friend could check nothing untoward was in the bowl – and nothing was in me. I understand they had a job to do, but it's so sickening to remember. I was that exhausted and that cried-out I just let it happen.

On the way back to the room I tried to ask when we were going to be released or charged. The women either didn't understand or didn't want to. They cuffed me and wandered off without a word. It didn't seem to matter to them that we hadn't drunk or eaten anything since breakfast. As for sleep, the chairs and binds made that impossible. Melissa had the added problem of being lassoed to the transwoman.

I hoped we'd be processed before the shift changed for the night. But nine o'clock came and we were still there, ignored, and our arresting guards were long gone. The ones who replaced them didn't even seem to notice we were there. There was a football game on a TV somewhere, by the sounds of it, so all eyes were on that. I didn't see a soul until two the next morning. Twenty-one hours after we'd arrived at the airport.

Sleep deprivation does crazy things to your brain. I started thinking about prison and dying in there. Then I started thinking about what I was going to eat when I got out. That was a mistake. As two became three and three became four, my stomach was going crazy with hunger. My tongue was dry and smooth as sandpaper. More than anything, I desperately craved a cigarette.

I was going stir crazy when suddenly a guy appeared at the door and unchained us all.

'What's going on?' I demanded through bleary eyes.

'Police,' was the only answer I got.

We were dragged to our feet. I tried to put my shoes back on but they were ruined by the knife cuts during the search of my stuff, so I opted for bare feet. We were led out into the main hall, cuffed just by our hands, then via a circuitous route we ended up in the staff car park. It was basically a dirt bowl, a desert. Any tarmac there once was had been buried under years of dust. There wasn't a clean vehicle to be seen.

Eventually a five-seater car swung around the corner. Our guard was driving but there were another four of his colleagues already in there – and it was only a five-seater. Somehow six of us squeezed onto the back seat, with two up front. I just hoped we weren't going far – particularly as the female guard in the passenger seat seemed hellbent on playing the same Bruno Mars song on repeat the entire journey.

About thirty minutes later we passed a fast-food joint that was open. I was half dead at the time but at the sight of that I knew I could eat a horse.

'Please stop, please stop!' I yelled.

The driver who spoke English said, 'Why?'

'We're hungry. We haven't eaten. We need food.'

'Not our problem,' he said.

'Come on, and I really need a cigarette as well.'

'Okay, then sing,' said the female guard in the front. 'Sing Bruno for me.'

'I'm not singing that crap,' I said.

'Then no cigarettes. No food.'

Just when you think these people can't get any more cruel. I'd already had selfies taken with people miming inserting a tampon, but this was a new level of crazy.

'Okay, okay,' I said, 'turn the van around and I'll sing.'

And that's what I did. To this day I cannot abide the sound of Bruno Mars' 'Lazy Song'. Because that's what I had to belt out. I really did have to sing for my supper – and a cigarette. And all the while the whole car was rocking with guards laughing. Even the transwoman joined in, the cow. But it worked. We pulled up next to the restaurant and the driver said, 'You have money?'

Shit. I didn't. His boss had wiped me out. Luckily, Melissa still had her €50 so she stumped up the cash.

'That should feed everyone.'

Here we go again . . . At least it wasn't my money being robbed this time.

It was so good to feel the cigarette on my lips. It felt even better to be standing outside the car in the night air. There was dust everywhere, in my hair and in my mouth, but the brief sense of freedom made it worthwhile. I'd have felt differently without my jacket. It was as uncomfortable as hell with its hacked lining but without it I'd have frozen in the winter temperatures. After the day I'd had, though, it could have been arctic conditions and I would not have swapped it for that awful, awful room in the airport.

When our food arrived, I was ordered back into the car and had to eat my fried chicken and chips perched on someone's lap. It was so stupid. We didn't even drive anywhere. Nothing the security people did seemed to make any sense to me. But eventually we got going again and an hour later we pulled up outside a large, dark building.

'Where are we?' I said.

The driver looked at me with what seemed like pity in his eyes.

'This is police station,' he said. 'You stay here now.'

CHAPTER EIGHT

SAY IT WAS HER

I didn't have a clue where we were. Somewhere in Lima, I guessed, from the journey time. What I did know was that we'd been up twenty-six hours and I was ready to collapse.

We were dropped off at a large, grim-looking building surrounded by armed police. There was a queue outside. The airport security woman marched me, Melissa and the transwoman past everyone and led us into a waiting room. We were still handcuffed by our wrists and ankles, so movement was slow and painful. We must have sat there thirty minutes. During that time, the men and women who had been on their feet, queuing for God knows how long, began filtering in. They didn't look too happy to be there and they certainly weren't offering us the hand of friendship.

Forty minutes of trying not to make eye contact later, I was summoned into a white room. Inside was a man in a long white doctor's coat. The good news was he spoke English. The bad news was what he said: 'Stand over there and take off your clothes.'

It wasn't a request; it was an instruction. He didn't even look to check I did it. When he turned round, and I was still fully dressed in my tatty jacket and jeans, he looked confused, frustrated, then mad.

'Clothes. Off. Now!'

'No way,' I said. 'You're a man.'

'Remove your clothes or they will be removed.'

'Okay,' I said, 'but I want my friend here.' I'd never called Melissa that before. I certainly hadn't thought of her as one up until that point.

'Fine,' the doctor said, and instructed the guard to fetch Melissa. Lucky her, she was then ordered to strip as well. I was worried that we'd be made to bend over again, like in the demeaning airport search, but thankfully he only needed to check us for tattoos, signs of self-harm, cuts and bruising etc. Satisfied we weren't injured, heroin addicts, or hardened criminals with prison tattoos, we were brusquely dismissed.

We passed that hurdle and were cuffed again and led out past the glaring line to our companions in the car. Then we drove through some gates and down towards another intimidating structure, housing what they called the Dirandro – the narcotics division of the Peruvian National Police. At least I now had some idea of the sort of criminals I'd be encountering. The worst of the worst. People one step down from rapists and killers.

Oh my God. People like me.

For a police station it was okay compared to where we had been kept in the airport. They had a seating area, there was a snack kiosk, even a sofa in the waiting room, which looked very inviting.

I said to the officer escorting us, 'Is this where we're going to stay?'

The guy laughed and said, 'Yes.' So I sat down on the couch, closed my eyes and willed on sleep. I'd have dropped off sooner but the officers started banging on an office door, yelling at someone to wake up. I didn't care. I was out for the count. I had twenty-seven hours of being awake to make up for.

I was woken – I don't know how much later – by a guy coming out of the office shouting. Through tired eyes I saw he was half-dressed with one boot on and his T-shirt hanging out, desperately scrabbling to get his act together at five in the morning. The way he was complaining, it looked like he wasn't used to visitors at this time. Of course, when one guard shouts the others come running thinking there's a breakout going on. We were suddenly surrounded by armed police yelling, 'Get up, get up! Let's go, let's go!'

Which we did. But why? I thought they said this was our final stop. How wrong I was. We were shuffled along a corridor, ankles still bound, the clanking metal echoing down the hall as we moved. They communicated only by pointing, either with their arms or their guns. They led us to a staircase and indicated we had to go down. It was pitch-black and terrifying. Like looking down into the jaws of hell.

Even in daylight I'd have struggled. I could barely get one step down without the chain around my ankles pulling the other foot. I didn't know at the time, but they were only allowed to chain the ankles of male prisoners. It was so dark I couldn't see where I was treading or how far I had to reach. Each movement was a step into the unknown and, in my case, a barefoot one. I had no idea what I'd be treading on next. Clinging onto the metal banister only made the exercise worse because both hands were cuffed together. But there was no way I was letting go. One slight miscalculation and I'd be down the stairs into whatever unknown hell lay at the bottom.

We inched our way down. The only sounds were our occasional gasps, heavy breathing from the guards and the eerie echoed clanking of our chains as they hit the steel handrail. And still I couldn't make out anything in the darkness. After what seemed like an eternity, I felt my foot touch solid ground.

Now what?

Melissa hobbled noisily down behind me, silhouetted by the faint glow of the upstairs corridor. The transwoman had been left with the doctor. It was just us and however many guards in the darkness. Instinctively, I edged closer to Melissa. At that moment she was my best friend in the whole world.

'Where are we?' I said.

'I don't know. But it doesn't feel right.'

We waited for the guards to give an instruction. We waited, and waited, and waited – and then suddenly the whole place was bathed in light. It sickened me to know they could've done that earlier. I could have broken my neck coming down those stairs. The three guards laughed. It was all a joke to them. What kind of people were in charge of us?

We were standing in front of a large black iron door. It couldn't have been more sinister if it had Hannibal Lecter's name written on it. One of the guards produced a giant key and heaved it open. On the other side was a large, gloomy corridor. Like the stairs, everything appeared to be made of concrete and metal. To the side there were gates, metal railings everywhere, then to the right an office. A couple of policemen were huddled round a television perched on a table. They didn't look up as we dragged ourselves in. In the next room half a dozen more men were asleep. I felt really insignificant, like we didn't matter to these people.

'Can I use the toilet?' I said to one of our chaperones.

He stared blankly back.

'*Servicios*,' Melissa translated.

He grunted, uncuffed me, and pointed to a door. I went inside and pulled my pants down when suddenly the door was kicked open. This woman, maybe late fifties, with glasses and dark hair, was screaming at me in Spanish. Mid-flow on a metal toilet you never feel more vulnerable. She just yelled and yelled. I didn't know what I'd done but she wasn't happy.

I tried to push her out, but she stood firm, ranting and raving. She didn't leave, so I had to finish up in front of her. I returned to the room and the guard who'd let me go in there was grinning. Whatever I'd done wrong, he knew about it. I felt wretched.

'Can I smoke?' I asked tentatively.

Nothing.

I mimed a cigarette and he nodded. Obviously I wasn't allowed to carry matches so I held out my cigarette, from the pack I'd had to humiliate myself to get, and mimed lighting it. He reached into his pocket and pulled out a giant lighter. I went to take it but he shook his head. He would do it. I leaned in. He pulled his hand back so I leaned further in, off balance now. Then he flicked the dial and this blast of fire shot up my face. I nearly lost my eyebrows. I let out a sound of alarm but the dickhead just laughed again. I wanted to cry.

Melissa managed to use the bathroom without offending the woman. When she came out the guards told us to get up. One of them, the dickhead, snatched my cigarette and threw it on the floor.

'*No fuma,*' he said.

His mates funnelled us into a hallway bathed in darkness. One of them hit a switch and my heart sank. We were standing in front of a line of eight jail cells. That's when it hit me.

We're actually going to be locked up.

The magnitude of our problem was finally hitting home. Being handcuffed was one thing. At least we'd been in an office with normal people. That was about to change. Who knew what – or who – lay on the other side of those walls.

The cell doors were solid black metal and very, very heavy. It took all the guard's strength to get the door to one of them open. It groaned and creaked as it swung back. When it was fully open, we were ushered inside. The guards didn't follow; they didn't tell us anything, they didn't show us anything. The second we were over the threshold, the door slammed shut, and we were plunged into darkness.

I thought I was going to wet myself. Then a little panel in the door was pulled back and a small ray of light cut through. I could see the room was tiny, and there were two cement shelves sticking out of the cement wall.

'I think those are meant to be beds,' I said.

'Well, I'm taking the bottom one,' Melissa said and threw herself on it.

There was no bed linen, not even a mattress. I was freezing but I had to take my jacket off to use it as a pillow. Then my feet got so cold I had to wrap my jacket around them. My head was buzzing. There were so many things I wanted to say to Melissa, so many questions to ask, starting with, 'What happened? What went wrong? I thought you said we wouldn't get caught.' I was so exhausted, but this was the first time we'd been alone, away from prying ears.

'Melissa,' I said, 'do you think we were set up?'

She made a grunting sound.

'Because they knew, I swear it, they knew who we were and what we were doing the second we stepped in that airport.'

She didn't say anything.

'Come on, you've got to admit it. We've been hung out to dry.'

Still nothing.

'Melissa, come on, you can't keep defending them.' She made another noise and I realised she hadn't heard a word. She was sound asleep. I think she passed out the second she lay down.

I managed to sleep, but I don't know how long I slept for. I woke up in the pitch black, shivering. I had no idea what time it was and it took me a few moments to remember where I was. When I did I started to cry. As my eyes adjusted to the dark I sensed something. Something ominous. The sliver of light through the door hole was casting shadows against my wall. What of, I didn't know. But they were moving.

I jumped off the bed so fast. My skin was crawling. I felt sick. These things were all over my bed. I could hear them more than see them. I couldn't help it – I started screaming. Melissa woke up and found me hysterical by the door trying to get out. From the other side of the wall came a shout. Not English. Just angry. Then another voice and another.

'Oh my God, where are we?' I said.

Melissa coaxed me back to bed. We agreed to share her bunk. I just wanted the security. I couldn't sleep, not with these creatures above my head. But they weren't only above my head. I was lying against the wall when I saw something trying to get past me. They were cockroaches, about forty or fifty that I could see, each about two or three inches long and all of them scurrying around my legs. I couldn't sit up without hitting my head, so I crouched away, hugging my knees crying as quietly as I could.

Neither of us could take our eyes off the bugs. Suddenly, there was shouting from the corridor and the door groaned open. A bunch of men in uniform came in, hollering at us, I guessed, to get up. I was grateful to get away from the cockroaches, so I was out of bed immediately. The floor was so cold on my bare feet. I remembered my jacket, still on my bed.

'Melissa, get my coat, will you?'

'Get it yourself.'

'Come on, please, those cockroaches are all over it.'

'Exactly.'

Eventually she grabbed it and chucked it at me. A dozen cockroaches fell on the floor. All of which made the waiting men laugh. They were trying to talk to us in Spanish. Melissa followed the odd word.

'I think they want us to confirm our names,' she said. So we did. It seemed the right answer. They gave us sheets of papers to sign and stupidly we did, despite not understanding a word. Then they tried to guide us outside. I could see a dozen or more unsmiling women hovering in the corridor. Not exactly a welcome committee. But I could also see the cockroaches diving into gaps in the cement. It was a decision. We went outside.

The whole corridor was lined with thin mattresses, little more than yoga mats, rolled up against the walls. Standing next to most of them was its proud owner. They couldn't make their minds up whether to stare at us or look away and pretend we didn't matter. A few mattresses at the end of the wall were unguarded.

'You have . . .' said a young Asian woman, pointing to the mattresses. 'You have. Women gone.'

'I think she says we can sleep on these,' I said. 'Although it wouldn't be the first time someone's played a joke in here.'

The woman introduced herself as Celine. Her English wasn't great but we grew to understand it. She'd been arrested on drugs charges a few days earlier. She was waiting to be charged and processed. The average time, she said, was fifteen days. She also said not to tell the police anything. They couldn't be trusted. That much I could agree with. Then there was a banging on the main door and everyone jumped up.

'*Desayuno*,' Celine said. 'Breakfast.'

We followed everyone else into a queue. When we got to the front the guard tried to serve us food.

'I need a plate,' I said. I made a shape with my hands. 'P-l-a-t-e.'

He pointed to everyone else and made the same shape. They were all holding their own plastic bowls or plates. Melissa and I had nothing.

He pointed to some stale-looking bread as if to say, 'That's all you're having, then.' As I picked up a slice another man appeared with two cups. The guard filled them with a scoop of watery porridge. It was horrible. But it was the closest thing to hydration I'd get all day.

The bathroom area was basically a hole in the grate with a small jug next to it, and a sink. If you wanted a shower you used the jug to pour water over yourself. When you used the hole to go to the toilet, you used the jug to wash it away. I tried the tap but it was off. Celine explained the water was only on for a brief moment every morning, hence the jug.

'What do we drink?'

Again, Celine pointed to the jug.

'You're kidding me? We can't drink that. It's filthy. And there's hardly any of it.'

She shrugged.

'Why don't we have water all day?' I asked. 'Is there a shortage? I mean, I know we're in jail, but still.'

Celine shrugged again. 'I think they just like to mess with us.' After the lighter and the toilet episode the night before, that sounded about right.

'They're dickheads,' I said.

'What is "dickhead"?' Celine asked. I had fun telling her.

Everything was so new my eyes were like saucers. There wasn't an inch of the squalor I didn't study. All the while Celine was running her commentary. What she lacked in vocabulary she made up for in enthusiasm. The only time she piped down was when we got close to some of the other women.

They weren't a particularly attractive bunch and there wasn't a smile between them. One of them, a pregnant woman holding a lit cigarette, had the angriest face I'd ever seen on anyone.

'What's her problem?' I said.

Celine kept on walking. 'Not good people,' she hissed. 'Not good. Walk.'

For a moment our tour guide looked scared. I realised she was getting as much out of being with us as we were with her. It was all about alliances.

When we were out of earshot, I said, 'That pregnant woman – she was smoking.'

'Yes, yes,' Celine said. 'Very bad.'

'No – I mean, yes, she shouldn't be smoking because she's pregnant, but where did she get her cigarettes from? I didn't think it was allowed down here.'

Celine rolled her eyes. 'The guards,' she said. 'They make deals.' What I would have given for a smoke that second.

'What kind of deals?' I asked. 'I've got nothing to trade.'

'You have this,' Celine said, and mimed a circle around my mouth. 'You use this, you get what you want.' It took a couple of seconds for the meaning to sink in.

'They give the guards blowjobs for cigarettes? Oh my God. Melissa, are you hearing this?'

She shrugged. 'Nothing would surprise me in this place.'

*

In the afternoon we were taken upstairs to a small office. It wasn't the Ritz but anything was better than being downstairs. It even had a window. More than that, it had a bottle of water on the table. Hopefully we'd get some. I hadn't drunk anything since the slop at breakfast.

This was Thursday. We'd been incarcerated since the wee hours of Wednesday with not a soul asking us anything other than our names – and to take our clothes off. Luckily, it was only the names again this time. There was a man and a woman. They asked Melissa first, in Spanish, what her name was.

She replied, 'Melissa Reid.'

'Ah,' the man said, '*Habla español?*'

She said, 'No.'

He repeated his question. Melissa repeated her reply.

Then he started getting angry. 'Don't lie to me, girl,' he said in English. 'How did you understand my question if you don't speak Spanish? Answer that.'

Backwards and forwards they went, him yelling yes, her yelling no. Eventually she jumped up and screamed right in his face, 'I don't fucking speak Spanish!' The cop looked like he wanted to hit her. Instead he yelled at another officer who grabbed Melissa and dragged her out of the room. I didn't budge. They'd have to carry me out to get me to go back downstairs.

The policeman asked me in English whether I spoke his language. I shook my head, anxious he wouldn't believe me. He was tired of that game now so he continued in broken English, explaining he was in charge of our case until a translator came in to help. The translator spoke even worse English than he did but between them they got their message across.

Then the awkward questions came.

He was clearly going to try and get two confessions out of us.

But then a little voice in my head said, 'What if he's just really angry that she shouted at him? What if he's out to get her? You need to distance yourself from her, pronto.'

'Come on, Michaella, just say it was her,' the policeman said. 'You know if I gave her this choice, she would say it was you.'

That decided it. He was playing us, I was sure. The guy wasn't going to throw away half of an open-and-shut case just like that. We'd already told the airport police that we'd been forced at gunpoint into doing it. If I changed stories now it would look bad, so I kept refusing to go along with his scheme and, for the second time that morning, he got frustrated.

'Okay,' he said, 'maybe you will think more clearly downstairs.'

I was escorted back into the gloomy, smelly pit. A dozen pairs of eyes studied me as I came down the stairs. They all turned away as I walked past. They weren't interested in me. I was nothing to them.

I found Melissa in our cell and relayed the policeman's offer. I wanted to check whether she'd been given the same deal. From the way she hit the roof I guessed she hadn't. She tore out to the stairs and tried to get up them but the guards wouldn't let her pass. She looked demented, she was screaming for the policeman to come down and explain himself. It was futile. Even if the policeman could understand her, the walls and doors were that thick there was no way she could be heard.

I realised why she was so angry: if I'd taken the cop up on his offer, she'd be screwed. As it was, I'd turned him down. But what if I hadn't?

'Celine was right,' she said. 'You can't trust them. They're just trying to split us up. Promise me you'll never make a deal like that. They'll just get you as well.'

'I know. It's horrendous,' I said. She was right. We couldn't trust anyone. We shouldn't have trusted anyone from the beginning – starting with Davey and Mateo. I went over the same questions I'd wanted to ask her the previous night, when she'd crashed out.

'It was just bad luck,' she said. 'Mateo wouldn't have done that.'

'But they knew, I'm telling you. They were waiting for us.'

'I don't know how much we were carrying but it had to be worth a million plus.'

'Easily,' I agreed.

'So why on God's earth would Mateo chuck that away and let us get captured?'

I couldn't explain. It just felt wrong. Wrong, wrong, wrong. Like everything in my life so far. When was my luck going to change? Not any time soon, it turned out.

We'd only noticed after we'd returned to our cell that the nice mattresses had vanished. The remains of a single torn-up one had been left in their place. Hideous as it was, made of scratchy fibreglass material, neither of us wanted to sleep without it. Climbing up onto the top bunk had shredded my jeans so much that I looked like a tramp, so we shared Melissa's bed. If anything, the cockroach party was louder than ever but knowing Melissa was right next to me allowed me to get some sleep.

*

We were woken at 5.45 a.m. again with the guards taking our names. They did this roll call at the start and end of each shift to make sure everyone was where they were supposed to be. After breakfast there was a ridiculous commotion as all the guards started shouting. There was no alarm, so I didn't think it was a fire. We found Celine.

'What's going on?' I said.

'I don't know. But they want everyone upstairs.'

We all had to line up and be handcuffed, then we were led up towards the holy grail of daylight. I was really surprised to see a load of men already there – probably sixty to our twelve. From the way some of them called across to the women they were either related or wanted to be. Celine pointed out one group of three generations of the same family, all busted when their house got raided and a shitload of drugs were found.

'How long will they be here?'

'Fifteen days,' Celine said. 'Same as everyone. I've been here a week. I haven't even been charged yet.'

It transpired the evacuation was for our own good. The entire downstairs was being fumigated. Good news for us, bad news for the cockroaches. The people doing it had thick boiler suits on – which was the only way they would enter the cells we'd been expected to sleep in. Everything I'd come to expect about human rights in

Europe did not apply in the police holding cells of the Peruvian justice system.

I spotted a chair over by one of the police desks. No one was using it so I plonked myself down. The seat was warm and the computer was on – clearly someone would be returning soon. A policewoman walked over, and I thought, *This is it.* She just smiled and sat down at the adjacent workstation. She didn't throw me out. On the contrary, she noticed me looking at the computer and said, 'Do you want to use it?'

'What?' I said, unable to process my good fortune. 'I mean, yes, please.'

'What do you want? Facebook?'

'Wow, that would be brilliant.'

She called up the page and I logged in.

'One rule,' she said, 'no talking.'

'Deal.'

I couldn't believe my luck. This was the single nicest thing anyone had done for me since I left Ibiza – *God, when was it?* – thirteen days ago. I was still doing the maths as my profile page loaded. I couldn't say I'd enjoyed a single one of those days. What I could say was that I'd barely thought about anything other than my family and friends back home. Judging from my Facebook page, they'd clearly been thinking about me too.

There were hundreds and hundreds of messages on there from my sisters, my brothers, my mum and my friends, all worried sick that I hadn't been seen for nearly a fortnight. I felt ill as I read through them. They hadn't a clue where I was. I'd told them Barcelona but they'd had no word from me in nearly two weeks.

I was the worst daughter in the world. The worst sister, the worst friend, the worst everything. Reading those messages was brutal. The first ones had arrived when I was still in Palma. They were casual, like, 'Hey, just checking you're okay.' Then, as the days had passed and I hadn't replied, they'd got more and more agitated. At one point my mother put an appeal on there for information about me. Then another one. Then another one.

And then she said she'd called the police.

There were links to newspaper articles about me, rewards offered, and ever more emotional pleas for me just to get in touch. I had been hoping that when I finally did get back in touch with my family, I could tell them I'd decided to go backpacking. They need never know what had really happened. That option was fading by the minute.

Oh, the shame. I couldn't bear to read it. But I had to. I had to know what they'd suffered. What I'd caused. Hands over my eyes, I peeped through gaps between my fingers, like watching a horror film. My heart was in my mouth. Every word made me feel more wretched. *I'd done this to them. Me. I'd caused all this pain. And for what? To earn a few quid.* Then I realised: it's only going to get worse.

If I didn't get home before they discovered I was in a police station my mother would die, I was convinced of it. I'd hurt her already. Hearing about the drugs would break her heart. If I actually went to prison it would finish her off completely.

Melissa had been in her own world but came over when she noticed my distress. When she saw I was online she cranked into action. When she read the notices she said, 'You have to reply. Update your status.'

'I can't,' I whispered. 'I don't want them to know where we are.'

'They're going to find out soon enough.'

'Yeah, but we haven't even been charged. What if they let us go? My mum will never have to hear about this.'

'Well, you've got to tell them something. They're going mental over there.'

'The policewoman said I wasn't allowed to talk on here. I think that means typing as well.'

'She may have told *you* not to talk but she's said nothing to me. Shove over.'

She squeezed onto the chair and started typing. It was a cursory message: 'Hey everyone, sorry for the silence. I've been through some crap but I'm okay now.' It didn't read like me at all but at least it should calm a few people down, allay a few fears.

All it did was make my family's anguish worse.

CHAPTER NINE

OUTSIDE MY REMIT

We were pulled away from the computers after that and spent the next couple of hours hanging around upstairs while the fumigation continued. But maybe our luck was about to turn. Melissa was being called to another room for something that sounded official.

'What's that for?' I asked.

'No idea – but you're coming, right?'

Of course, I said yes. Anything to escape the infernal boredom of hanging around doing nothing. We were shown into an office where a woman in a smart suit was waiting.

'Melissa?' she said, offering her hand.

'Yes. And you are?'

'I'm from the British Embassy. We understand you're in a spot of bother.'

'You could say that.'

They sat opposite each other across a desk. The only other chair in the room was five or six feet away, by the wall, so I sat there. They started chatting. Just pleasantries. I was happy to eavesdrop. It was so refreshing to hear a conversation in English – especially one that wasn't threatening. Eventually, though, I had to leap in.

'Excuse me,' I said, 'how do you know about us?'

The woman paused. Checked her notes.

'A flag came up via Interpol,' she said. 'Your families are very worried.'

That made sense.

'Yeah,' I said, 'but how did you know where we were?'

'You were arrested at Jorge Chávez Airport. Whenever a British national is arrested abroad, the UK embassy has to be informed and . . .' she paused for dramatic effect. 'Here I am.'

In a way it was reassuring that such protocol existed; on the other hand, if the embassy knew I was in jail, then my family would also know soon enough.

Melissa and the envoy spoke for I don't know how long. I was in a fug, too busy worrying what my family would be thinking. Perhaps it could still all be explained as a terrible mistake. We hadn't been charged or convicted yet. Whatever, it was unlikely I could use my cover story of going backpacking.

When I came out of my own thoughts, my entire focus was on the table. Or, more accurately, what was on it. Standing proud just in front of Melissa was a bottle of water. Clear, still, unpolluted water. Two days into this hellhole and I'd had nothing but slurry for breakfast and pond water for hydration. My throat felt like sandpaper. We were in midwinter but I'd never known thirst like it.

As far as I could tell Melissa was relaying the same 'we were held at gunpoint' story that she'd said at the airport. It was embarrassing but at least our stories would be on the same page.

The meeting concluded with the envoy giving Melissa a bag of crackers and promising to do everything in her power to alleviate any suffering in the police holding facility and to expedite her release. She'd get access to proper lawyers, proper specialists and constant supervision. South American prisons could, she admitted, cut the occasional human rights corner. The envoy would also act as a conduit between Melissa and her family. It was great news. Fantastic news. And for me as well. We were both as guilty or as innocent as each other. The same rules applied to the both of us. Or so I thought.

Melissa left the room after her interview and I moved over to her chair. I couldn't take my eyes off the bottle of water in front of the embassy woman.

'You're Michaella?' she said.

'I am. I overheard most of what you said to Melissa, so you don't need to repeat yourself.'

'Actually,' she said, 'there's a bit of a problem there.'

'How so? We were arrested together.'

'Yes, but I work for the British Embassy.'

'I know. And I'm British.'

'Not according to your passport.'

'What?'

'Your passport was issued by Eire. That's outside the UK's jurisdiction, as you know.'

'Are you kidding me? I live in Northern Ireland. The last time I checked that was as British as London.'

'Yes,' she said slowly like she was talking to a child, 'but that's not where you acquired your passport. And in these matters that is all we have to go on.'

'I only got an Irish passport because it was quicker!'

'Well, that's not for me to comment on. But if you had waited for a British passport I could offer you legal and some financial assistance. As you didn't, I can't.'

'What can you offer me?' I said, just shy of getting hysterical.

'Um . . .'

'You gave Melissa a box of biscuits and a bottle of water. Can I at least get those?' She instinctively reached out for the bottle in front of her.

'Again, I apologise. If it were up to me . . .'

I nearly tipped the whole table over as I stood up. I couldn't believe it. I wasn't even worth the price of a cracker or a bottle of Evian. I'd never felt so low. It was like Superman swooping in to save a family from a burning building then taking one look at you and going, 'Er, no, not you, you're not one of us.'

I fled the office in tears.

Before I had time to reflect on the unfairness of everything, we were summoned by the dodgy cop who'd tried to get me to lie about Melissa. He led us out of the police station and into a waiting car. Melissa managed to bite her tongue and the cop didn't speak except to say we were being processed. I had a face like thunder.

'Whoa, what's up?' said Melissa.

'That embassy bitch says I'm not British, so she won't help me.'

'We're in the same boat, then,' Melissa said, 'because I asked her not to contact my family.'

'Really? Are you out of your mind? Don't you want them to know you're safe?'

She shrugged. 'No. I'm going to wait and see what happens. It's not like I was checking in with them all the time, like you.'

She shut down the conversation and the journey continued in silence. We arrived at another facility in the complex, where our fingerprints and prints of our feet and entire body were taken. All the time this was going on I was brooding on what to tell my family. I was racked with guilt. I had to let them know I was safe, but what twenty-year-old girl wants to call her mum and tell her she's in jail for trying to smuggle cocaine?

When we arrived back at the station the fumigation was finally finishing. I tried not to dwell on the sheer number of cockroaches and other bugs that had needed exterminating. Melissa went back downstairs but I was paralysed with emotion and stayed upstairs in the office with a couple of the cops who had so far been okay to me. After everything that had happened, it was like a dam had burst inside me. I started crying. And then it was uncontrollable. The tears poured out of me until my cheeks were hot and raw.

I was crying about my mum and my family, but also at how stupid I'd been. I'd been so naive. I felt depressed, confused, *abandoned*. The policeman on duty in there must have got the gist of what I was going through, because he let me sit there for a while and cry in relative privacy, separate from the rabble downstairs. I couldn't even wipe my face properly because of the handcuffs. The policeman came over.

'I need to call my family,' I sobbed.

'Family?' he repeated.

'Yes, my family. *Familia*.'

He sighed, then reached into his pocket and handed me two soles.

'What's this?' I asked.

'For family,' he said, and he then led me up a characterless staircase, the sort you would expect to use as an emergency exit. We passed various men in suits going up and down. I was the only woman. And the only one in manacles. We emerged in a corridor featuring a bank of payphones. There was no one else there apart from a guard. The policeman said a few words to the guard, then left without a glance backwards. My hero.

I was a bit overwhelmed. I'd not seen the phones before, but they were on an upper level of the building. I mean, who uses payphones anyway? Despite the old technology, I was so grateful. I grabbed the receiver and – and stopped. I had no idea how to reach the UK. I'd heard about international dialling codes but had no idea what ours was. My mobile had always done all the donkeywork for me.

I looked at the guard. 'UK?' I said.

He shook his head.

I couldn't help it. The tears gushed out again. I was so close to speaking to my family and yet again the opportunity had been snatched from me.

The guard, bless him, was another good soul. He showed me his own mobile and opened Google. He was letting me look up the dialling code. Gingerly, I keyed in the digits and my home number. There was a pause, silence, and then a muted ringing sound. Thank God! At least I'd navigated this far towards being able to make contact. I waited and waited, my heart pounding with anticipation. And then someone picked up.

Juggling the handset and the coins with my cuffed hands, I managed to insert the soles.

'Hello?' said a voice. It was tiny, distant.

'Mum!' I shouted. 'Mum, it's me, Michaella.' There was nothing in response but a muffled sound, and then Samantha came on the line.

'What happened to you? Where are you?' she asked, a huge tone of urgency in her voice.

'I'm so sorry . . .' I paused, as all thoughts of stories of backpacking dissolved. 'I'm in jail.'

'What d'you mean, you're in jail?'

'I'm in Peru. I'm in jail.'

That's all I had time for, as that's when the connection ran out. *Beep. Beep. Beep. Beep. Beep. Beep.*

The sound echoed in my head for ages. I couldn't call back as I didn't have any more money. It was wonderful to hear my mother's tiny hello but why hadn't she said anything? Was she in shock? At least she now knew I was alive. All I wanted to do was to walk out of this nightmare as quickly as possible and get back to her. But because I'd been so stupid that wasn't going to happen. What kind of future lay ahead?

The guard who had looked up the dialling code escorted me back to the office. The tears were still flowing, and I must have looked terrible, because, yet again, the policeman let me sit in the office and gather myself a bit before returning back downstairs. I was lucky these guys were being so nice and not like the officious bullies at airport security.

I sat there for about an hour when the duty cop – whose name label said 'Esteban' – took a break from his computer. He left the room and came back with some snacks from the kiosk. To my utter surprise he handed one to me – a sort-of burger bun with ham and cheese. He must have known how bad the food was in that place.

'Thank you so much,' I wept. And I then remembered a tiny bit of Spanish from Ibiza: '*Gracias.*'

He smiled and, while I had his attention, I pointed at the sandwich: 'Is possible also for my friend?' I still felt some loyalty to Melissa. We were a ramshackle team of two and, although she hadn't exactly shown much emotion, we were in this mess together.

To my surprise, Esteban nodded his head and disappeared for a few minutes, returning with another sandwich that he'd paid for himself. I stuffed it into my jacket pocket and felt some degree of positivity – that I'd managed to call home, that people had shown me kindness, and that I was now going to pass that kindness on to Melissa.

We sat there for a while then Esteban said he needed to go on patrol, which was my cue to return to the cells. When I got back downstairs, Melissa was hanging off the bars. She had wound herself up into a fury. It wasn't the reception I'd been expecting.

'What were you doing up there?' she spat. 'You were ages. Were you stitching me up? Were you selling me out? Were you? Were you?' She was mad, on fire, paranoid. And right up in my face.

'No! Of course not,' I shouted in reply. 'I was upset. I called my mum, that's all. They gave me a few soles to call my family. On a payphone. It was nothing to do with you.'

'Oh, that's nice that you called your family,' she replied, sarcastically.

'I asked you earlier and you said you didn't want to!' I shouted, incredulous. 'Don't get mad at me just cos I spoke to my mum who has been worried sick about me!'

'Why were you so long? What have you been doing in that office? Have you been talking about me to the cops?'

'No, no, your name hasn't even been mentioned, for fuck's sake!'

Backwards and forwards we went. It was a right old-fashioned ding-dong, a slanging match, no question. We were screaming at each other, with all the pent-up blame-game of the past few days pouring out over a one-minute phone call. It was horrible. I hated it. But it was Melissa who backed down first.

'I can't do this,' she said. 'I don't want to see you right now.'

I couldn't argue.

She banged on the door long enough for Esteban and a colleague to arrive.

'I need a different cell,' she said. 'Let me out.'

I wasn't bothered when the door to our block was unbolted and she left. It had been that kind of day. I felt my way over to my bunk. Even in the dark I recognised my bits and pieces around my pillow. I was just about to close my eyes when I remembered the sandwich.

The sandwich I'd begged for Melissa.

I sat bolt upright and reached over to my jacket. There it was, spicy chicken and a wee bit of salad. I'd already eaten my own upstairs. And it was late. But Melissa had really pissed me off.

I opened the wrapper and shoved that sandwich into my face as fast as I could. It was only when I'd finished chewing that I got a grip of myself.

Is this it? I thought. *Is this what I've become? Am I reduced to this sort of behaviour out of spite and revenge?*

As I looked at the crumbs from the sandwich on my pillow I thought, *Yes. Yes, I am. This is me now. This is Michaella 2.0.*

CHAPTER TEN

PLEAD GUILTY

A night's sleep actually did me the world of good, although my family were the first thing I thought of on waking. Had Samantha told my brothers I was in jail? Did Uncle Gene know? Then I remembered the row with Melissa.

My immediate emotions lasted only as long as it took the hardship of the day to kick in. There was nothing edible for breakfast and nothing worth drinking if you didn't want ditch water in your system. On top of that I was sick of my clothes. They honked, really stank. I'd been in the same gear for four days. My body wasn't much better. I'd not seen a shower since our hotel. Celine offered me some face soap for my clothes but what could I wash? I didn't have any replacements. In the end I just did my underwear. It was a start. The torn jeans, ripped jacket and summer top would have to wait. It's not like everyone else didn't stink either.

Just when I thought things couldn't get worse, two girls came by drinking from water bottles. *Clean* water bottles.

'Please,' I said, 'where did you get those?' I pointed to the bottles.

Neither woman looked like she'd had a wash since arriving, maybe not even for a while prior to that. It didn't stop them having attitude.

They looked at me like I was something they'd trodden in. Then they laughed and went to walk off.

'Come on,' I shouted, 'please can I have some water?' Even as I was begging I was reaching out for one of the bottles. The woman holding it smacked my hand away like I was a kid stealing sweets. At least she stopped walking.

'*Agua?*' she said.

'*Agua?* Oh, *agua – si!*'

I watched like a hawk as she unscrewed the top. She held the bottle out towards me. As I went to take it she tipped it upside down. Even before the water hit the floor I had my hands cupped underneath, trying desperately to catch every drop. She wasn't having it. She waved the bottle around, spraying the contents everywhere but near me. When she finished, she chucked the empty bottle at me and laughed. I was so shocked. *Who wastes water in a place like this?*

Melissa appeared. There was an awkward tension at first, but she broke the silence, although she didn't apologise for her outburst the previous evening. She just carried on as normal.

'What's going on?' she asked, looking at the wet floor. She was shocked when I told her. Celine less so.

'They get it from the guards,' she explained.

'Which guards?' I said. 'No guards are giving me water.'

'They will if you pay,' she said. 'And I'm not talking money. There are ways to get everything in here.'

I remembered our first night, when she told us that guards traded cigarettes for blowjobs.

'Maybe there are,' I said, 'but that's a price I won't be paying.'

The rest of the day passed without incident – or water. I couldn't help but notice it everywhere, though. Even the pregnant woman who'd been smoking had a bottle. The idea of someone dropping to her knees in her condition sickened me. If only there was another way to get the odd home comfort or two.

Maybe the universe heard me. Towards evening, a guard clicked his fingers in my direction.

'What?' I said.

'Upstairs. Your boyfriend.'

'My boyfriend is upstairs?' I confirmed.

'Yes. Come.'

I looked at Melissa. 'I don't have a boyfriend.'

'You do now,' she said. 'Let's go.'

For once the guard didn't chain our hands and legs. Whether word had come down the line that we weren't dangerous, or whether the embassy had arranged it, I couldn't say. It was bloody luxury, though, compared to hobbling up with an arm and leg tied behind your back.

We were shown to a meeting room. I couldn't imagine who would be in there waiting. The man inside was no one I'd ever set eyes upon before. And it was certainly not my boyfriend. Not that I let on. Not immediately.

The man stood up, arms out, declaring his delight at seeing me. Except, given Melissa was alongside me, I don't think he was 100 per cent sure which of us was which. So he played it safe, looked between us both, and did just enough to fool the guard into leaving us alone.

All three of us were smiling at each other with forced grins. As soon as we had the room, I said, 'Who the hell are you?'

The guy was maybe double my age, so in no way was he boyfriend material, and dressed in a casual suit. He looked both smart and scruffy at the same time. Behind his chair were half a dozen large bags.

'It's such a pleasure to meet you both,' he said. 'A lot of people are worried about you.'

'Look, I don't know who you are. Who the hell are you and what are you doing here?'

He got straight down to it. He was a journalist from the *Daily Mirror*.

'How'd you find us?' Melissa asked.

'I have my ways,' he said. 'But I think the real question is: what can I do for you?' The way he put it, the whole of Britain had been reading about us. I was horrified. The last thing I wanted was publicity. He showed us a handful of newspaper cuttings as proof. We were big news. Front-page news on some days. And that was when no one had a clue where we were or what we'd been up to.

I was mortified.

'Trust me,' he said, 'I'm giving you the chance to put your side of the story before the lies come out.'

I had no desire to publicise myself. I was ashamed, head to toe, about everything. I didn't want a single person looking in my direction if I could help it.

'Look, nothing bad can come of this,' he said. 'Maybe this will show I'm on your side.' He dragged over one of the bags and pulled out a dozen Mars bars and a couple of boxes of Ferrero Rocher.

'My favourite!' Melissa said about the former, exactly as I was thinking it about the latter. On top of that he had a duvet for each of us – proper ones – a dozen bottles of water, loads of tins and cartons of food and various other bits and pieces. If we'd had an Amazon wish list he'd somehow bought the entire lot.

'I actually brought you a lot more food,' he said. 'But the guards helped themselves to that. Some kind of visitor tax, I think.' I couldn't complain. What had got through the grabbing hands of security was amazing.

'How did you know we liked all this stuff?'

He tapped his nose. 'It's my job to know. So how about your story?'

I looked at the presents. I wasn't sure that talking to a journalist would ever be a good idea but Melissa said I was being silly. We huddled together to whisper to each other while he feigned disinterest.

'Look, I don't want my parents to know either,' she said. 'But if this guy is right, and more reporters are on their way, then we're going to be written about whether we like it or not. We should get our version of events in first before people start making shit up.'

Eventually, I agreed.

Melissa did most of the talking while I dreamed about Ferrero Rocher. She told the story about us being kidnapped at gunpoint, having our passports taken, being forced to become drug mules on pain of death. And I went along with it.

'Is this your story as well?' the reporter asked.

'Yes,' I said. 'That's what happened.'

Sat in that office, with a guy I'd never met before in my life, being asked all manner of questions when all I could think about was how to survive the next twenty-four hours, it's fair to say I didn't think about the consequences of exaggerating our story to the tabloid media. The UK was a long way away. I'd had no help from anyone in an official capacity, and all I wanted was some basic provisions and to know what was going to happen to me. It was so much easier to say yes than to backtrack and tell the truth. We hadn't even been charged yet. And I wasn't about to contradict everything.

He left, pleased as punch with his exclusive, and we struggled downstairs with our booty. There was no doubt every single item would change our lives for the better. There was also no doubt we could never have managed the journey handcuffed and chained. Maybe the guards knew all along.

A lot of the other girls were jealous of our swag, especially the bedding. Not only did we have duvets, there were pillows and blankets, everything you could want for a cold winter night on a slab of concrete. What we'd had to do in exchange for it all was out of my head before I'd even put my duvet down. I'd only been incarcerated a few days, but already the only world that mattered to me was the one below stairs. I looked around at all the other women hardened by the system and a life of hard knocks. I didn't want to become like them. I'd make sure I wouldn't.

*

Sunday began like all the other days: stupid o'clock for the pointless roll call then inedible gruel for breakfast. I went through the motions of queueing with my begging bowl more for the chance to stretch my legs than anything else. I didn't eat though. I just couldn't face it. I went back to my cell and snacked on the goodies left by the man from the *Mirror*.

Mid-morning, things changed a little. Esteban said I was needed upstairs. Melissa was busy with Celine and some others, so I went alone, once again without cuffs. The policewoman who'd logged me onto Facebook was waiting up top.

'You have nice hair,' she said. 'Do mine. And, by the way, my name is Maria.'

I don't know what I was expecting but it wasn't that. She pointed to my hair, which I'd made an attempt to plait, and asked for the same. She plonked herself down and waited for me to get on with it.

'Okay,' I said, as much to myself as her. 'We're doing this, are we?'

I enjoyed it. Concentrating on anything took my mind off the horrific reality I'd fallen into. When we were done, Maria found a mirror and beamed a smile of satisfaction. Then she went out back and beckoned me over. There, awaiting me, was my suitcase. I hadn't seen it since the airport. It was tatty and torn but it looked like my stuff was intact. For the first time since I'd arrived, I could put a pair of fresh pants on.

Melissa's was there as well, so she was summoned up. I told her what had gone on. 'Thank Christ you did a good job,' she laughed. 'If you'd messed up her hair we'd never have got this.'

We went to drag our cases to the stairs but another officer stood in our way. 'Cases stay,' he said.

I looked at Maria, with her freshly plaited hair. She shrugged. 'Evidence,' she said.

It was amazing everything was still there. I put on what clothes I could then tore the packages of cigarettes open and stuffed the individual packs down my trousers. I looked lumpy as hell, so I tied my jacket around my waist then headed for the stairs. As we got there, Maria said, 'Tomorrow you interview. Okay?'

We nodded. It was weird how we hadn't yet been spoken to officially. Anything that moved the process out of the limbo we found ourselves in had to be positive, though. I just wished the conversation could happen when I wasn't smuggling cigarettes in my knickers.

'Listen,' she continued, 'say "guilty", okay? This kidnap story . . . not good. Police not like this.'

'But . . .' I went to contradict her, but Melissa elbowed me in the ribs.

'Thanks,' she said, 'you're really kind', and she dragged me towards the stairs.

Esteban escorted us down. Waiting for us at the bottom was the old witch who'd searched us on our first day. She made it clear she was going to do it again. I desperately shifted the cigarette packs around my trousers and held my breath while she patted me down. I swear she was only interested in being able to prove she had power over us. This time she seemed satisfied enough and waved us off.

Esteban watched it all. When the woman was out of earshot he said, 'You need a light?'

'Oh my God, do you have one?'

I was so grateful. He produced a lighter and flicked the flame. Life was improving in very small ways. We continued the short walk past the other cells to our room. Esteban never left our side. When we were outside he put his hand on my shoulder and said, 'You say "guilty",' and repeated, almost word for word what our friend upstairs had said. 'You say "guilty" or,' he said – and then he made a cutting motion across his throat. 'Everyone guilty who want to live.'

That put a dampener on the day. 'No way,' I insisted. 'I'm innocent!'

He raised his eyebrows.

'Okay,' I said. Message received. I zipped it, thanked Esteban and shuffled inside, focusing on unpacking the contraband from my pants. I was going to be very popular. Cigarettes were currency in here.

'So, we get interviewed tomorrow, then,' said Melissa.

'They're bound to make us sign something. Put our names to the story about being kidnapped and forced. Then it'll be serious.'

'It's the best chance we have. If they think we went into this to make money they'll throw the book at us.'

'We're not bad people. We haven't hurt anyone.'

'I wish I could think like you. They don't care what we're like as people. We broke the law. And if you ask me they're not going to be satisfied till we admit it.'

We were still debating the whole business when a hubbub in the corridor got our attention. The chat got louder, then women appeared in our doorway.

'Michaella, Melissa!' they shouted. '*Familia, familia.* You have family. You come. You come. Family.'

There was a bunch of them over in another cell. About five feet from the floor was a brick-sized window that looked out onto the car park and main entrance. We were enticed over for a peep. Outside there must have been two- or three-dozen people, mostly men. They were all looking a bit tired, all a bit dishevelled in their crumpled, dusty suits, and plenty of them had large cameras. They were making a right racket, but two words stood out: 'Michaella' and 'Melissa'.

'See?' the pregnant one said. 'Family.'

'They're not any family of mine,' I said.

Melissa was silent for a sec. 'I wish I could say the same.'

'What are you talking about?' I asked. 'They're journalists, right?'

'I guess,' she sighed. 'But see that guy at the front, the one walking towards the gates?'

'Yeah.'

'That's my dad.'

The fuss outside caught everyone's attention. Every single journalist and cameraman out there was desperate to get inside. They were shouting and shoving, some of them really pushing it with the armed guards. It took a good while for me to appreciate they were trying to get to us. They wanted pictures, they wanted words. They wanted *the full story*.

'They know,' said Melissa. 'Everyone knows.'

'Knows what?'

'About us. About what we've done. About what's happening.'

'People get arrested all the time.'

'I guess. But maybe not young British females with a shitload of cocaine.'

It didn't make sense to me. I genuinely couldn't see their agenda. Why was what we'd done worth writing about? I'd seen worse things back home and no packs of journalists were fighting to cover that. I'd *lived* through worse.

Melissa was in no mood to talk about it. The sight of her dad among the pack of jackals sent her spiralling. Not knowing if or when she'd be allowed to see him was driving her spare. A couple of hours later we were finally summoned upstairs to meet him. As a bonus we got to see Melissa's older sister as well. Pretty impressive, she said, considering that the only sister she had was much younger than her.

It was the 'boyfriend' scenario all over again. It turned out the 'sister' was a journalist from the *Daily Mail*. It didn't take a genius to work out she was expecting something in return.

We were ushered into an interview room and Melissa and her dad got to hug. That was lovely to see, although it made me upset, thinking of Mum. Melissa got so emotional. And there was one other mitigating factor: her dad was carrying chicken and chips for everyone.

No wonder the guards had let him and his bogus daughter in without any checks. They'd got their portions first, no worries. We were happy for anything at that stage. Melissa hugged him hello but fell on the food seconds later. I too was tucking in like it was the last supper. Then I realised Melissa's dad was crying.

It was such a sad and surreal meeting. And quick. Reluctantly, we had to return to our bunker while our guests were escorted back outside. I was glad to get the chance to lie down. I hadn't eaten so well – and so heavily – for a couple of weeks. I'd had that much sugar I just wanted to nap. In any case, we had our interrogations to prepare for – our first legitimate opportunity to put our case to officials. As I fell asleep, the words of Maria and Esteban played over and over in my head.

'You must say "guilty". You must say "guilty".'

Oh no! I just don't know what's best.

*

Monday morning began like all the others. We had guards shoving clipboards under our noses, lumpy water thrown into bowls in the name of breakfast, and antagonistic noises lobbed in our direction by various other inmates. That was usual, but today seemed worse than ever.

There was a small TV screen at the far end of the corridor. Half a dozen or so women were huddled around it. They were all pointing and shouting. I drifted over, took one look at the screen and froze. I was looking at myself. It was footage of me and Melissa in the airport being stopped. I looked like shit. My hair was terrible. My clothes looked disgusting.

And I was being arrested on national TV with eleven kilos of cocaine in my possession.

I'd never felt so ashamed. The other women saw it differently. They were smiling at me, patting me on the shoulder, rattling away in numerous languages, and obviously highly entertained. Celine appeared next to me.

'You've impressed them,' she said. 'None of us got on the news.'

It was weird to imagine strangers seeing my story. I couldn't understand what was being said but the pictures spoke for themselves. The only consolation was the fact this was local TV. The idea of my family seeing these images was too horrible to contemplate.

It was custom to sit in the corridor during the day because it was the only place that had lights. After the TV exposé I just wanted to bury myself away. For once I didn't mind being on my bunk. Unfortunately, I wasn't there for long. I heard Esteban's voice echoing along the corridor. Eventually he found me in my cell.

'You have visitor upstairs,' he said. 'Come, come . . .'

'Who is it this time, Esteban?' I asked. 'My long-lost cousin? Another boyfriend?'

He laughed. I'm not sure what he understood but it was obviously enough to make a joke. 'It *is* a father,' he said. 'Father Sean.'

Interesting . . .

Father Sean Walsh was a priest from Ireland. He was involved in a Catholic mission in Peru, where a lot of Irish people did community work. He'd heard about our predicament and taken it upon himself to check on my mental and spiritual well-being. I was as bemused as I was grateful. What sort of person dedicates their life to visiting people in Peruvian prisons? Father Sean was one of them. And I was so happy he did.

He bore gifts like all the visitors who'd been before. He also brought wisdom, and a representative from the Irish Embassy. He explained that the Irish Embassy no longer had an office in Peru. The nearest one was in Mexico, from where this guy had flown in. After we'd exchanged polite greetings, I tried to assess the situation. At first I was suspicious of them. Were they journalists, masquerading as a priest and a consul?

'It's a shame you don't have a British passport,' said the embassy guy.

How many times had I regretted that? Although his next advice was just as familiar.

'When you're tried,' he said, 'I recommend you plead guilty.'

'That's what everyone's saying. What if I don't believe I am?'

Father Sean puffed out his cheeks. 'I'm no legal expert,' he said, 'but I've been around these parts a while. People who plead guilty seem to get treated better by the system. Don't ask me why. That's just the way it is.'

The consulate rattled through some of the processes of the Peruvian justice system but I found it hard to take everything in. Actually, I barely took anything in. But it proved to me they weren't journalists, and the meeting was actually really useful.

The visit was cut short because Melissa and I were due to begin the process of interrogation. I was strangely relieved it was happening. I couldn't wait to put over my point of view. Yes, I had cocaine in my suitcase. Yes, I put it there. Was it mine? No. Did I conjure up the whole plan? No. Was I tricked into helping some South American cartel? Yes, I reckon I was. And that's what I was going to say.

*

Midday came and went. The only activity in our direction was a message saying I had a visitor and had to go upstairs.

'Who is it?' I asked.

The guard shrugged and wandered off.

'Is Esteban around today?' I called after him. He pointed towards the other end of the corridor. Off I went. I found my favourite guard manning the payphone area. A place where you heard more arguments than conversations.

'Esteban,' I said, 'I'm told I have a guest. Can you check if it's some nosy journalist?' He looked relieved to get a break. One call later he said, 'Your brother. '

'Really?' I wasn't buying it. 'Which one?'

He shrugged again.

'Can I see him?'

'No. You have interview.'

And that's how it stayed. One o'clock passed, then two, three and four. As Melissa pointed out, I'd only spoken to my mother on Friday. There's no way anyone from Ireland could have upped sticks and reached us in the back of beyond so soon. I hadn't even said where I was being held.

It was torture just waiting, waiting, not being told anything, followed by more waiting. Being locked up is one thing. Being kept waiting for a meeting is another. It drives you crazy.

'Do you think they do this to everyone?' I said.

Melissa shrugged. 'Totally. Bastards.'

Five o'clock rolled around and we were both at our wits' end. We'd gone over every version of the story so often it was beginning to sound dodgy even to Melissa. Esteban finally appeared in our block, smiling, if a tad out of breath.

'Michaella,' he said, 'you go up now. But not for interview,' he said. 'No interview today.'

'What? Why not?'

'No translator.'

'Why do you want us then?'

We were escorted into an interview room by two guards filling their faces with pizza. They couldn't have been more distracted if they'd tried. I was so annoyed by their attitude I barely looked into the room. When I did, I nearly fell over. In front of me was Keith, my real flesh-and-blood brother. Not a journalist, but my genuine kith and kin, large as life, twice as beautiful – and looking inconsolably upset. That set us all off. Melissa didn't know him from Adam but even she was crying at the sight of our reunion.

Keith was all over the place. He's twenty-eight, a macho man, he could arm-wrestle Godzilla and win. Yet here he was, tears streaming down his face as hard as they poured down mine. So many emotions were coming out. I had no idea I'd been bottling so much up. I hadn't seen anyone I knew for nearly two months and I poured all that emotion onto him.

We hugged for ever. It seemed the right thing, the only thing. I was sobbing into Keith's shoulder the whole time. He was drenching mine. It was a beautiful, close moment. We'd never been more connected. Eventually, he told me that as soon as the family knew I was in Peru he'd volunteered to fly out to see me. A quick Google search had unearthed more details from newspaper websites that were beginning to pick up on the story.

'You've been all over the news back home,' he said.

He had a satchel with a dozen or so newspapers inside. They all ran stories about me being missing – the kind of articles one sees about missing young women before they're found dead. I scanned the pages and images, aghast at the level of interest being shown.

It was only after I'd digested the press cuttings that I realised Keith wasn't by himself. He had arrived with a guy called Peter Madden, a high-profile Belfast lawyer whom my family had contacted to see what could be done to help me. He had knowledge of South American jails, having previously represented three Irish Republicans who had been held without charge in appalling jails in Colombia. That case had been quite controversial. The men had been accused of helping train Colombian guerrilla fighters, the FARC, in urban warfare. So Peter was a legal heavy hitter, and he had travelled out to see me with Keith. But all I wanted to do was talk about my family with my brother.

Peter took down some basic details of what had happened to me and wanted me to be confident when I was finally interviewed – when they managed to find a translator. But my attention kept wandering to my mum, and what she'd think once the more up-to-date stories about me and Melissa – and drugs – began appearing in the tabloid press. The only thought in my head was my family. And how ashamed I was to be letting them down.

'I really didn't want yous to find out about all this until I was back,' I said. 'But now you do, I need to know, how is Mum? Does she hate me?'

Keith coughed nervously. 'She's not been well,' he replied, staring at his shoes. 'She had to go to hospital.'

'No! I just spoke to her on Friday. What's wrong?'

'*What's wrong?*' he repeated, fixing me with his eyes. 'You're asking me that, Michaella? She's been so sick with worry that when you rang it gave her such a shock she had a mini-stroke. We were lucky people were home with her at the time. She's okay but all the stress of you being missing has really taken its toll on her. It could have been the end.' He leant forwards and, with a sob, said, 'She thought you were dead. We all feared you'd been murdered in Ibiza or something.'

I stared at him, processing the words. All the discomfort of the previous days meant nothing compared to hearing the trauma I'd put my mum through. It really hammered home how stupid and selfish I'd been. I'd caused my mother a stroke . . . what kind of daughter was I?

I wanted the earth to open and swallow me up. Whatever hell the Peruvian judiciary had to throw at me, nothing would ever compare to this. I hated myself, black and white. If I could have taken my own life there and then, I'd have done it. I'd never felt so low.

I have Keith to thank for resuscitating me. Bringing me back to life. Clearly he was as shaken as me about our mum's brush with death. But he'd still made the effort to visit me. He'd leapt on a plane with a lawyer and a ticket he couldn't afford. Whatever he said to me, I was honour bound to listen.

'Right,' he said, 'whatever you've done, we're here for you, you know that, right? All of us. I'm first here but we're all coming. And I mean all. Mum doesn't care what you've done. We're just all so relieved that you're alive and well.'

'God, no, don't let Mum travel all this way. I'll be home soon, I'm sure. I'll see her soon enough.'

'You don't know that,' Peter interjected. I'd forgotten there was a legal mind sitting there. 'You haven't had your trial yet,' he continued. 'There are complex systems here, and complicated sentencing. There's something like three thousand foreign nationals in Peruvian jails for drug trafficking – most of them drug mules – and a lot of them are women. Don't think you'll be set free just because you're young.'

I sat immobile, dizzy from guilt and dehydration and regret. The reality of my situation was being fast-tracked into my consciousness.

'You gotta listen to him,' said Keith. 'He's your lawyer. He's on your side. He's the fella bringing you home.'

'As soon as I get interviewed I'm going to tell them it's not my fault. They can't keep me after that. They have proper trials here. Don't they? Can't they see I was set up? I was forced into this.'

Keith didn't ask me about the kidnap story that was being reported in the news. He didn't even ask if I was telling the truth. We spent all our time together talking about Mum and the family. All the while, Peter was getting agitated, pressing to talk about the hard reality of the process. Just before the visit ended, Keith took a short video of me on his phone. I put on a brave face for Mum, sent her good wishes and said I was well. The guards really didn't give a damn, and probably couldn't understand what I was saying in any case.

There are only so many times and ways a person can apologise. We were both sick of the sound of my 'sorry' when the rap on the door came. It was time for Keith to leave. I was allowed to follow him back upstairs. The guards by the exit looked happier to see him than anyone I'd ever seen.

'I should have told you,' Keith said. 'I brought you pizza but the guards said as I hadn't brought them anything they'd look after it. I'll get you something tomorrow. And I suppose I'll have to bring them something again as well.'

I smiled, Keith smiled, the guards smiled, we all smiled. It was frustrating, it was wrong. But it was life in Dirandro. And – as far as all the advice I was getting went – it was a life I needed to get used to pretty damn quick. What was it everyone was saying?

'*Plead guilty, plead guilty, plead guilty.*'

CHAPTER ELEVEN

THAT'S WHAT THEY WANT TO HEAR

'**O**kay, you two, upstairs.'

We knew the drill. The only difference being that I was in the middle of washing my clothes. Don't imagine for a moment that we had washing machines. The only way this was going to get done was with a bar of soap under a dribbling cold-water pipe over a tiled sink. All I had to wear was a long summer dress that I'd pleaded for from my suitcase. I tried to explain to the guard that I just needed to finish my washing, but it was no go. He just made an obscene face and pointed towards the stairs. 'Up, up, up!' he said and ran behind me, threatening to touch my ass. I legged it. He wasn't getting that kind of satisfaction. Like a lot of the guards in Dirandro, he was overstepping the mark, using every opportunity to be 'handy'. There was an underlying sexual tone to many of the guards' interactions with female prisoners.

Esteban and another guard were waiting by the staircase. Out of habit we went to walk past them. Esteban grabbed my arm.

'*Lo siento*,' he said. 'I'm sorry. Your hands.'

'What the—'

He seemed genuinely sad to be affixing the cuffs around my wrists. '*El capitan*,' he said – *the boss* – and gestured his head upwards.

'What's going on?' Melissa said. 'I thought we were beyond this. It's barbaric.'

There wasn't another word from the guards, not even the friendly ones. I was just grateful our ankles remained unshackled. We emerged through the heavy door at the top of the staircase. I happened to see our friendly neighbourhood lady cop, Maria. She was out of speaking range, so I held up my bound wrists and pulled a face. She saw me and looked away. Then I guess something got the better of her, so she turned and walked over.

'What's going on?' I asked. 'I thought we were okay.'

'That's what I thought,' she said, 'so why you do this?'

From nowhere she produced a copy of an English tabloid. There was a massive picture of Melissa and her dad with her birthday cake plus hundreds of words describing how we were living in luxury. I only had a chance to see a snatch of text but none of it resembled anything I'd said to any visitor. No wonder she was spitting feathers. They were under instruction from on high to make life very uncomfortable for captured drug smugglers, and here we were in full colour being shown having a soft time of it. In her police station.

'It's all lies,' I said.

'Yes,' she agreed. 'Lies. Very bad. Now go. You two: *finished.*'

I knew it. Melissa's dad had signed a deal with the devil and they'd spun the piece to make it look like we were being treated leniently. God knows what other horrors were around the corner. I could see the pack of hungry reporters outside the window. If they'd stood a chance of getting in before, this article had blown it for them now. So at least one good thing had come out of it.

Hopefully they'd get the message and give up sooner rather than later. I couldn't face another sneaky reporter lying his or her way in, even if they brought me all the Ferrero Rocher in Peru. But I wouldn't hold my breath. I'd seen what the guards would do for the smallest bribe – a pizza, a packet of cigarettes. I'd seen how a tiny bit of information could be distorted across two pages. All I could control was myself.

I just need to bite my tongue.

That applied inside and out. We were led into the interview room, but it stank to high heaven. There was a desk covered in pizza boxes. From the smell alone I pitied anyone who'd eaten the stuff. Our court interrogator arrived with his errant translator. They looked us both up and down, like we might be responsible for the aroma, then retreated into an antechamber just past my shoulder.

They were assembling their papers and files when there was a commotion in the corridor. *Come on, guys, what now?* I couldn't really follow it but when the door opened to reveal Keith again, I gasped with surprise. I was so pleased to see his familiar face. But he looked deeply troubled. The sight of his little sister in handcuffs sent him spinning. He didn't know who to shout at first. One guy he ran to didn't speak English. The second understood enough to tell him to shut the hell up.

'Englishman, be quiet.'

'She's not an animal, let her go!'

'Englishman want handcuffs?' he threatened, and went for the pair on his own belt. Still my brother didn't get the message. I'm not sure what was worse – the sight of me in cuffs or the guard calling this proud Irishman 'English'.

'Keith,' I yelled, 'please don't. They're not messing. They'll lock you up as soon as look at you. Mum doesn't want two of us in here.'

He was proper enraged. 'It's not right,' he said.

'Come on, don't ruin the time we have.'

He huffed and puffed and finally settled down but still couldn't take his eyes off my wrists.

'How can you put up with this?'

'I'm lucky it's not my feet as well. You've got to remember, we're not even people in here.' As hideous as it was, being cuffed wasn't as bad as not having free access to running water.

I said to Keith, 'How did you even get in here? I'm meant to be interviewed today. There's no visitors allowed.'

'The power of pizza,' he replied, pointing to the Margherita boxes on the table. 'You'd think they'd be sick of it by now.'

'I hope it tastes better than it smells,' I said. 'Something's well off.'

'Trust me, it does. I've got one for you as well.' I gave it a sniff. It was cold but it smelled fine. It was very welcome.

'By the way,' Keith said, 'Peter's here as well. With another lawyer called Meyer Fishman, who is Peruvian but speaks fluent English. He recently helped some American girls who were in a similar position to you.'

So I now had two lawyers. Maybe things would start to move in my favour. Keith told me my family had got Peter to liaise with Fishman, as he was local and knew the justice system, and the language, better than Peter could ever manage. He would effectively hand the baton to him once we'd had our hearing.

We barely had two minutes to catch up when Melissa was summoned to the interview room. I say 'room' – there was no door, no wall, no obvious separation from where I was sitting with Keith. Melissa, the interrogator and translator were literally on a table about six feet from us. I could hear every word.

Keith got clued in soon enough. He wanted to chat but as Melissa went through the motions of our well-worn story, I gave him the shush sign and he started listening as well. She was able to speak freely. Neither of the cops in the room had ever uttered a syllable of English in my presence. In any case, they were too busy stuffing their faces with pizza. The only time they looked alive was when a third guy entered the room and went to put his unfinished Margherita down on one of the boxes. The other guys leapt up, mouths and hands full of dough and cheese, and started gesticulating like madmen till they could speak. They were pointing at the box like it was cursed. A second later they were all laughing.

There was no way I could hear Melissa with that row in my ear.

'What's going on?' I asked.

The cops ignored me but the American translator revealed what was happening. Another drug smuggler had been brought in but nothing was in his luggage. Any drugs he had, they reckoned had been swallowed. In a situation like that there was only one way to get your hands on them and that was to wait for nature to take its course. Apparently, that had happened, no problem. But the cops had needed somewhere to stash the stash – and they'd chosen a pizza box. Hence the less-than-pristine appearance. And the appalling smell.

It beggared belief.

'Why the hell's the box still in here?' I shouted. 'I could have touched it. I could've put my hand in . . . what's wrong with these people?'

'They're animals,' Keith said quietly. 'There's no other word.' I watched as his eyes fixed again on the handcuffs.

'Some of them are all right,' I said, thinking of Esteban and the lady cop Maria. 'They're just people trying to do a horrible job, but these guys are pretty bad.'

'It's chaos here. Just trying to get through the security is like a test. You don't know who to trust. And now they let me come and sit with my sister with human shit in the same room? Oh my God. I don't *ever* want you to get used to this. Nothing in here is normal.'

I stared at his earnest face. The tears weren't far away. My big musclebound brother was struggling, no doubt about it. But I had my own problems. 'Keith, I love you, but what choice do I have?' The only question was: for how long?

*

Two hours Melissa was batting questions this way and that. When she finished I was confident the interrogator knew less than when they'd begun. I wasn't looking forward to the cross-examination, even if I had just overheard the most detailed version of the kidnap story yet. I took my place with Peter and my new representative, Mr Fishman – a curious-looking, mild-mannered guy with thick glasses – to my side.

'Did you do this of your own choice?' I was asked.

'No.'

'Are you sure?'

'Yes.'

'Explain.'

'There was a man with a gun.'

'And he forced you to do this?'

'Totally. Absolutely. One hundred per cent.'

And that's how we carried on. My fingers were crossed the entire time.

Fishman interjected when he needed to. The rest of the time I spouted the same story Melissa and I had rehearsed. There'd only been a couple of moments during the whole pizza debacle when I couldn't hear her answers, but I managed to wing it well enough. That's not to say the process wasn't thorough. Our BlackBerries had been taken and analysed, they said. They asked me if I knew the names of my captors. I said no. On the BlackBerry, Mateo was identified by one letter alone: 'C'. Even Mateo was a false name.

Our interrogator wasn't a bad fella, if I'm honest. He was tall, slim, and to the point. He asked the questions on his list and followed up with others of his own when appropriate. I felt guilty for not being totally up front with him, but we couldn't backtrack now. I had no idea how our story would play out in the long run.

He went out of his way to explain – via Fishman and the American interpreter – the legal process and ramifications as best he could. His job, he said, was to get our stories down on file as accurately as possible. They'd be passed to the state prosecutor who would decide whether there was a case for us to answer in court. If he thought there was enough evidence we'd get a trial. If he didn't, we'd be free to go. It was good of him to throw us that bone. But even without the Peruvian CSI cracking the BlackBerry there was no shortage of evidence.

By the time we finished it was 8.50 p.m. According to the rules, our cell doors would be locked at 9 p.m. Melissa was dragging her feet but I ran like the wind. I had my laundry to collect. I reached the bathroom, but I couldn't see anything resembling my clothes. I had a quick look in the corridor in case some angel had hung them up there to dry. Nothing. I started to panic. I rushed around asking everyone if they'd seen my stuff but I was met with blank looks and snarls. Not speaking Spanish just made me look ludicrous in their eyes. When I told Melissa what had happened, she replied with her trademark, Scottish sarcasm, 'Jesus, if you can't trust thieves and criminals, what's the world coming to?'

When we woke up the next morning, the entire corridor was empty, save for us two and Celine. Everyone else had been processed and shipped out in the wee hours. Whoever had taken my stuff had timed it perfectly. They knew they'd be gone before I even woke up. After some persistence on my part, Celine eventually told me that the pregnant woman had been the culprit. No matter how bad my situation was, there were plenty of people worse off than me. But it still didn't alter the fact that the little bit of comfort I'd been looking forward to – a few basic clean clothes – had been denied me, and I was deeply miserable.

*

The interviews continued over three days. Peter was there for the entirety. Keith was there for some of it. Melissa's dad and his friend sat in for one session as well. A virtual transcript of the first session appeared in the papers shortly after he left. Was it a coincidence? I don't know, because what really annoyed me was the appearance of our mug shots in the same rag. We weren't exactly Chanel fresh by this stage. For them to appear anywhere else was an indication that hard cash had changed hands. By the looks of things, a whole load of it.

When my time with the interrogator was up, he closed his file and I went to leave. Through the interpreter he told me to stay. He wanted to impart some advice.

It turned out it was the same advice I'd been getting all week.

'I have to say, from what I can see, I think you will go to trial.'

Okay, I thought, *that's not the end of the world. I have a fighting chance with a good jury.*

But that wasn't the bombshell.

'If you do go to trial, I recommend you plead guilty.'

Not you as well.

What was it with everyone telling me to throw my life away? I said as much and, once it was translated, he tried to calm me down.

'I believe you will get a fair trial,' he said. 'That is not the issue here. Judges in Peru do not like liars or people who waste their time. So if you admit your charges there is a very good chance the judge will be lenient. It is your first offence, and you've no history. But if you try to fight the charges and you are then found guilty, which I have to say is a very real possibility, then from my experience you should be prepared to never see daylight again.'

Was he serious? 'You're saying people who plead guilty get shorter sentences than people who plead innocence but are then found guilty anyway? That makes no sense.' I looked at Peter who was desperately making calming gestures.

The interrogator continued. 'Also, consider this. The wheels of justice turn very, very slowly in this country for people who plead "not guilty" when the state prosecutor thinks they are. You could be looking at a considerable wait just to get a trial. If you plead "guilty", you might see a court in a year. The delay will be taken off your sentence.'

The interviewer's eyes never left me as I drank in the interpreter's translation. I got the feeling he was trying to be decent.

'Michaella,' he said, 'please plead guilty and let justice – Peruvian justice – take its course.'

He packed up his stuff and Peter and I were left in the room alone. If my lawyer spoke I didn't hear him. The enormity of the situation was sinking in. Finally, you might say. I felt faint. All those numbers. A year if I did this, two years or three years if I did that? What the hell? It was the first I'd heard of any of it.

I'd put so much effort into trying to keep my head above water that I'd ignored what was actually going on. Guilty or not guilty, what did it matter? Whichever way I looked at it, I wasn't going home any time soon.

How did I not see this coming? How did I not realise I was stuck there?

What have I done?

*

If Celine's prediction of fifteen days in the holding cells of Dirandro proved true, then we had another week to go before anything else of significance happened. I knew more women would be arriving to fill the spots left by the others, but for twenty-four hours us three had the run of the whole downstairs.

Eventually a few new arrivals were thrown in. The gobby ones made a row and the timid ones looked at their feet to try and be invisible, just like the last lot. Some of them pissed me off, some of them didn't. I wasn't bothered either way. My time there would be up soon and I'd be long gone by the time the cells were anywhere near maximum capacity again. In the meantime, we just had to make the most of every opportunity.

One afternoon I was upstairs, having braided Maria's hair again. After I finished she was out in the corridor by the kiosk, which we had avoided looking at, as we had no money and no way of buying anything. But today we happened to take a look, and there, on the counter, was a tray of the fluffiest, freshly baked doughnuts – all sugary and absolutely mouth-watering. Melissa and I were literally wailing. We stood awkwardly for a minute or two and then, to our surprise, Maria asked if we wanted one.

'Er, yes, please!' I said, wondering if I'd heard her correctly. I couldn't believe she was so kind as to let us have such a treat, but she was. It was partly being in the right place at the right time, but I realised this was a modest but very welcome 'payment' for my hair-braiding skills. It struck me how this bartering system may come in useful in my near future.

We were in seventh heaven with our doughnuts when another cop came in and announced we had company. As we were already upstairs, he suggested bringing these guys straight in. I was sugar-drunk. I didn't care who he brought in as long as my sugar rush lasted. It turned out to be two Peruvian journalists, one of whom spoke pretty good English. They started asking us questions but we really didn't want to talk to them.

'I've been doing all the talking to these guys, it's your turn,' said Melissa.

'Well, I've been supplying the cigarettes and it's my work that got us the doughnuts.'

'Well, I don't wanna talk to them.'

'Neither do I.'

We went back and forth, eating our doughnuts and bickering while one of these guys filmed us on his ancient-looking video equipment. We gave them some perfunctory answers that I don't remember. There were long silences. The blurry footage of our interaction is still online somewhere.

The next day passed with low-level tetchiness simmering all the while. I guess we were stir-crazy by this point, not knowing what was going to happen to us. We locked horns a wee bit and eventually I walked away. There were enough empty bunks in the corridor to find my own space. My head was whizzing, though. Every bad thought I'd previously had about Melissa came back. I'd not really clicked with the girl from the moment we'd met in Palma. It was only as we were thrown into the legal system that I'd begun to depend on her as a friend. Without all the bravado and the posturing Melissa could be a sweet girl. She meant no harm, I was sure of that. At the end of the day she was as scared as me.

Was this how it was going to be from now on – me and her arguing every day and no other friends? For the first time I thought about learning Spanish to improve my chances of interacting with others. Maybe this would be possible once we were moved out of Dirandro. Would there be books? Better shower facilities and somewhere to wash my clothes? I had so many questions and fears. The game was survival and I was determined not to go under.

CHAPTER TWELVE

STOP SMILING

'**U**p! Up!'

It sounded like at least two men shouting. I couldn't see for sure. The flashlight in my face was blinding.

'What is it? What's going on?'

'Up,' they repeated. 'Up.'

I swung my legs over the bunk and paused to get my thoughts together. My head was foggy. If I didn't know better I'd say I had a hangover. Sadly, no alcohol had passed my lips for more than two weeks.

Two weeks! The penny was slow in dropping but I got the message.

That's it. That's what's going on. Our fifteen days must be up. I'm being moved.

I was virtually hauled to my feet. My clothes and other possessions, most of them brought by Keith and the *Daily Mirror* guy, were being scooped up by the guards. I tried to intervene. He was making a right hash of packing, if that's what he was doing. Turned out it wasn't.

They were forensically going through everything I owned. About as thoroughly as the customs guys had searched us at Jorge Chávez.

At least this time I knew there was nothing to raise the alarm. They must have known that as well. Either way, they weren't holding back.

I watched, horrified, as they pulled apart my clothes and possessions. My jacket – my poor jacket – was being inspected like it was radioactive. Why the laundry thieves hadn't taken it I couldn't say. It was warm. It was mine. And I really hated watching them tear it up further.

I felt so alone. Not for the first time I wished I hadn't fought with Melissa. I'd only wanted to make a point. We might never be soulmates, but at that moment, in that country, in that police station, we were all each other had. We shouldn't have been fighting. We should have been united.

The handcuffs were out. The guards were even carrying ankle chains. I begged them not to put them on me. I kicked out a little. Not much, not enough to suggest I was any kind of threat. Just enough. I guess they took pity on me. I was led upstairs with just my hands bound. Melissa was already there. She glowered at me. I gave her the eyes back. Then I took a breath and said, 'I'm sorry.'

She blinked a couple of times. 'Me too.'

'Do you know what's going on?'

'No. Maybe court?'

'At this time?'

'They're messing with us. Don't give them the satisfaction of being annoyed.'

The whole search and intimidation exercise took ages. By the time we were pushed out the front door, hands cuffed behind our backs, it was 7 a.m. A female police officer led the way.

'You see state prosecutor now,' was all she said. Her English wasn't good enough for any more details. My head was spinning. Perhaps Peter had arranged this – or maybe Fishman. We didn't have a clue.

The policewoman was flanked by a couple of army dudes in camouflage fatigues. Each of them had a machine-gun swinging casually around their necks like a shoulder bag. Overkill without a doubt. We weren't murderers; we were barely out of school. What were they thinking?

Outside the main door of the Dirandro office it got worse, as we were greeted by another handful of heavily-armed military bodies. Plus about a hundred members of the media. *Where the hell did they come from?*

Suddenly, I was grateful for the armed escort. Flashes were popping in our faces, arms were stretching out, waving cameras and Dictaphones in our direction, people were pushing others out of the way to get a second with us, diving at us as though their lives depended on it. It was horrible. So claustrophobic. Even more so with my hands tied. I was flinching and ducking every inch of the way to the car. I kept thinking I was going to be mobbed, and if that happened there was nothing I could do to protect myself. My heart rate must have been going through the roof. Luckily, the military wall was impenetrable. I don't know how many cameras were trashed or wrists snapped, but no one got through the green shields. And that was without using their guns.

What no one could prevent, though, was the yelling. Above the sound of my own panic I could make out my name being shouted again and again and again. I hated it. Not because I was scared. But because I was coming to terms with a truth I couldn't escape. Whatever was happening was out of my control.

This isn't my secret any more.

Not since that night fleeing from Michael have I ever been so relieved to get into a car. At least this time the driver didn't stop and kick me out. If he had I'd have been torn apart. As we pulled away hands thundered against the roof and windows, my name echoing in the air. Progress was slow. There were bodies every which way you looked. I could barely breathe. My heart was in my mouth. It hadn't beat like that since the arrest. From the look of it, Melissa was enduring something similar. I wouldn't know for sure. I couldn't speak even if I wanted to.

We inched our way through the crowds and eventually the driver was able to put his foot down. After an hour or so we arrived at a building tucked behind giant gates. I was horrified to see a phalanx of photographers already waiting. Their camera flashes were going off across every inch of the car windows. I honestly thought they were mistaking us for someone else. People get arrested every day. Why were we such a big deal to them?

Then I remembered the newspaper cuttings, the pictures of the birthday cake and the mug shots from our arrest and the penny dropped. Clearly a picture of us was worth a euro or two back home. The journalists banging on our windows weren't concerned with telling our side of the story. We weren't public interest; we were cash cows. They were parasites, making money out of our misery. It made my blood boil the more I thought about it. They didn't care about us; they were just trying to make as much money as possible.

We managed to get inside the grounds without running anyone over, unfortunately. When we pulled up the lady officer said, 'Now you see state prosecutor.'

There was a pause. Clearly she was expecting a reaction – a positive one at that. She got nothing from either of us. Even if my mind wasn't elsewhere, the interviewer had already as good as told me our chances. There was nothing to get excited about as far as I was concerned.

We hung around inside the building, waiting in anonymous corridors before we were eventually led into this incredibly fancy office where the state prosecutor was waiting with his female translator, an impressive, striking-looking woman, with long dark hair and amazing dark eyes. Her name was Andrea. She was American, she said, from Miami, where she had lived for over half her life. She was originally from Colombia but had been educated in America and was bilingual. She seemed to be assuming a bigger role than simply a translator. She launched into an explanation.

'This is a big deal,' she said. 'Do you know how rare it is to get a personal audience with the state prosecutor?'

Neither of us had anything to say in response.

'No one meets him this quickly, so you are very lucky. He reads your files, makes his decision, end of story. You are getting a chance to influence that decision.'

I thought of everyone who had advised us to plead guilty. That was assuming we got a trial. If what Andrea was hinting at now, then we might not need one. Maybe certain strings were being pulled in our favour . . .

The SP looked businesslike, as befitting his occupation. He had our files on the table and, judging by the questions he asked, he had obviously read them.

'You say you were kidnapped?' he said.

We nodded.

'Are you sure?'

We nodded again.

He took a breath and puffed out his cheeks. Then he looked us both in the eyes. 'You are sure you want to continue with this story? You don't want to tell me anything else?'

I think he was trying to say, in as subtle a way as he could, that he didn't believe our crock-of-shit story for one minute and was giving us every chance to come clean. But we stuck to our guns. Even if we didn't agree on much else, that was about all he was going to get from us. Was it the right approach? I don't know. Melissa seemed convinced. More importantly, changing our story at that late stage could only have looked dodgy. Even I could see that.

The truth was, this guy across the desk held our fates in his hands. We had to make him believe we were unwitting accessories. If he had any doubts, we'd get the full nine yards in court. And even that would not be straightforward.

'I have to tell you something about our legal system,' the SP said. 'It works slowly. And it was not designed for so many cases. We have prison spaces for maybe twenty thousand criminals. You know how many inmates are in those prisons? Closer to forty-five thousand. And how many of those have faced a trial? Less than half. So let me say again, if I decide you have a case to answer, your trial will not be tomorrow, it will not be next month, or even next year. If you see the inside of a court within four years you will be lucky.'

Four years? Four fucking years!

It really was all to play for at that stage. Our goal was clear. We just needed to convince him of our plight. First, though, we needed to convince our own lawyer. At one point, Andrea asked me why I was smiling.

'Oh no, am I? Sorry,' I said. I must have looked like an idiot. I can't help it. It's a nervous reaction. When I'm in stressful situations, the corners of my mouth go up in a kind of smirk. I had it at school, I had it with my mum when she was angry, and I had it with boyfriends. But if there's a time and place to look like you're not taking someone seriously, it's not when you're sat across from the state prosecutor of a South American country. The problem is, the more you try not to do something the harder it gets. I basically had to think about cockroaches for five minutes to get my face to behave.

I was amazed how many ways the SP found to try to convince us to tell the truth. The news of the four-year waiting list had been a bombshell. But he had others up his sleeve.

'Peru has many prisons, some much, much nicer than others,' he explained. 'Ancón Two is okay, very modern. Others are not so nice. You are foreign women accused of drug offences. There are various places we send foreign women accused of drug offences. The one that takes the most is a prison in Chorillos, Lima, called Santa Monica.' He paused and waited for Andrea to catch up.

'You do not want to go there,' she warned. 'Santa Monica is a female-only prison, that is the good news. But let me be clear: it is not nice. It has poor sanitation, poor hygiene, inedible food and the other inmates will try to kill you. They give you no blankets, no cutlery, no plates, no cups, no toilets, no showers. What you have you buy and then you fight to keep. There are people in there for their entire lives. They have nothing to lose by killing one more person.'

'We'd only go there if we're found guilty, right?' I asked.

Andrea conferred with the SP. 'No,' she said. 'Most of the people who go there are awaiting trial. Just like you will be if he decides it so.'

For all the horror stories he was sharing, I got the feeling the SP took no pleasure from our fear. If anything, he was still hoping it wouldn't come to that. But, as he kept repeating, that all depended on the answers we gave.

We were there a couple of hours, going over and over the same old ground. I'm not sure how much that was to do with the SP, though. Apart from his couple of speeches, generally the questions he asked in Spanish lasted about two seconds, then his interpreter, this Andrea, would translate them into English – except her translation would last half a minute or more. It got funny in the end. He'd go 'blah blah' and she'd spin it out for ever, probing this and that, really digging in for the detail. And as far as I could work out, she'd relay hardly any of it back to him.

The situation was so scary we were looking for anything to take our minds off what was at stake.

Eventually, the state prosecutor started collecting his papers together, signalling that the meeting was ending. I wondered if we'd done enough. He said a couple of words but, instead of translating, Andrea got her phone out. There was a distinctive pop of light.

'What the hell?' Melissa said. 'Are you taking pictures of us?'

The woman looked embarrassed, but she didn't answer.

'Why are you taking pictures?' I said. 'Are you going to sell them? Everyone thinks they can just make money out of us.'

I was fit to burst. We were that tired of other people using our situation to line their own pockets. We were ready to go to war with the next person who tried it. But sometimes you have to pick your battles. While I was freaking out, Melissa was listening to Andrea, who had completely shut down the issue of the photos. We were to wait in the corridor for the state prosecutor to make an assessment of our story. He wouldn't be sleeping on it. He would let us know the outcome within the hour.

As the clock ticked on, I felt like a defendant in the dock, awaiting the jury's verdict. But this would be a jury of one – a middle-aged, world-weary legal expert who had seen and heard the woes of criminals more hardened and wily than us. When Andrea emerged from his office, I knew what she was going to say before she opened her mouth.

'Girls, I'm sorry, but the state prosecutor has made up his mind. He didn't believe you,' she said. 'You're going to trial.'

*

Head spinning. Nausea. An echoing in the ears.

I felt like I'd been hit by a truck. My obsession with the paparazzi and Andrea taking our photo had been my brain's way of protecting me, of not making me face up to the more serious facts. We were going to trial. A trial that could see us locked up for ever in some hell called Santa Monica. A trial that wouldn't even take place for another four years. A trial that basically signalled the end of my life.

I don't know how long I stood there trying to process the reality. The weight of the last few weeks came thundering down on my shoulders and my body responded in a way my brain still couldn't. My knees felt weak; my empty stomach was ready to erupt. If there had been any food inside me it would have come out there and then.

How was this happening?

Why was it happening?

Why was it happening *to me*?

It wasn't a game any more. It wasn't some big adventure. The last few weeks had felt like a massive comedown from a ketamine high. Like my senses were just settling back to normal. And that's how I'd been treating it. The cockroaches in my bed, the freezing nights, the ripped jacket, the hacks pretending to be long-lost relatives to make a dollar: none of it had been pleasant but it hadn't felt real, either. It was just a stage you had to go through before you felt better.

It had been like watching a movie of my life, not actually living it. At some level I believed my family would just come and get me out. I'd been so naive, so upbeat and positive, and with no reason whatsoever. No two ways about it, I had been conning myself start to finish. There was no hero in this story. As far as I could tell, there wasn't even an ending. Not for a long, long time.

I sat in silence as we were driven away from the prosecutor's office. Next stop was the courts, where we would be processed, whatever that involved. What did it matter at that moment? The swarm of faces and cameras outside the car windows made no impression. The hands banging on the roof, fingers feverishly pulling at the door handles to get in didn't terrify me any more. How could they hurt me more than I'd already hurt myself?

I didn't know what Melissa was going through. I can't honestly say I'd thought about her or anyone else for what felt like a long, long time. But as I slowly came down from my personal cloud of misery, and saw her staring blankly out the window, I realised how grateful I was she was there.

We'd had our problems, but at that moment Melissa Reid was the most important person in my world. One thing was certain: I wouldn't be able to get through the next phase of my life without her by my side.

CHAPTER THIRTEEN

AS LONG AS WE'RE TOGETHER

I looked out of the car at the horde of sweaty men waving their cameras above their heads, jostling over each other for prime position. I couldn't tell where one greasy head ended and the next began.

The court building was about ten metres away. There was no obvious path between us and the entrance, but I could see my lawyer Peter Madden waiting there. Why hadn't he been at the state prosecutor's meeting? I couldn't follow what was happening behind the scenes. My immediate concern was how to get from the car to the court. A couple of military guys wielding machine guns were maintaining a perimeter around us as we emerged but that was it. After that all hell broke loose.

The noise hit me first. So many people were shouting my name. I wanted to close my ears, close my eyes, jump back into the car and get out of there. The guard pushing me in the back told me that wasn't an option. I put my head down and shuffled as close as I could behind the lead guard, and every step of the way I felt hands all over my head and body.

'Michaella! Michaella!'

Dozens of strangers were clamouring for my attention. I wanted to fall to my knees, to curl up and hide. I knew if I stopped moving for a second, I'd be crushed. And the worst of it? It wouldn't be the worst thing that could happen.

It took two guards to force the court doors shut. Even the size of their guns hadn't tempered the journalists' desire to get a piece of us. But we were now inside and away from the baying mob. Peter seemed strangely buoyed by what was unfolding. He was quite comfortable with all the media attention. He said he got the call late the previous night with no time to brief us or even warn us of what was happening. He'd high-tailed it over just in time to meet us at the door of the court. When he got his breath back, he introduced us to a new figure, an Irish missionary called Father Maurice Foley. The priest had been back in the old country the previous month, where he'd seen us on the news. Knowing he was due back in Peru, he'd sought out my family.

'That was a challenge, I can tell you,' he said. 'Their whole yard was full of reporters pretending to be your friends.'

Father Foley had a very comforting air about him. He said my mum was looking strong. She was praying for me, not blaming me. I'm not sure I fully appreciated what a remarkable thing this elderly priest had done for me at that stage. The fact he'd gone out of his way to help a family of strangers was wonderful. He was like a superhero, at a time when I was giving up hope on everyone.

The second he left the room another pair of guards arrived to join the two already with us. After a curt chat, Peter said, 'You're being taken to a cell.'

'How long for?'

'Until the court calls you to be processed.'

'And when will that be?'

'It should just be a couple of hours. I'll try and get some food sent down.' We were shoved out the door so hard and fast I never got the time to say goodbye to Father Foley.

Okay, I thought, *I can do this.* And then I saw our cell and I knew a couple of minutes would seem like a lifetime. I say, 'cell', there was that much crap inside it looked more like an abandoned office. The kind of office you'd give an employee you really hated. There was an old filing cabinet in one corner, alongside boxes of papers. There was even an old fridge. Which obviously didn't work.

It was about seven foot by seven, solid walls on two sides and bars on the other two. No windows anywhere. The stationery took up half the floor space. Half the rest was filled by the slumped body of one of the scariest-looking women I'd ever seen in my life. She was almost certainly Peruvian, nearly as wide as she was high, and covered in the most bizarrely gruesome tattoos of Disney characters. I'd never seen Cinderella look so intimidating. And I definitely wouldn't want to bump into her Minnie Mouse in a dark alleyway.

As the guard clanged his keys into the door lock, she didn't take her eyes off us for a second. But she wasn't the worst of it. Not even close. Directly on the other side of the bars was another cell filled with even nastier-looking men. Dozens of arms reached through the bars, waiting to cop a feel of me and Melissa as we entered.

'We can't go in there! Please, don't make us!' I shrieked. I started to back away and got precisely nowhere. As the door swung open, heavy hands shoved us inside to the raucous catcalls from the killers and rapists next door. With the baying neighbours, the stench of God knows what, and the unforgiving airless heat, it was an all-out assault on the senses. I wanted to close my eyes, cover my ears and hide. But if I did, I'd never survive.

It was all I could do to avoid the eager, clutching paws. But where to go? The woman was taking up the safe wall. And she didn't look like budging. In fact, no sooner was the guard out of earshot than she made a point of standing up and blocking our path. In one step she was so close to me we were actually touching. But if I moved back even a few inches I'd be mauled by the animals in the cage behind.

And, that, obviously, was her plan.

Panicked, I studied the room. The only other space was at the back where there was a hole in the floor. The toilet. The area around it was filthy but at least it wouldn't hurt me. I moved towards it, but the woman blocked my path.

'She wants us to get caught,' Melissa said.

'I know. What are we going to do?'

'I think we're going to fight. And then we're going to die. But at least we'll go together.'

I couldn't see any other outcome. The guards had disappeared. No matter how loud we shouted, they weren't coming back. We were on our own.

Just as Miss Disney lifted her arms to give us the push that would send us to hell, the main doors opened and the distinctive aroma of fried food filled the room. I nearly cried when I saw Peter carrying boxes of chicken and chips.

'Thank God you're here,' I said. 'This place is dangerous. It's beyond belief what we're dealing with down here.'

In one glance Peter read the entire situation. He looked horrified. He said something but the cacophony from the male half of the unit drowned him out. He wasn't allowed to stay down there with us. But the men couldn't give a damn about me and Melissa any more. All they had eyes for was the chicken.

Colonel Sanders was working the same magic on our cellmate. The second she heard footsteps she'd retreated back to her wall, but her dark eyes never left the food. I snatched one of the chicken boxes from Peter and held it out.

'Would you like some?' I said. She looked wary, like a stray dog being summoned by a stranger, not knowing whether to beg or bite.

'Take it,' I said. 'Please.'

She took the box and sat back down, gesturing us to join her as she did so. Eager not to ruin the peace, we did. And immediately wished we hadn't. The sight and sound of the woman tearing into piece after piece of chicken was the most hideous thing I've ever witnessed. Spots of greasy saliva rained down on her arms and legs. I wanted to gag.

She took her fill and offered me the box to finish what was inside.

Oh God, no. The thought of even touching the carton made me feel sick.

'It's okay,' I said, and waved my hands to convey it. She got the message, I think, because she sat back and polished off the remaining portions. Afterwards she burped, wiped her fingers over her filthy shirt and started chatting again. Non-stop, unintelligible.

Melissa did her best to pick out the odd word, but the rest was lost. The more we didn't understand, the angrier she got. She leapt to her feet and began shouting into the air, waving her fists in total fury. I thought she was going to smack us. But she didn't. She smacked herself. Right-punched her own face. When that didn't work, she headbutted the wall. Not once, not twice, again and again. I could see the blood coming off the brick.

The men opposite laughed like it was the funniest thing ever. It wasn't. It was just sad. I think all she wanted to do was communicate with us. I don't know when she'd last had a conversation with anyone.

Eventually she sat down, rocking on her backside, hugging her knees, all the while still muttering a hundred miles an hour. Melissa and I didn't say a word. We didn't want to set her off again. It was only when Peter returned that we dared move.

'Any news?'

'About another hour, I'm told,' he said. 'Don't get too comfortable.'

'Somehow I don't think that's going to be a problem.'

He left again and I sat back down and felt my eyelids get heavy. It wasn't just food we'd gone without. I'd barely slept in the last twenty-seven hours. I didn't want to go before some official hearing feeling groggy, so I didn't fight it. I thought I'd get forty winks, tops. We made some space on the floor and tried to make our minds go blank to blot out the horror show around us. When I finally stirred, nearly three hours had gone by. And we were still stuck there.

By the time Peter returned, the whole afternoon had been and gone. He couldn't have been more apologetic. The court had made promises it couldn't keep. 'But you're definitely next in the queue,' he said. 'You'll be in by ten o'clock.'

'Wow, they work late here.'

'No, not ten tonight. Tomorrow morning.'

'You're saying we have to sleep here?'

'I'm sorry. If there was anything I could do . . .'

There was no point blaming Peter. It was the system and we just had to get on with it. I needed a pee, but the sight and smell of the toilet hole was just too off-putting. I asked a guard if there was anywhere else I could go. He laughed in my face.

'Try and sleep,' Melissa said. 'The urge will pass.'

It took ages but eventually I dropped off. Our cellmate was not about to join us in slumber, however. I woke up to an unearthly sound. When my eyes focused, I could just make out the Disney woman crouching over the hole, fingers down her throat, vomiting into the void – and all around it.

Just when you think your senses can't suffer any more. What with her caterwauling and the hellish aroma, it was all I could do not to throw up. But at least any idea of peeing had completely left my head.

I guess I must have fallen back asleep at some point because the next thing I remember was being woken to the chimes of a guard smacking his truncheon against the metal bars – that and the noise of about fifty men and one psychotic woman telling him to shut up.

I'd slept sitting up, my bag containing everything the thieves back at Dirandro hadn't stolen clutched to my knees. When we didn't jump to attention the second the guards arrived, I was dragged to my feet so fast I could only watch as the bag fell to the floor and rolled dangerously close to the latrine hole.

I went to grab it but two guards virtually lifted me towards the door. I'm five foot eight, maybe an inch or two taller than most of the men in uniform, but they were solid. Even so. That bag was my last link with the outside world. All the bits and pieces Keith and everyone had brought me were in there. There was no way I was leaving it behind.

I don't know how, but for a second I had the power of ten men.

I lunged backwards into the cell, catching both men off guard, and managed to snatch my precious bag before I was caught.

We were marched upstairs, no information as to where we were going. Situation normal, of course. I guessed it was to court, to be processed, whatever that entailed. We were first dumped in a side room. Two minutes later Peter showed up with Fishman, who had our notes and records and quickly ran over our stories before checking our plea for the hundredth time.

'Not guilty,' we parroted in unison. It was getting boring, even to us.

'You think it's boring now,' said Fishman, 'you're going to be asked questions today that you've answered a dozen times already. Do yourselves a favour and keep to your stories.'

'You believe us?'

'I believe that if you start contradicting yourselves or each other it won't reflect well.'

He went on to explain that we'd be in an open court. Which meant that any media who got there early enough could get in. It was the first time this had ever happened at a hearing in a case like ours – most likely due to the international interest in us. We should expect a bit of attention, he said. In fact, he'd been asked if we wanted to do any live TV interviews.

I looked at Melissa. Melissa looked at me. Then we looked at him. 'No!'

'Then we're done here,' he said. 'Let's go.'

He banged on the door and guards arrived to handcuff us for the walk to the chamber. I was sick of being dragged around. Before they could get organised, I said to Melissa, 'How about you wear this?' and I handed her my tatty leather jacket. She was totally on the same page and threw over her top for me to put on. Knowing all those cameras were going to be pointing at us made us want to get some kind of control of the situation, however small. If just one or two journalists got our names confused because of our clothes that would make our day.

As we reached the door I said to Melissa, 'I'm glad you're here.'

'Me too.' And then out we went.

The corridors were packed with cameras as we shuffled in. When I finally looked up we were in a massive room filled with rows of chairs full of random people and journalists and, at one end, a stage with half a dozen seats like you'd see at a school prize-giving ceremony. We had a complete meltdown at the sight of it. We were facing the full force of the Peruvian justice system with the nation's TV cameras trained on us, and they would do with us as they saw fit. I'd been thinking this would be a discreet affair in an office like the one in which we'd met the state prosecutor. This couldn't have been more different. They were gearing up for a showpiece. We looked and felt awful. And vulnerable. We hadn't been able to shower or change our clothes after a night in a vomit-strewn cell. Things couldn't have been much worse. We tried to refuse being at the centre of this parade, but there was no way anyone was backing down.

We were forced to walk in and sit down opposite the stage area, alongside Fishman and a translator. Once the whole room was filled up, the judge and a local prosecutor took their places at the top table. We were mortified.

Fishman was right. The questions came thick and fast but there were no curveballs. What our lawyer hadn't prepared us for was the atmosphere. It was as intimidating in its own way as the cell downstairs had been. The magnitude of our situation was finally hitting home.

I was thrown completely. Even answering the question 'How old are you?' had me tongue-tied. I must have sounded totally dodgy. Melissa and I had agreed to answer alternate questions, which was a bit of a lottery. She seemed to get the easy ones whereas I was grilled with more difficult questions, such as: 'Why are you saying you were kidnapped?' Implicit in their phrasing was the accusation that we were lying. Then, 'If you were being forced, why didn't you alert the policemen who had asked to have their picture taken with you?'

They were referring to our sightseeing charade at Cusco. They took a dim view of why we'd done such touristy things if we were supposedly under threat from gangsters. Every time I bumbled or hesitated, the questioner would say: 'Come on, answer the question!' There was no let-up. They knew the kidnap story was a crock of lies but we'd come so far with it that we couldn't backtrack now, and the authorities were running out of patience.

On paper my answers probably read okay. To see me standing up in court trying to say the same things, I must have sounded and looked as guilty as sin. I was visibly shaking. The ordeal lasted about an hour. When it was over, I collapsed on a seat, exhausted, and said to Fishman, 'What now?'

'Now you're in the system. This is where it gets difficult.'

'What, this *hasn't* been difficult?' The lawyer shrugged. He'd seen worse, clearly, and reading between the lines that's what we should expect for the next four years.

'I'm going to do everything I can to get an early trial date,' he said. 'Until then you just have to stay strong and hope for Ancón 2. If you're lucky you won't get sent to Santa Monica.'

'I don't care,' I said emphatically. 'As long as we're together, we're okay.'

Melissa smiled weakly. We'd had our ups and downs but we both knew our only chance of surviving was as a pair. We had to use that to our advantage. It was the only card we had.

*

By rights, now we were in the prison system we should have been shipped out immediately. After speaking to the journalists all Fishman could tell us was, 'They'll move you when they move you. I'm not being funny,' he insisted. 'It's just the way they do things.'

That was it for our contact with the outside world for the rest of the day. Fishman left and we were, once again, at the mercy of our captors. There were no friendly faces here – no Esteban or female cop to buy us doughnuts.

When we returned to our stinking cell beneath the court, Disney woman was gone but there were still the guys behind the bars opposite, stripping off and miming what they wanted to do to us if they got the chance. They were permanently fighting or masturbating, and making sure we knew about it. It was the very worst of what could barely be labelled humanity.

When the guard next appeared, I caught his attention and, in stilted sign language, told him I wanted a cigarette. The problem was, I had no lighter. There was no smoking in my cell, he mimed, but he gestured to the other side of the cell, to a bathroom area where it would be possible. He had a lighter, and he would show me where I could smoke.

I quickly regretted trusting him. No sooner had he lit my cigarette and I was smoking it, sitting down on my haunches, than I felt a hand ruffling my hair. And then it got worse. My head was being pulled towards his crotch.

'Melissa, Melissa!' I shouted at the top of my voice.

'What's going on? What are you doing?' she shouted.

He obviously thought it wasn't worth his while getting embroiled in a scene with us two infamous prisoners, so he left. I was mortified to have trusted him and was dreading he would take some kind of revenge. Celine's warning came back to me: 'You can't trust them!' I would have to be more careful in future.

Some time later we were marched to another cellblock where the guards' uniforms were different. Their attitude, too, was sterner, more militaristic. These were the INPE – the *Instituto Nacional Penitenciario* – the government agency behind most of Peru's seventy-one prisons. Our first experience of them was horrible. I'd been given about sixty soles by Father Foley – all the money I now had in the world. One of the INPE came over. He'd spotted it. He starting shouting at me with full military bearing, demanding I hand it over to him. I burst into tears and was powerless to stop it being taken. A female police officer had been watching and immediately came over to check with us what had happened. She then got it back for us.

We were into a new cycle of lawlessness, it seemed, where you couldn't trust people just because they wore a uniform. Some were fair, and decent; others – the men, mostly, of course – were opportunistic at best and downright brutal and sadistic at worst. This new reality went to the core of my misery. To think we might be facing four years of this before we even got to trial. I didn't think I could suffer it for even four weeks.

We were marched to this new cellblock and manhandled along more corridors and into another faceless room. For at least ten seconds we were left alone before an internal door opened and a guy in a white coat beckoned us in. Using no English whatsoever he invited us to strip. He seemed to be writing down descriptions of our bodies, checking it against stuff written on other bits of paper. The fact he was dressed like a doctor seemed to make it okay. For all I knew it could have been the janitor in fancy dress.

When he was done two nurses strolled in and they got a bit more personal. They produced a clipboard holding a month-by-month calendar. One of them started tapping it and pointing to my crotch and babbling away in Spanish, all the while staring casually over my shoulder at a TV on the wall. Then she handed over the clipboard with a pen. If she'd been looking my way, she'd have noticed I had not the slightest clue what she was on about.

'Any idea, Mel?'

'Fuck knows,' she said. 'I can only make out what sounds like "sangria".'

When the nurses took their eyes off the TV and saw nothing was written they started doing these big theatrical movements, jabbing at particular days on the calendar and pointing again between our legs. All the while this 'sangria', 'sangria'.

'Oh, I get it,' Melissa suddenly said. 'It's "*sangre*". Blood. I think they want to know our cycles.' She paused. 'Do you remember yours?'

'Are you joking? I couldn't tell you what day it is today.'

'What about at the airport?' She was right. How the hell could I forget that? When the hell was it? The 6th of August, or the 7th. 'You'd better write something down. Number two's getting a bit crazy.' She was right. It was like she'd been possessed by Disney woman. She was shouting and grabbing at me.

'Please, give us a break,' I said. 'I don't even know if it's day or night right now.'

But it wasn't the clipboard bothering her now. I was spun round to the opposite wall – the one with the TV on it. It was showing footage of me and Melissa being manhandled into the court earlier that day.

There's something about seeing yourself onscreen that knocks the wind out of you. I looked terrible. I was pale, my clothes a size too large and I was clearly exhausted. The image changed to scenes of us being arrested at Jorge Chávez. I was wearing the same outfit except my jacket was still in one piece.

To my horror, a couple of male guards blithely walked in, dressed in the same fatigues as the guys earlier. It was only when they started going through our dirty clothes that I kicked off, realising how violated I felt.

'Hey, come on, leave it alone,' I said, desperately covering myself with both hands. 'I need to put those on.' Language barrier or not, they knew what I wanted all right. One of them smiled, exposing a broken row of yellow and gold teeth. Instead of putting my clothes down, he held them out towards me, just out of my reach. He knew what he was doing. The only way I was getting anything was to stop covering one half of my body.

'Please,' I begged, 'put it down', but he just waved my tattered jacket and pants like he was teasing a cat with a ball of string. Both men were looking now, leering and waiting. One of them sat on the table. He was settling down for the long haul.

'Ah, what the hell,' I said. I flung out one hand and snatched my jacket before he could whip it away. While the guy's eyes were busy I grabbed the rest of my stuff as well and ran to the corner to get dressed. When I turned back, they were by the door with all our belongings in their hands, including my precious bag.

'Hey, that stuff's mine. Where are you going?'

There was no answer. Just a shrug. Then a laugh. Then a door slamming.

Melissa was still traumatised by the ghosts of ourselves on the telly.

'Did you see that?' I said. 'They took our bags. They could plant any shit on us now.'

'You really think they need any more evidence?' she said. 'They're just scum.'

And, of course, she was right. We never saw our bags or their contents again.

*

Rage is a great distraction. I was fuming for so long about being robbed I lost track of time. I remember us being sent to a cell with bunk beds, being glared at by another mob of disgruntled inmates, all female, thankfully, then being hoiked out again a couple of hours later. The INPE didn't like letting the grass grow under our feet.

This time was different though. We were taken outside and shoved against a wall. If a firing squad had materialised, I wouldn't have been surprised. In the end it was just Peter who appeared.

'Thank God you're still here,' he said between heavy breaths. 'I have news.'

'I hope it's worth it.'

'I just wanted you to hear it from me,' he said.

Oh no, hear what? I felt my insides tighten. I knew exactly what he was going to say. 'We're not going to Ancón 2, are we?' I said.

He shook his head. 'I'm really sorry. Fishman and I did everything we could, but they've decided to send you to Santa Monica.'

I took a gulp of cold air. All the stories, all the rumours about how bad the place was, ran through my head. How much worse could things be? Melissa looked at me and, from her expression, I could see she was forcing on her tough-girl persona.

'We'll be okay. As long as we're together we'll get through it,' she said.

Instinctively, I reached out for her hand. She squeezed mine back.

'That's the thing,' Peter said. 'I've just been told.' He paused. Looked like he was going to burst. 'You won't be together. They're going to split you up.'

CHAPTER FOURTEEN

HABLA ESPAÑOL?

'**W**here are we?'

Not even a grunt in response.

It must have been six or seven in the morning, on a day in August 2013. In front of us was a sprawling low-level compound. I assumed it was Santa Monica. And I assumed that's where we were going to be split up. But all I could really see was the dust. Everywhere you looked had this corn-coloured film over it. The roads were yellow, the buildings were yellow and, after just a few minutes in the open air, my jeans were threatening to turn the same colour.

We were standing outside the transit van we'd arrived in. It was painted black, very badly so, and its windows had been blacked out also. It had obviously been enough to fool the paparazzi. We were on our own in the cloudy morning air, just us and half-a-dozen unsmiling INPE guards, who wore the same dark fatigues as the ones back at the court. They were heavily armed and brutal. The one who'd tightened my handcuffs had laughed when I winced. They'd openly leered at my crotch on the journey over. And at least one of them had my personal belongings in his locker.

'Walk,' one of them said in heavily accented English. Then, in a language that needed no interpretation, he indicated forwards with his gun.

The most positive thing I'd heard about Santa Monica was that it was all female. That wasn't saying much, but at least we'd be separated from male prisoners. We were taken inside the closest building and searched. Again. That killed some time, at least. Maybe not four years, but I was grateful for every second we were above ground. The room we were in was small, made smaller by the ridiculous number of guards staring at us, but it had a window overlooking a garden that contained the first bit of genuine grass I'd seen for weeks. There were even flowerbeds. Beautiful ones, well tended by the look of it.

I'd experienced enough of the Peruvian sense of humour not to get too excited. For all I knew the window was a fake. But no, I went over and pressed my nose against the dusty glass. There were people out there, inmates by the look of it, sitting and talking and enjoying the space.

'Wow,' I said, 'they're wrong about Santa Monica, Mel. This place doesn't look as bad as we've been told.'

'That's because it's not Santa Monica.'

We spun around. In the doorway was Fishman.

'Trust me,' he said, 'if this were Santa Monica you'd know it. And,' he added, 'I'd still be trying to find you.'

'Where are we then?' Melissa asked.

'Virgen de Fatima,' he said. 'Not as modern as Ancón Two, but not quite the hellhole of Santa Monica – although don't let the pretty flowers fool you. You've got some of the country's worst criminals here.'

Fatima wasn't short of its share of scary people. It took the majority of serious cases awaiting trial. Terrorists, murderers, abusers, you name it. They were sent there then shipped off after sentencing. Drug smugglers were looped into the same category. In fact, after terrorism, drug-trafficking was regarded as the next worst crime.

'The state prosecutor asked for you to come here. This is very unusual, as this is not usually a foreigners' jail. Only Peruvian women here.'

'So is Santa Monica, isn't it?' I asked.

'Santa Monica is all female but there are many foreigners there. And it is so bad, so bad . . .' he paused, then added, 'It would be worse for them if you were in Santa Monica. You have journalists observing your treatment who could report it all over the world. There could be . . . bad press if you were sent there.'

'Look, Peter said they were separating us. Can you stop it?'

'It's out of my hands,' Fishman said. 'They'll make their mind up what do with you while you're here.'

'So, it could happen any time?'

He nodded. 'You could have a few hours together, a few days or a few weeks. They do things differently here.'

Suddenly, there was a commotion outside the office. The door flung open and there stood Keith, followed by Melissa's dad. Both looked like they'd run through a prickly hedge backwards. Getting past the INPE when you don't have lawyer credentials was obviously not straightforward.

I was so happy to see my brother. Especially when Fishman said, 'We don't have much time. You're going to be moved soon and after that visitation rights are down to the discretion of the guards.'

Me and Keith looked at each other, then embraced. Even with everything going on I managed a smile. I was so lucky and grateful he was there.

Fishman explained that he'd be badgering the courts for an earlier trial date but, since we were pleading 'not guilty', not to get our hopes up. Then he said, 'Keith, did you get them?'

My brother fumbled in his pockets then handed over a phone card containing 200 soles. Enough, he said, for a month's daily use.

'Look after those,' Fishman said. 'They're like gold in here. Do not let them out of your sight.'

'You'll need this as well,' Keith said, and handed over a bunch of actual notes.

'What do I need that much money for?'

'Don't you want to eat?'

'Are you kidding me? You have to pay for food?'

'Everything in Fatima has a price,' Fishman said. 'And you don't want to be paying for it the way a lot of the inmates do.' It took me a second to process what he meant. I felt sick at the prospect. But he was right: I didn't want to be owing anyone favours.

'Keith,' I said, 'I'm desperate for some new clothes. My others were stolen. Can you get me a few things before you go?'

'I'll do my best,' he said, 'but I've only got one more day here.'

'Don't remind me! Just get what you can. Anything will do.'

A shout from one of the guards indicated our time was up. I hugged my brother and thanked our lawyer. The second they were out of sight I felt my lip start to tremble. Suddenly the beautiful garden seemed a mile away. The endless grey corridor walls were all I could see now. And it felt like they were closing in, suffocating me. *Four years,* I thought. *Four years in here. And that's just waiting to get a trial date.*

'Melissa,' I said, 'I can't do it.'

'You can. We both can. We have to.'

'Until they tear us apart.'

'Don't. Even. Think. About. It.'

There were four INPE crowding outside our room. Suddenly, they parted to reveal a small, smartly-dressed woman behind them.

'*Habla Español?*' she asked.

We shook our heads.

'*Vale,*' the woman said. 'Okay. English.'

Bless her for trying, but her accent was so thick and her vocabulary so limited that I struggled to make out more than a handful of words. She seemed to be saying that she was the prison's director, but that couldn't be right, could it? Why the hell would she be meeting us personally? In my fifteen days in the Peruvian system I'd been treated like a nameless piece of meat. This woman knew our names. I didn't know whether that was because she made it a point to know all her inmates' names, or just the names of the high-profile ones, like us.

Maybe it isn't going to be so bad here after all.

We were led through a series of corridors, the director chatting the entire time like some excited estate agent showing off a property. I barely made out a word she said but Mel was nodding along. I'd ask her later. We walked for ages turning this way, then that. If I had to find my way out of that maze, I'm not sure I could have done it. We ended up at a large doughnut-shaped area. The 'rotunda', she called it, had five gated corridors coming off it. 'Minimum security, maximum security, B1, B2 and B3,' the director said.

'Which one are we?' I asked.

'For the moment,' she said, 'you are here. Tomorrow . . .' she paused. 'Tomorrow we will see.'

The gates were all electronically sealed, but one had five INPE waiting outside, four guys and one woman. The woman, it turned out, was the head of security. She was in charge of us now. Any problems we had, the director said, we were to ask her. Just one problem: she didn't speak a word of English. Then came the familiar question: '*Habla español?*'

'No,' we replied. She shrugged and started speaking Spanish anyway, at machine-gun speed, as the director and her guards disappeared.

Our corridor took us out from the centre, along one of the spokes of the bicycle-wheel layout. We went down some stairs, through a couple of checkpoints and emerged by a patio. A bunch of smokers were braving the cold. It looked like the scene from outside any office. You could forget it was a prison. From behind them, inside a large lobby, an almighty hubbub spilled out.

There must have been four or five dozen women leaning against the walls or sitting on the floors, basically doing nothing but talking. There was the slightest of pauses when we walked in while they considered their responses. Some of them went out of their way to make it clear they were ignoring us. Others made throat-slitting signs and signals of a more sexual nature. It was terrifying, but I tried to concentrate on the three payphones screwed to one of the walls. The card Keith gave me was burning a hole in my pocket. First chance I got, I'd be phoning my mum.

I thought we'd be taken to our latest cell but the guards stopped at the foot of another staircase. The head of security rattled off some more quick-fire Spanish that she knew damn well we'd not understand, then shoved us forwards. The way she was gesturing I guessed it was time for the next stage of this pass-the-parcel game we seemed to be part of. Sure enough, there was a woman waiting who beckoned us over. She wasn't dressed like INPE. She wasn't dressed like any security I'd seen. In fact, she was dressed just like us. Worse even.

She was small, about five foot four, quite chubby with short, dark hair and dressed in cut-off denim jeans and a short-sleeved check shirt. Her arms were covered in tattoos. When I got up close I noticed her eyebrows were printed on too, as was her lipstick.

She smiled, revealing more than one gold tooth. '*Habla español?*'

Like the head of security, she didn't take the fact we replied 'no' as a reason not to babble on in Spanish. Melissa followed enough to make out the woman's name was Gonzales, which sounded like a man's name to me. But then maybe that was the look she was going for.

'So, why's she pointing to herself and saying, "*Delegada*", then?'

'Prison nickname?' Melissa suggested. 'Maybe surname. I dunno.'

Gonzales or '*Delegada*' led us up the stairs and into a giant hall with a bunch of doors coming off. I'd like to say I was alert and took it all in but I felt like I'd been on this magical mystery tour for hours. It was all getting a bit much. What I can remember is that no one was spitting at us. Everywhere looked clean enough, the women seemed tidy, if hideously aggressive-looking, some of them. The worst part was the not knowing. I didn't know why someone dressed worse than me appeared to be in charge, I didn't know where we were going or for how long. To be fair, I got the feeling Gonzales had told us what was going on – but in a language I couldn't understand. It wasn't her fault we couldn't understand a word.

'Mel,' I said, 'we really need to learn Spanish. They could be doing anything to us.'

We both understood the underlying meaning of that admission. I hadn't bothered with Spanish before because I had no need of it beyond '*Hola*' and '*Gracias*'. On some level, I knew that learning the language was admitting to myself that I wasn't getting home any time soon.

But the time for denial was over. Even I could see that. We were looking at four years until a trial. That fact wasn't going to change. And if we wanted to stay alive for that time we needed to play the game. To do that we needed to be able to understand the rules.

I think Gonzales got that. A few women were taking more of an interest than the others and she called one of them, Rosa, over. She was a tiny thing, and clearly terrified of Gonzales. She looked like she'd jump at her own shadow. But Rosa had one thing going for her that made her the most important person in the room.

She spoke English.

Okay, not the best English, but she didn't ask if we spoke Spanish so she was already my all-time favourite Peruvian.

Gonzales continued the tour talking nineteen to the dozen as the head of security had before, and Rosa did her best to translate. The four doors led into four cell blocks. Each one slept a hundred women. Two of them looked packed near to capacity. One was empty and one, judging by the belongings next to the bed, had only one occupant.

'*La Diosa del Amor*,' Rosa said. 'Or as you say, "the goddess of love". You'll meet her. She is very special.'

At the back of the hall was a small kitchen area. Basically, a microwave, a sink and a table. Again, it was strangely well maintained. Although I did notice all the pans and knives and even the microwave were chained to the wall. A few women were playing cards, a couple were reading, mostly they were doing make-up. Each other's and their own. It was nice to see. I didn't know how long any of them had been there but the fact they still cared about their appearance gave me hope.

Maybe you can get through this. Maybe don't give up on yourself.

Gonzales was getting bored now. She marched us back to the empty cell and then left.

'What's her story?' I asked.

Rosa looked at me blankly.

'Who made her boss?'

'Gonzales is *delegada*,' she said.

'What does it mean? Does she work here?'

The best Rosa could explain it was that South American prisons don't have enough staff, so the inmates get to nominate someone in charge. They don't get paid, they don't have weapons, but they do make the rules and run their own little fiefdom. I hadn't noticed but there were no guards in the hall. We hadn't seen any since the head of security took her detail away with her. Apparently, the guards only left the rotunda for roll call four times a day and for lights out. The *delegada* was expected to handle everything on the other side of the door. If there were problems on the inside, she was the one who'd get in trouble on the outside.

'What kind of trouble?'

'*El calabozo*.' Quite literally: 'the dungeon'. In other words, solitary confinement. Losing your freedom would be bad; a loss of face among the inmates obviously worse.

'So, Gonzales is a bit scary?'

'No. But she has scary people with her.'

Good to know.

We'd only merely glanced in the cells before. Rosa explained we'd be staying in the empty one, at least until the director had done all the paperwork. Inside felt more like a dormitory than a cell, with its rows and rows of metal bunk beds. There was a window, which I hadn't expected. From the chattering and laughing I could hear through it, it sounded like the cell next door was having a party. I looked out and realised I was staring onto the main street where we'd come in. The prison was such a maze I'd lost my bearings. I watched as local people went about their daily business, walking past the prison oblivious to the horrors on the other side of the wall. I couldn't decide if being able to see the outside world was a treat or greater torture. Time would decide.

A big steel door was operated remotely from outside. Lights suspended from the high ceilings worked similarly, as they had in the last couple of places. But compared to those this was paradise. This had a TV.

And a bathroom. Sort of.

At the back of the cell was a makeshift shower, which was basically a pipe sticking out of the wall. I'd have been happy with that but what made the place five stars was an actual toilet next to it. I'd almost forgotten what one looked like. There was no screen or privacy of any kind, so in the other cells there could be ninety-nine other women watching your business. Those in the beds closest to it suffered even worse, I suppose. But considering Mel and I had the run of the place it was as close to luxury as we were going to get.

Rosa asked us if we wanted to know the *delegada*'s rules, but before she could get going a woman ran into the cell and rapped me on the back with a rolled-up newspaper.

'What the hell?' She was babbling something as she hit me.

'Rosa, what does she want?'

She's saying, 'It's you, it's you.'

Melissa grabbed the newspaper and the woman calmed down. She pointed to the front page. There were our mugs, large as life, and hundreds and hundreds of words.

'*Famosa, muy famosa.*'

'She says you're very famous.'

I didn't have time to reply. A voice like a foghorn blasted out from the entrance. The person it came from filled the doorway. Nearly six feet tall, built like a brick outhouse – with just a stained vest stretched thinly across a huge chest that merged with an even bigger belly – she looked like a wrestler gone to seed. As the newcomer came closer, our translator all but buried herself at the rear of one of the bunks. The woman with the newspaper backed away as well, finally silent.

The giantess had tattoos on every inch of visible skin, including her face. Dark teardrops ran from under her eyes all the way down to the rolls of her neck – a prison code meaning she'd killed people. Her arms and legs were a mosaic of shapes and colours. Beneath the drawings were clear wounds from self-harming and, I guessed, stabbings. It was not a healthy picture. By now the woman was close enough to snatch the newspaper from Melissa.

'*Famosa*,' she repeated, and looked from the front-page picture to me then back to the picture then at Mel.

I was close to retching. Not out of fear – although I was definitely scared, I won't lie – but the stench. I don't know if it was her vest, her pants, her sweat or just her breath – it was too pungent to analyse.

Melissa was that bit further away and asked Rosa to translate. This was one person we didn't want to antagonise by not understanding. But it turned out our guest didn't want to talk. She leant down right into my face and sniffed, like I was the one with the odour problem. Then she smiled and kissed our pictures on the paper.

'*Famosa*,' she said again and, smiling, waddled back out of the room. No one spoke for a minute. I'm not even sure we remembered to breathe.

'What the hell was that?' I said.

Rosa emerged from her hidey-hole then skipped over to the doorway to ensure our visitor was out of earshot.

'That,' she said quietly, 'that was *La Diosa*.'

'*That* was the Goddess of Love?'

Rosa nodded solemnly. 'Not funny. She's evil.'

'How?'

'I can't say.' The woman was clearly terrified of crossing the great goddess.

After much cajoling, eventually Rosa spilled the beans. I wished she hadn't. *La Diosa* used to be married. The husband had an affair and eventually had a baby with his girlfriend. It's hard to keep these things quiet and *Diosa* found out. She didn't say anything to him and carried on as normal. One night he came home from work and she fed him a stew, like she often did, but this tasted different.

'What meat is this?' the husband asked.

'Yours,' she replied. She'd murdered the girlfriend, killed the nine-week old baby and served it up in a dish. If we didn't feel sick before, we did now.

How the hell were we on the same planet as someone like that, let alone sharing a hall? If that lunatic didn't qualify for maximum security, then who the hell did?

*

We'd started our tour about 8.30 a.m. At nine o'clock there was shouting, and the place emptied, Rosa included. I watched from the cell door as all the inmates trundled towards the staircase.

'Do you think we should follow?'

'I guess they'd tell us if we had to.'

'Fair enough.' As if to ram the point home, there was a buzz and the door to our cell slid shut.

Another day we'd have got angry, at least indignant. Right then we were so tired we let it happen. In any case, we had a home to make. Melissa and I agreed on two beds at the back of the room, furthest away from the door. It was only us two, so the bathroom issue wasn't a problem. I just wanted to have as much notice as possible if *La Diosa* returned.

The following day was my brother's last in Peru, so I wanted to write a letter for my family for him to take back. I hadn't spoken to my mother since I caused her illness. I had so much to apologise for. I'd barely completed a paragraph and the tears were rolling down my cheeks. I must have looked like a clean version of *Diosa*, except the tears were real, not etched on.

An hour went by, then two, then three, and suddenly the doors opened again, coinciding with the inmates reappearing in the block.

I had no interest in going outside, not even when I heard them clearly eating.

'Do you want to go out, Mel?' I asked.

'Not really.'

'Good. Neither do I.'

Courtesy of Keith we both had a packed lunch, which I was determined to make last as long as possible. Avoiding our neighbours and keeping our noses clean was the order of the day. Tomorrow we'd be braver. Right then, we couldn't wait for the doors to close again to get a few more hours of safety under our belts.

It must have been nearly six when I realised everyone was back in the hall. Not for long though. Our door was opened and once again I saw the inmates file downstairs. Twenty minutes later they were back, and the aromas of some nondescript foods wafted in. If anything, it made me less inclined to eat. I thought of exploring the patio where we'd come in but then I had a better idea.

'Hey, Mel, remember those phones?'

'Yeah, damn right,' she said. 'Let's go.'

We hid our few belongings as best we could and ventured back outside and down the stairs. There were women coming and going from the rotunda carrying plates of food, but no one was using the phones. I was so excited to finally get a chance to speak to my mum. But I couldn't get the phone card Keith had given me earlier to work. Melissa couldn't get any sense out of it either. 'Use mine,' she said. 'Keith can sort yours out tomorrow.'

I'd committed the dialling code to memory this time and I was so excited to hear the faint hum of the overseas call connecting. I didn't even consider what unearthly time it must have been back home. I just wanted to hear my mother's voice. There was a click as the phone picked up.

'Mum,' I shouted, 'it's me!'

But that was all I managed. A hand came down on the receiver and cut the call off. I turned round and saw we were surrounded by a dozen angry-looking women. No one said a word. They just stared.

A kerfuffle broke out at the back and the *delegada* emerged, dragging Rosa with her. I was distraught. What business was it of theirs if I was calling home?

'What's going on, Gonzales?' I said. 'I'm just trying to call my mother.'

'Not phone time,' Rosa said.

'What?'

'Phone time finished today. If you use phone, then punishment.' She looked at Gonzales, who rattled off some instructions. The group of women surrounded us and took our arms. I was suddenly very frightened.

'Rosa, where are we going?' I couldn't see her in the crowd. I was vacillating between fear and a burning sense of injustice. There were no guards, so who was this woman to make up the rules? And where the hell were they taking us?

At the top of the stairs I realised we were being pushed towards the cell doors. But we didn't stop at our cell. We were shoved past to the door on the opposite side. The door for the cell with only one inmate.

The cell of the Goddess of Love.

'Oh my God, Mel, we're going to die.'

None of the women came inside with us. The doors could only be operated by guards, so they formed a human wall at the entrance.

The cell smelled as bad as you'd imagine. And from the noises I could make out the tenant was home. For whatever reason, she decided to ignore us. The women made no sign of leaving so Melissa and I sat down on the bed furthest from *La Diosa*. At some point a klaxon went off and I saw the confusion in our jailers' faces.

'I think it's curfew time,' Melissa said, 'but they don't want to leave us.'

'Well, if they don't get back to their cell before the INPE arrive they'll be the ones in trouble. The second they leave we're legging it.'

The sound of voices broke through the high-pitched chatter outside.

'Mel, it's the INPE!'

'Thank God.'

We both yelled for help. The women didn't budge. Just smiled. I heard Gonzales' voice in conversation with them. Finally, the inmates dispersed to be replaced by two women in INPE uniform.

'*Habla español*?' one of them asked.

'Noooo, but . . .'

She laughed. 'I have some English.'

'Great, can you let us out? We're in the wrong cell.'

'*La Delegada* says this is right cell. You broke rules.'

'We didn't know.'

She shrugged. 'You should know.'

'Look, I'm sorry, we won't do it again. You've got to help us. This woman is a monster. Please, please!'

'Okay, okay,' the INPE said. 'I tell you what to do.' Her voice was drowned out by the electronic metal door sliding noisily across. I started banging on it, screaming, praying she could still hear us.

'Come on, what were you saying?' I yelled. 'What should we do?'

Her voice sounded distant but clear. '*Don't. Fall. Asleep.*'

CHAPTER FIFTEEN

THE WORST-LOOKING CHETO

I could hear the laughing, even from behind the steel doors. It had been a set-up. Yes, we'd broken the rules and had to take a punishment, but no one would risk putting newbies in the same locked room as the Goddess of Love. Not for more than a couple of hours anyway. The INPE had been in on it. That's obviously what I heard Gonzales explaining. This whole delegate thing meant she was a law unto herself. Able to mess with people's minds. And safety. What kind of bullies were in charge of us?

Luckily, we hadn't had time to sleep. At 8 p.m. the same INPE who'd locked us up led us back to our original cell. At first I had been relieved to see the bunk beds, but their design hid a sickening surprise. The hollow metal tubes were alive with scratching and clawing. I knew it was only cockroaches, I knew they couldn't hurt me, but the sound of them by my head, by my arms, by my feet, was too much. It was so loud, so unnerving and so close. I cried the entire night.

At six the next morning two new INPE yelling, *'Rapido! Rapido!'* burst in and basically lifted us out of bed. Melissa was groggy as hell. She must have been having a nightmare because she just screamed and ran in the shower like they were out to kill her. I was a zombie, awake but feeling half dead. I wasn't running anywhere. They hauled us downstairs to the patio and I didn't have the energy to fight it. Two hundred or so women were already gathered. The ones who didn't laugh at us made it clear they were not happy. I got the feeling it was with us. Rosa made her way over. She'd been told to pass on a message.

'Roll call,' she said. 'Head count. You have to be here. Or everyone punished. Gonzales says.'

Some notice would have been nice. August is the coldest month in Lima, average temperature about seventeen degrees at midday. This was the crack of dawn and I was in short sleeves and flip-flops. Within ten minutes my feet were freezing, and my arms were turning blue. I really hoped Keith would be bringing some jumpers with him on his final visit.

Some of the women were smoking, so we tried to cadge a cigarette. Some of the girls didn't want anything to do with us but a few saw an opportunity to turn a profit. The price offered for one ciggie would have bought a packet back home. At first, I shook my head and walked away. *I'm not going to be blackmailed.* Five minutes later it's all I could think about. I hadn't tasted nicotine since the dodgy guard with the lighter. I needed to make a deal. And fast. Obviously by the time I went back the price had doubled but hey-ho. I had my drag. All was well.

'What a shakedown,' I said to Rosa. 'They're obviously playing "let's fleece the rich European".'

'They did not charge a high price because you are European,' she said.

'What? Why then?'

She looked surprised. 'You are drug dealers. Drug dealers have money.'

'Is that what you think? Is that what everyone here thinks?'

She made a 'duh' face, which I took to mean 'yes'.

About 6.20 the show began. The guards called out a series

of names and one by one we answered. And that was that. The INPE left and most women drifted off. A few that remained made threatening signs to us. It had to do with more than tardiness.

We traipsed back to the cell chastised and confused. I wanted a shower but there wasn't any water. Not just hot water, no water of any kind. Rosa said it was only turned on for two half-hour periods a day. Aside from washing ourselves, if we wanted to flush the toilet or drink or clean our dishes, we'd need to fill up pans during that time for use throughout the day.

'Where can I get a pan, Rosa?'

'You buy.'

'What about a bucket?'

'You buy.'

'A cup?'

'Buy.'

There were big metal doors at the back of the main hall, and at some point one of them opened and large metal vats of porridge or gruel or some other non-descript slop were brought through by people dressed like the rest of us. Were they prisoners too?

They set the containers down and started to dish out portions to the queuing masses. Everyone had their own bowls or mugs. We had neither but that wasn't new. In Dirandro, someone had taken pity on us. Would they again?

Sure enough, as soon as word got round that we had no crockery or cutlery, a gaggle of women surrounded us offering theirs. None of the bowls looked too clean.

'It's okay, it's okay,' I said, overwhelmed by the generosity. 'I just need one.'

'Er, Michaella,' Melissa said, 'I don't think they're *giving* them to us.'

'Oh no, not the drug dealer thing again . . .'

What choice did we have? Melissa knew enough Spanish to say, 'how much?' – *cuánto cuesta?* – and one woman held up five fingers. Another held up four, another three, another two. Their bowls were all as filthy as each other's, so I went for the cheaper option. I got out

Keith's cash but as soon as the woman saw the bundle of notes she snatched the bowl back and held up ten fingers. Everyone else did the same.

So that's how it's going to be.

*

Between six to nine in the morning, everyone was allowed to do their own thing. Apart from *La Diosa* – who remained in her cell – and us. When we got back to our cell an INPE materialised outside. For at least five minutes he wouldn't let us go in. Our belongings were all over our bunks, clearly having been forensically gone through. I assumed it was a random check. It was horrible being turned over and scrutinised all the time.

For the subsequent two and a half hours we had to listen to the hubbub and chat of everyone else enjoying their downtime together. At nine, I heard Gonzales' unmistakable voice yell something and everyone started drifting back outside to the patio. Everyone, that is, except the Goddess of Love and the two European girls dominating the national front pages. Two burly inmates blocked our door when we tried to get out. We weren't allowed to socialise with the others, apparently, although I couldn't work out why.

I enjoy my personal space, but once our minders had gone the echoing silence in that huge empty hall was a bit creepy. The whale-like groans coming from *Diosa* didn't help. I was actually relieved when everyone returned just before midday. We were kept apart again until the roll call. I got the impression that they were being protected from us, which was ironic, because among them were murderers and violent women. We were no threat to anyone.

When we did get together outside for the next head count, I managed to ask Rosa where everyone had disappeared to. I've never seen such a nervous-looking woman. Every minute she spent near me got her all jumpy. Still, she stayed long enough to say, '*Trabajan.*'

'What's that?' I asked.

'They work.'

'What kind of work?'

'Making. Selling. Cooking.'

'Are they paid?'

'*Sí.*'

Bizarre. *Is anyone here an actual member of staff?*

It turned out there were also classes prisoners could take in things like social studies, home economics and languages and a bunch of other stuff. I thought about it and realised that lessons or jobs would fill a huge chunk of the day. And we had more than 1200 of them until we could expect to see a judge, let alone daylight.

'How can I get a class?' I asked.

Rosa looked nervous, more so than before, if that was possible.

'Gonzales,' she said. 'Ask Gonzales.'

For whatever reason, I could tell it was painful for Rosa being seen with us, so I let her go back to what she was doing. In any case, I wanted to get as close to the doors as possible. The second they were unlocked I made straight for the phones. As soon as I got there, I remembered my dodgy card. Luckily, the head of security was overseeing the transition from outside to in.

I showed her the card and pointed to the phone and made a kind of 'broken' sign. She looked at me stonily then held out her hand for the card. I handed it over and she held it up to the light, examined it this way and that, then put it in her pocket.

'What are you doing?' I said. 'That's mine.'

'Cellphone. For cellphone,' she said. 'Not work here.'

Stupidly, I tried to reach for it. She grabbed my wrist with both hands like she was going to snap it.

'Jesus, okay, I'm sorry! I just want my card back.'

She held up one palm as if to say 'wait'. *Okay,* I thought, *she's going to sort it. That's fine.* When the last of the inmates were inside she smirked at me and walked out. I didn't see her again all day.

There was 200 soles' worth of calls on that card. Keith must have got confused and bought the wrong type. It was so unfair! But I wasn't in a position to ask for a refund or swap. I thought of my poor mum, not understanding why I'd been cut off. I couldn't bear to think of her worried all over again.

*

Lunchtime was the same story as breakfast. The same procession of fake staff lugged in giant containers full of the same shitty food. A bit of bread, a bit of rice, some mushy veg, possibly some meat – it was hard to tell. I had my overpriced bowl but I couldn't bring myself to use it until it had been washed. And God knows when the water was going to be turned back on again.

But I was starving. If I didn't eat something soon I'd get ill. The question was, would I get more ill from using the bowl? Eventually, I gave in and wiped it with my shirt as best I could. It wasn't exactly pristine but at least it was mine. I lined up with the others but instead of being served I was asked for cash. I didn't see anyone else paying but what choice did I have?

People were starting to drift back to their jobs when I managed to grab Rosa walking by. I wanted to ask if us being cooped up and searched all the time was customary.

'Yes,' she said, 'for drug dealers.'

'God, we're not drug dealers!'

'Of course,' she smiled pointing to a crowd of women, 'and that woman did not kill her husband and that woman did not rob her boss and that one . . .'

'Yeah, I get the point. No one here is guilty.' She was about to scurry off when she saw my scummy bowl.

'Can you not afford new ones?'

'Where am I meant to get one of those?'

'The kiosk,' she said matter-of-factly.

'What do you mean, "kiosk"? What kiosk?'

She nodded to the far side of the hall. I followed her gaze beyond the kitchen area. Without a ton of people in the way I could make out a little window, like a post office counter, and a bunch of stuff inside. Even from a distance I could see plates and food and drinks on shelves inside. It was an Aladdin's cave of treasures.

'Are you telling me there's a shop here that sells food and I've been eating this crap? *Out of these bowls?*'

Rosa shrugged.

'Can I go there now?'

'No.'

'Why on earth not?'

'It's closed. *La Delegada*'s orders.'

*

With so much to take in, time didn't pass as slowly as it might. In the afternoon, two INPE took us back through the rotunda to the main block. They'd told us nothing about why or where we were going. When I saw the director step out to meet us, I had the sinking feeling that the time had come for us to be split up. Luckily, it wasn't. Not on that occasion at least. But I realised how heavily it was weighing on our minds.

Instead the director had a list of questions – in English, thank goodness. Were we okay? Did we understand what was going on? Did we need anything? When I rattled off a shopping list she pointed me in the direction of the kiosk.

Yeah, a bit late now . . .

She asked if we had husbands or boyfriends because on official visit days anyone not on our permitted list wouldn't be allowed in. We had neither, so that was simple. I told her about Keith, though, and Melissa described her dad. Then she looked at our notes and told us to settle in because for all she knew we'd be there until our trial, however many years away that was.

We were about to leave when an INPE whispered something in the director's ear. 'Good timing,' she said. 'You have guests.'

I knew it wasn't a visitor day, so it had to be Peter. To my relief, Keith was alongside him – carrying four bags. Our lawyer had got him in somehow. It was so great to see him. Knowing it was the last time for God knows how long was a kick in the stomach. Still, I had to make the most of the time we had.

I think the director was on the same wavelength. We were allowed to use the meeting room for a while but when I said I had a letter for him to deliver she said I could take my brother downstairs to collect it. I don't think he knew what he was letting himself into. From the moment the INPE left us at the patio he was bombarded by bum pinches and women blowing kisses. If the majority of the inmates hadn't been at work or classes he'd have been lucky to escape fully clothed.

In the sanctuary of my cell we tucked into some fizzy drinks and snacks Keith brought. As we did he got more and more quiet. In the end he just burst into tears.

'I can't stand the idea of you living here. It's barbaric. You're not an animal. You shouldn't be in here.'

'They don't care what you think, what anyone thinks,' I said. 'There's nothing I can do. I'm in their hands. At least we have our own room. And it's not as chaotic as Dirandro.'

'Okay,' he said, 'but why were there men out there as well? That's not safe.'

For a second, I didn't follow. Then Melissa said, 'He means the chetos.'

For every dozen inmates there were two or three who had their dark hair flattened into a neat sort of military comb over. They wore trousers and a shirt and serious shoes. To all intents and purposes, they looked and acted like the young men I'd seen on our travels around Machu Picchu. Except these were women. I could tell Keith wasn't 100 per cent convinced by the explanation. We hadn't been either when Rosa had told us. But it wasn't worth dwelling on.

'Four years till you see a judge?' Keith said. 'That's a crime in itself.'

That I couldn't disagree with. I looked at Peter who just puffed air exasperatedly.

'I've done everything I can to speed things up. If you get lucky, then Fishman will take care of it.'

Peter was flying back to Ireland with Keith the next day, so we'd just be in the hands of Fishman from now on. From the sound of it, most of the prep work had already been completed by Peter.

An INPE appeared at the door to show our visitors out. I flung myself at my brother and we both started blubbing. I was so grateful he'd come. It couldn't have been cheap, and he'd spent so many hours and days queuing to get just five minutes with me. The idea of my guardian angel not being on the same continent was terrifying. He was leaving the room when he suddenly remembered the bags.

'I got you your clothes,' he said. 'Had to guess your size but I hope they're okay.' And with that he was gone. Gone from Virgen de Fatima, gone from Lima, gone from Peru. Gone from my world. My last connection with home removed.

And I was still holding the letter I'd written for my mum.

I sat down on my bunk and nothing Melissa could do or say could stem the tears.

*

The final roll call of the day – the fourth – was the excuse I needed to leave the cell. It was a full house this time, as the workers returned ready for dinner. I had my own bowl now. I also knew not to pay for food I was entitled to. Of course, they tried to get a few soles out of me but I refused and grabbed one of the serving spoons myself. That could have gone terribly wrong but I got away with it. The woman behind the counter took back the ladle and dished me out my portion without another word.

When we got back to the cell, I couldn't believe it. There was another raid going on, this time about six or seven of the guards ripping the place apart. But that wasn't the worse of it. Oh no, *that* was seeing my new wardrobe collection from Keith.

I'd been too upset to open the carrier bags earlier. Now the INPE had saved me the trouble. I picked up the first thing piled on my bed. It was pair of large, red tracksuit bottoms. Not my style, my colour or my size. But that was okay, there was plenty of other stuff. Next item: a jumper, polyester, multi-coloured, XL and hideous.

Melissa was pissing herself. Every single thing was horrible. Even the stuff that might have fitted me was for men not women. He must have walked into the shop with his eyes closed. And as for the underwear! I couldn't even bear to open the packets. The picture of the granny with a perm on the front told me everything I needed to know about the target audience.

By the time we hit the hay I could see the funny side of Keith's incompetence. Less funny was how we were being targeted by the INPE and the other prisoners for being drug smugglers. It made no sense to me. We were the worst drug smugglers in the world. We'd only tried it once and got caught. We were hardly the female versions of Pablo Escobar.

How long was the silent treatment going to go on for? And why were we considered bigger threats than anyone else? According to Rosa, her cellmates were murderers, child abusers, gun runners, all types of violent thug. Even the women who'd killed or hurt their partners in self-defence had still killed or hurt someone. I hadn't even managed to kill a cockroach. It made no sense to single us out. Unless we were being singled out for some other reason.

'Mel, you think they're picking on us because we're in the papers?'

'Maybe. Or they're just hoping to find some drugs to use themselves.' That sounded more plausible. Despite the intimidation, there had been no further mention of us being split up. Maybe they'd changed their minds. I certainly wasn't going to mention it.

Some of the women in Fatima were, like us, awaiting trial – many of them in their second, third and fourth years of limbo. Others were already serving their time. Apart from the fact they were all Peruvian, they had one other thing in common: they were all obsessed with their looks. I thought the kiosk must do a roaring trade in cosmetics because everywhere you looked there were people applying lip-gloss or brushing their hair or brushing someone else's.

The women in Fatima were poor, yes, but what money they did

have went on their appearance. Their hair, their clothes, their make-up. What else was there to think about? You couldn't have a pet, you were on your own most of the day, and any physical possessions were liable to get nicked or broken. Make-up, clothes, beauty, they were the obvious outlets. Ironically, it was the chetos, the ones who seemed to go out of their way to appear the least feminine, who looked like they put in the most effort.

It got me thinking. 'If you started doing facials and whatnot, you'd clean up in here.'

'Good luck with that,' Melissa laughed sleepily. 'You'd be better off selling weapons to this lot. Or drugs. They think we're doing it anyway.'

'I don't want to make money,' I said almost to myself. 'I just want to go home.'

*

I was up a lot of the night scratching. The cockroaches were tap-dancing inside the bed poles again, but the worst part of it was that the tubes of the bed frames were missing their caps, so the horrible things could emerge from the holes with alarming speed and crawl anywhere they wanted. The mattress itself seemed to have its own breed of inhabitants. I'd just get comfy and then I'd feel something on my foot, on my elbow, on my neck, on my shin. It was never-ending. Whatever I smacked or scratched at was never the end of it. The itch just moved somewhere else.

Melissa could sleep for Britain. She woke up ten minutes before the first roll call, still giggling at my new range of male prisonwear displayed on the bunk next door.

'He thinks you're a cheto.'

'I'd be the worst-looking cheto here . . .'

We were on time for the day's first roll call, which is more than can be said for the INPE. After a few minutes of waiting, I plonked myself on a long bench no one was using.

Gonzales was straight over.

'*Diez soles*,' she said, and held up ten fingers. Ten soles? For sitting down on an empty bench? What next – a fine for having your period? Told off for breathing?

I was fuming. Everywhere you turned there was a rule. You could only use the phones at certain times, you could only use the microwave at certain times, you could only use the TV at certain times, and even then, you could only watch certain channels. And why? All because Gonzales – *La Delegada* – decreed it so. It was so weird everyone doing what this tubby middle-aged woman said. What must it be like to have such power?

We were expected to head back to our cells afterwards, but I needed to look at this kiosk. Sure enough, there was everything you could need inside, including phone cards – which of course I was desperate to buy – as well as a new plate, plastic cutlery and a mattress for my bed. It didn't look box fresh, but it would have to do. The woman running the place looked familiar. I realised she'd been standing next to me at roll call that morning. She was an inmate, like us. How the hell was she running a shop?

I pointed out everything I wanted and got out my money. The woman looked at the cash and sighed. Then she pointed to a sign on the door.

'*Cerrado*,' she said.

'What?'

'*Cerrado*.' She made a crossed gesture with her hands to suggest 'closed' and the penny dropped. She wasn't going to serve me. The kiosk was shut. I'd just have to return later. As I walked out, I passed half a dozen inmates going in. If I spoke the language, I'd have told them not to bother. And yet, when I turned back a minute later, they were all emerging with new purchases.

That pissed me off. Not as much as getting back to the cell and finding Melissa outside, powerless, as another search of our stuff was going on. There was so much I needed to learn. Unfortunately, our cell door was closed more than it was open, almost as though someone didn't want us snooping around.

*

Make-up and makeovers were all the rage that morning. Saturday was visiting day for male friends and relatives and the whole hall was filled with coiffing and primping and preening from everyone, chetos and princesses alike. I pulled on the least offensive ensemble I could find among Keith's supermarket sweep and shuffled out to watch the commotion.

One by one the inmates' names were called, and they'd give a little squeal and run down to the patio where chairs and tables had been put out. Watching them all getting excited reminded me of how far I was from home. I knew no one in the country now apart from Fishman and a couple of priests.

I distracted myself from all the jollity by returning to the kiosk. Melissa said if the woman refused to serve me this time I should go straight to the director. That was Plan B. I thought I'd try something else first.

I pointed to a bowl and asked, *'Cuánto cuesta?'*

Before she could answer, I pulled out my entire wad of cash and thumbed casually through the notes. I could feel her eyes burning into it. Ten minutes later I had all the essentials for prison living, including a brand-new phone card. But first I wanted something to pass the time. Four years, ideally.

There were dozens of books out the back, all in Spanish, but the woman running the joint found me a handful in English – which was good of her. Now she'd seen I was flush, she couldn't do enough for me. I chose something called *Big Girl* by Danielle Steele and trotted back to my cell armed with all my goodies. Melissa was out mingling with the locals. I admired her spirit. She didn't speak much more of the language than I did but she had the balls to try. Being surrounded by people talking a foreign tongue was not my idea of fun. I just wanted to be alone.

Back in the cell I went through all my purchases then plucked up the courage to look more closely at Keith's. I made two piles: 'hideous but possibly wearable' and 'hideous and last resort'. Then I climbed onto my bunk and opened my book. Amazingly, two hours passed before I realised. Even then I only noticed because the director of Fatima entered the room. She didn't look or sound happy.

'You lie,' she said.

'What?'

'You lie to me.' I swung my feet over the bed and jumped down. Toe to toe I was still considerably taller, but she was the one in charge.

'You say you have no husband. You say you have no boyfriend.'

'Yes.'

'So why is he here?'

'What?'

She showed me a note in Spanish. I could make out the words 'Michaella' and 'Caesar'. She jabbed at another and said, 'He's your boyfriend, isn't he? Admit it.'

It was a big leap from the romantic world of Danielle Steele to the harsh realities of the Peruvian prison system, but I did my best to catch up. Apparently, someone had arrived and logged in as my boyfriend. I'd like to say it was a mistake, but past experience told me otherwise. The fake suitors that had queued up at Dirandro came flooding back. Despite all the gifts they tended to bring, I wasn't falling for it.

'He's not my boyfriend,' I insisted. 'He's probably a journalist.'

'No,' the director said. 'I've seen him. He's no journalist.'

'Well, whoever he is, he's no friend of mine. Can you send him away?'

'Really? You don't want to see?'

'No, really. I just want to be left alone.'

Finally, I think she believed me. She made some conciliatory noises, possibly even apologised, and left with her heavily-armed entourage. Hopefully she went to kick this 'Caesar' out of the state. Presents or not, whoever he was I wasn't interested.

Saturday night in the block had a different vibe – excitable. Clearly a lot of women had enjoyed their visitors. I would only learn later just how and why.

Night-time for me was another bout of torture. Lining up for

Sunday roll call I couldn't help looking for the bites and bumps I'd got on my arms and legs. My body was on fire with itching and there was no remedy.

*

Sunday was female visitors' day. Again, I didn't have anyone, not even fake girlfriends. We were confined to our cell, so I read my book and caught up on sleep. For some reason, the bugs didn't attack during the day. And, if you climbed quietly enough into bed, you didn't disturb the cockroaches either.

I may not have had any physical visitors, but I had the next best thing. Straight after roll call I'd put my name down to call my mum. By early afternoon my timeslot arrived. It was with trepidation that I dialled the number in case my new card didn't work, but the second I heard my mum's voice all hesitation was out the window. I was too choked to say anything at first. Hearing her was enough to send me over the edge, which of course set her off. Eventually we pulled ourselves together and spoke a bit about Keith, who was probably still in the air. She also brought me up to date on the rest of the family. My cousin Ingrid was getting married the following Friday and I felt so terribly homesick. I desperately wanted to be there. I said I'd call if possible.

It was so crushing being out of the loop and unable to do anything about it that I forgot the time. Suddenly, a hand crashed down on the phone and cut me off. It was Day 1 all over again. Only this time the punishment was worse. The *delegada*, as her name suggested, delegated phone regulation to one of her helpers. It was her hand ending my call because I'd overrun. She took me over to the booking form and turned to the following day. She found my name and very deliberately put a line through it.

'You can't do that!' I cried. 'I need to speak to my family.'

She scowled at me and turned over to Monday's page. That was empty so she carefully copied my name onto the top line – then crossed it out again. Every time I opened my mouth she banned me for another day. The only thing in the world that really mattered to me was communicating with my family – and she was taking it away. I stormed away from the phones and ran straight into the head of security. I had to confront her. I was out of my depth, but I just couldn't let it go. She'd ripped me off.

'Hello,' I said, 'where's my phone card?' I knew full well she didn't speak English. That didn't mean she wouldn't pick up on the body language.

She pointed up the stairs and rattled off some command. I didn't budge. I held out my hand like Oliver Twist and again, more politely, asked for my phone card. It didn't matter how many times I asked, her face didn't budge. Eventually, burning with the injustice of being banned from the phones, I pointed at the pocket she'd put my card in. That was it. A firm forearm raised up in my face while another hand reached for her gun.

'*El calabozo*?' she shouted. '*El calabozo*?' That brought me to my senses.

'No, no, no,' I said, throwing both palms up in surrender. 'I'm sorry, I'm sorry, er . . . *lo siento*'. Rosa thought I might need that phrase and she was right. The woman released her grip on the pistol and pointed once again up the stairs. Not needing to be asked a third time, I let it go. She'd stolen 200 soles' worth of calls from me. At least I was still alive.

The question was, was it going to be worth it?

CHAPTER SIXTEEN

OH, DIOS MIO!

Monday 26 August saw us eat like queens – thanks to a visit from Billy, Melissa's dad. He always brought treats but this time it was a proper meal. Afterwards, we had to listen to a film in the main hall being enjoyed by the rest of the inmates. For some reason we weren't allowed to join in. We wouldn't be able to follow a word, but I was weary of being treated differently. I was already banned from phoning home. Now I couldn't have contact with our neighbours.

Billy was meant to return that Thursday but was refused entry due to a public holiday or some excuse. It was hard to believe anything given how we were being ostracised. Melissa was beside herself. Expecting a visit and not getting it was the cruellest thing in Fatima. The pain was compounded by knowing he was leaving Peru at the weekend. Luckily, he was able to come on Saturday, on 'men's day'. Watching Melissa in bits during the visit and after he left broke my heart. For once I wasn't thinking about my own torture.

Billy may have left the country, but his contacts stayed close. I was surprised to get a visit from Andrea, the woman who had been our translator for the state prosecutor. Turns out she was much more than that – and had been all along. She had been brought on board by the

Daily Mail as their new reporter on our case after the original one was 'let go'. She told me she'd worked in Europe, on TV shows here and there, and was an all-round reporter, journalist, translator and fixer. This explained the photos she'd taken of us in the SP's office.

Away from the intensity of the court buildings she was able to open up. Yes, she wrote for the *Daily Mail*. Yes, she wanted to get 'exclusives' from me. But she promised never to write anything without clearing it with me first.

It wasn't long before I had reason to take her up on the offer. The head of security rarely entered our block, but when she did, she made a beeline for me. I think she thought we were pushovers. At the very least, after stealing a month's worth of phone calls, she always saw a chance at the next profit. One day, she caught Mel off guard and said the wrong thing. Mel was considerably more hot-headed than me and, as usual, the threat of '*calabozo*' soon followed. Luckily, Rosa was nearby to talk her down – and pass on the head of security's terms for not sending Melissa to solitary.

'She wants a DVD player,' Rosa said.

'She what?'

'A DVD player.'

'Yeah, I heard, I just don't believe it. Where am I going to get one of those?' Rosa spoke to the head of security then scribbled a note.

'She says to send the machine to this address. You have one week.'

Andrea came good on the DVD front and would prove helpful many times more. To her credit, she actually wanted to do more. She told my family that she would see me all right for money, for basics, even for luxuries in exchange for first refusal on stories. She was totally upfront about that. She'd write nothing without permission. It would all be above board. They considered it, but declined. I was their daughter, their family, and they didn't want to be doing deals and selling stories to the English tabloid press. Whatever I needed, they'd get it for me. Melissa's family, however, made a very different decision.

I half expected never to hear from Andrea again. But she returned again and again to visit Melissa as part of their deal. She helped out a lot with supplies and advice. It was another visitor, however, who helped address a larger problem. Saturday brought a visit from Father Foley. He offered me the chance to pray with him, but I passed. I'd never been religious – which made the sectarian violence our family had attracted back home all the more preposterous. Something I was grateful for, however, was the little Spanish dictionary and phrasebook he brought.

I'd devoured four novels by then but now the fifth was put aside as I pored over my new reading material. Morning, noon and night I studied it. The other inmates laughed at me mouthing my new vocabulary as I read. Gonzales went one further. When she saw what I had she sat down next to me and we studied together for half an hour a day. I practised my Spanish, she her English. Some of the learning was off-book. She noticed I would say 'Oh my God' a lot, so she taught me how to say it in Spanish: '*Oh dios mio*'. I couldn't say that Gonzales was particularly friendly, or that I ever felt comfortable in her company, but it was good having a study partner. Despite the huge number of people around me I felt excluded, lonely. Melissa preferred to wing it with the locals and pick up the language that way. She had the confidence for it, whereas I didn't.

'Just talk to people,' she said. 'You'll learn quicker than with some book. And,' she added, 'you won't have to spend your days with Gonzales, of all people.'

'You know that's not me.'

'Why do you want to learn it all anyway? I'm getting better every day. I can help you out.'

'Yeah, but you don't mind being screamed at when you can't understand something whereas I hate it.'

For me, learning the language was the key to fitting in. Surrounded by dozens of women with short tempers, I couldn't cope with them being annoyed at not being understood. The less you understood the angrier they got.

'In any case,' I continued, 'you know what they say: knowledge is power.'

'So?'

'So? How many fines have we paid because we didn't understand the rules? How many times have we nearly got punched because we didn't understand what someone was saying? I'm sick of being treated like an idiot. I want to be making decisions for myself, not having this lot do it for me.'

'And I suppose it's got nothing to do with not being able to understand the TV?'

I laughed. 'Yeah, maybe that as well.' I liked how we could find some humour in a topic, considering our circumstances.

'Seriously though, Mel,' I said, 'in four years' time we're going to go to court, and some judge is going to make a decision that will affect the rest of our lives. I just want to make sure I know exactly what is being said on my behalf. I don't want anything left to chance. I don't want some translator cocking things up that I would have spotted.'

'Not a bad plan,' she said, 'but you reckon you can do it in just four years?'

'I want to do it in two. No – one. Or six months. How hard can it be?'

'Well, all I can say is *buena suerte*.'

'What does that mean?'

'Look it up in your precious book. Or ask Gonzales!'

I had plenty of time to study because for the majority of most days the whole block was empty with people either working or in classes. I enjoyed the peace and quiet. It drove Melissa nuts. She begged the head of security to be allowed to join in but the bitch said no, not yet.

'Why not?'

'Security,' she said, and laughed. Then she made the sign of 'money' with her hands.

'Fuck you,' Melissa muttered, and let the subject drop. We both knew she'd virtually guaranteed another invasive inspection. They were happening so often, what was another?

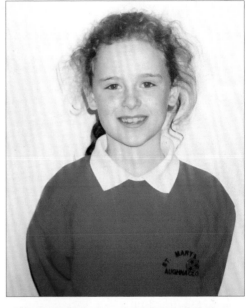

Top left: I was four years old here, so young and innocent.

Top right: On my first day at primary school.

Below left: With my mum, at my first communion.

Middle right: With my brother, Glenn on his tenth birthday.

Below right: With my beloved Uncle Gene, I miss him so much.

Can all of my facebook friends please like and share this post.
My sister Michaella Mccollum Connolly has been non contactable for the last 9 days .
Her phone is off and her facebook page has had no activity.
Michaella has been living in Ibiza in San Antonio bay for the last few weeks.
The last reports of michaella was that she may have been in Barcelona or Madrid
These reports may or may not be true!
Michaella would have contacted home at least every 2/3days to let us know she was ok.
None of Michaella's new friends in ibiza have been able to contact her also.

Above left: I left for Ibiza at the age of 19 and threw myself into life there. *(© Author's own)*

Above right: When I made the dreadful decision to go to Peru, this was the Facebook message my sister put up, thinking I was missing in Ibiza.

(© Author's own)

Centre: The infamous photo at Jorge Chávez Airport just after we'd been arrested.

(© Shutterstock)

Left: We were kept here, at Dirandro, the headquarters of the Peruvian Drug Enforcement Division (DIRANDRO) when we were first arrested.

(© CRIS BOURONCLE/AFP/ Getty Images)

Left: Arriving in court for the first time in Peru, I was absolutely petrified. *(© Martin Mejia/AP/Shutterstock)*

Below right: I couldn't believe my brother, Keith flew out to be there. His support was incredible. *(© Martin Mejia/AP/Shutterstock)*

Above: Michaella and I were handcuffed together in court, sat next to Fishman (left) and our translator (right). We had no idea what was being said.

(© CRIS BOURONCLE/AFP/Getty Images)

Right: My solicitor, Peter Madden, talking to the media scrum that had amassed outside the Dirandro head-quarters, when we were first arrested.

(© Mark Large/Associated Newspapers/Shutterstock)

Left: We were moved to Virgen de Fatima prison, where we spent our time waiting for our trial. *(© INPE/Shutterstock)*

Right: It was always so shocking seeing how people lived in parts of Peru. The outskirts of Virgen de Fatima was so poor.

(© INPE/Shutterstock)

Left: We were taken to Sarita Colonia prison for our trial. After thinking we were going to get 15 years, it was almost a relief to be sentenced to 6 years and 8 months in prison.

(© Ernesto Benavides/AFP/Getty Images)

Right: I was overjoyed when my mum came to visit (seen here with my sister, Samantha) but I hated what she had to go through to get to me. *(© RTE)*

We were soon moved to Ancon II. These pictures only give you a rough idea of the conditions we had to live in.

We had to take comfort where we could, joining in with the various activities on offer or watching TV. But I was always wary of my fellow inmates. My friendship with Melissa was so important and we became close during our time in Peru.

(© Top: (© CRIS BOURONCLE/AFP/Getty Images)
Bottom: Author's Own)

Below: After being in prison for almost three years, I was finally free. Here I am hugging my Mum and brother, Glenn

(© Author's own)

Finally celebrating my freedom with my family, it was like a dream come true!

Bottom right: A still from the interview I did with RTE the day after I was released. I didn't want to do it but I'm glad I did, and was finally able to tell my story.　　*(© RTE)*

It was a shock when I found out I was expecting my boys, but I just feel so lucky to have them. Everything really has turned out exactly as it should.

(© Author's own)

'You know what,' she said. 'Next time she gives us shit we should just let her stick us in *calabozo*. We're virtually on our own anyway.'

Even when I wasn't studying, I still preferred the four walls of my cell to the hustle and bustle of the main hall and the patio when everyone was around. Melissa was the opposite. She loved being in the thick of things. The very idea of being surrounded by people I couldn't understand made my skin crawl.

Speaking of which, the bug problem didn't get any better. Two weeks in and I'd barely slept more than three or four nights. I was so wired during the days I convinced myself I could see bugs crawling under my skin. I had to wait overnight to find a guard who spoke English. Even then he just laughed when I told him I needed a doctor.

I got headaches too. The lack of sleep might have had something to do with it. Constant hundred-watt bulbs in hideous strip lighting from dawn till dusk contributed. Still, I wasn't allowed near a medic.

My worst complaint was closer to home. In early September I made the mistake of going over some letters sent by my family. As I read their words, I could picture their loving faces laughing at my jokes, but then confused and hurt by my actions. For some reason, what with the physical weakness, I just caved. I hadn't cried so hysterically since the night I'd fled my deranged boyfriend with his samurai sword. I couldn't stop. Nor did I want to.

I never wanted to show my frailties to my family, though. They had enough to contend with. The day of my cousin's wedding I made good on my promise to her and rang her mobile. She was at the reception. She sounded so happy. Listening to the party going on in the background, I desperately wanted to be there. When she handed her phone over to Uncle Gene all pretence at happiness dissipated completely. I crumbled, he crumbled, we both just sobbed until my ten minutes was up. I felt terrible for ruining Ingrid's day. I was a blight on the lives of everyone who knew me.

But some things were improving. With the language barrier getting that wee bit lower day by day, we finally started to get involved more in the community. Gonzales told me about a class we could join. It taught cosmetics – *what else?* She figured the international language of beauty would get us through the early weeks. I decided to go along just for a change of scenery. The INPE had other ideas. I was stopped at the door due to 'security issues'. I could only imagine who was responsible for that.

It was Andrea again who smoothed the issue. A bundle of cash – sent by my family – found its way to the head of security's address, and soon we were back on track. In fact, we were finally allowed to mingle more freely, and the daily raids dried up. Even so, I was nervous about asking to join the class. I quickly wished I hadn't bothered. The first day the teacher didn't show up. The second day, same story. The third day she did, and I couldn't follow a damn word. I may as well have been deaf.

Classes weren't free. You either paid for them or worked for them. I had money, but since work was compulsory under Gonzales' rules, Melissa and I said we'd do our bit. I was hoping to become phone monitor so I could nip on when the room was empty. Instead, I got canteen assistant. Starting with evening meals, we were part of the squad designated to walk over to the kitchen block and wheel back the giant canisters of whatever the inmates in there had concocted. Back in our hall we ladled it out. If I hadn't fancied eating there before, I really didn't now. So far, I'd got by on microwave packets from the kiosk and whatever treats our visitors brought. Unless Jamie Oliver suddenly appeared in the kitchen, I couldn't see that changing.

The money I earned either went on my classes or to other inmates doing jobs for me. Everything ran on cash, everything had a price. You were only allowed one phone call a day, and only during certain hours, and only then if you'd put your name down on the list. I'd learned that the hard way on Day 1. Whereas I could have spent all day talking to Ireland, some women had no one to contact. One by one they came to us to 'sell' their slot on the phone list. That was an offer I could not turn down.

Another time, on one of the rare occasions our door was open, this woman came in saying, '*Limpio, yo limpio.*'

She wasn't aggressive or scary-looking but she did look desperate. Like everyone else in the building. Desperate enough to come into a cell with two people who clearly weren't meant to be mingling with the masses.

'Mel, you have any idea what she's saying?'

She didn't, but that never stopped her. She threw every word of Spanish she knew at this woman, all hand gestures like a local. In the end they were both miming.

'I think she's offering to clean for us,' Melissa said. 'For cash.'

I looked around our empty, cavernous space. 'Unless she can kill cockroaches, I don't think we need her.'

When that gambit failed she grabbed some of my clothes.

'*Te lavara la ropa?*' She made a scrubbing gesture, apparently offering to wash them.

You could pay anyone to do anything. All the cleaning duties for the mutual areas like the hall, the patio, the phone room, were done on rotation. If you didn't fancy doing your share one day, you could always find someone else ready to trade for the price of a meal or some toiletries.

For all her weird rules, *La Delegada* appeared to be trying to help everyone get along. She organised a volleyball competition one weekend, which I chose to ignore. Didn't matter, there were plenty of other events on the horizon. Yoga, aerobics, big film nights, a kind of sports day, even a 'peace parade' one Saturday. I couldn't get excited about any of it. The ideas came from a good place but I hated being reminded of where I was. The idea of 'joining in', of being part of the gang, filled me with dread. In my heart, I didn't belong there. By participating in bonding exercises, I felt I'd be admitting I did.

You'd be forgiven for thinking I didn't enjoy human contact. Certainly this 'Caesar' must have thought that. Every Saturday he made the pilgrimage from God knows where to line up with all the other husbands and boyfriends and claimed he was there to see his beloved – me. And every Saturday I refused to see him. I wasn't averse to strangers though, far from it.

An angel had come into my life in the form of an Irish missionary called Maureen. One Sunday, she arrived out of nowhere as I was sitting in the patio area. She looked so lovely, tall and slim with white hair – ethereal, almost. She'd lived in Peru for about forty years and was in her sixties or early seventies. She was so pure and calm and good-hearted. And very spiritually minded. She was with another nun called Claire, and they'd brought me amazing fresh, home-baked rolls and fruit. They'd heard about me on the news and had made it their business to offer pastoral care. The best part of being with them was they didn't want anything in return. All the journalists had their agendas, and Caesar clearly wanted something. But not these lovely women. It was a pleasure to see them every time they came. Especially as Maureen would do special meditation sessions with me.

I don't know why it is that Irish people like to connect with their own, but I was touched and proud of my fellow countrymen and women. Some visitor days I could be downstairs for hours with the nuns or other random Irish visitors – backpackers and the like – so we made a pact early on that we'd share each other's visits. Otherwise we'd go insane with just ourselves for company upstairs.

It wasn't just my people showering us with attention. Shortly after arriving at Fatima I got four letters from complete strangers, Peruvians who'd seen me on TV and wanted to reach out. Every few days it was a similar story. I had people from all over the world telling me they felt like they knew me, which I wasn't happy with at all. I'd only seen a couple of stories in the press and they'd all been lies. Whoever these people thought they were writing to it wasn't me.

Some of the letters, obviously, were basically descriptions of what men and occasionally women could do for me in exchange for love. But you don't need to be in prison to get that kind of attention. Others were written from a better place. People were praying for me. Some even sent gifts: chocolates, flowers, clothes.

Writing was one thing. Making the arduous slog over to Fatima to visit a stranger was a different level of madness, especially considering the rigmarole of getting through security. For my own safety, I refused to see any single men. I made an exception one day for two backpacker loons who arrived asking for me and Melissa. They were English, about twenty years old, and off their heads on acid. They were so excited to see us. I had to ask: 'Why?'

'We've done all the sights, seen Machu Picchu, you were next on the list.'

'So, we're a tourist attraction now?'

'You better believe it. You should start charging.'

Most of everything else they said was incoherent babble. It made me think: was I that annoying when I was taking all sorts back in Ibiza? Very likely.

That still left plenty of women who wanted to reach out. A few were Irish tourists who interrupted their holidays to see if 'one of our own' was okay, but I often got a chance to test out my *español*. A few of them were girls who felt sorry for me being cooped up there. Some were blatantly intrigued by these so-called infamous celebrities and fancied a day out. I only had one bad encounter and that was more my fault than theirs. It had been a rough night. The cockroaches were tap-dancing in my ear, the bed bugs treating my body like a racetrack. When I went outside to see some mystery guests, I was scratching like a dog with fleas. Three young Peruvians were trying to talk to me when I swear I saw something move under the skin of my arm.

'Look,' I said, '*¡Mira! ¡Mira!*

They pored over my arm, but it annoyed me they saw nothing. I got up, said goodbye and ran indoors. They didn't come back.

So many bizarre things happened. One of the English-speaking visitors brought along some pages from a British tabloid, showing an article on how I was the latest fashion sensation. Apparently, our story was so big back home that girls were rushing out to buy copies of the jacket I was wearing when we'd been arrested. Shops all over the country were selling out. It was mind-boggling.

Apart from the lovely nuns there was no shortage of other religious folk dropping by. Most, like Father Foley, were Irish. Others spoke limited English. The thing they had in common was wanting to help me. Sean Walsh dropped by occasionally to read the Bible to me, but I wasn't the most attentive student. However, when Sean announced he was going to North America for an unspecified amount of time, I knew I'd miss our sessions terribly. I was certainly becoming more spiritual. I began to find Gonzales' yoga classes helpful, and the meditation they advocated alongside was really calming. I remember one Sunday feeling low and praying. I didn't want to be one of these people who calls on God only when they've got a problem, so I directed my thoughts at the universe. I imagined angels up there listening, watching, helping. I told them that I'd do the best I could for myself and others and hope that would be enough for them to look out for me. It seemed a fair trade.

Give and take was the way of the world in Fatima. *I'll give you this if you give me that.* Everyone understood the rules. No one arrived on visitor days empty-handed. I was happy with a warm loaf and a dictionary. Other inmates had greater expectations. Week after week I'd see some of them walk back to their cells after a visit armed with radios, perfume, legs of ham, you name it. Some of their bunks looked like Santa's grotto. And that's without the cash they seemed to acquire.

On the days when I didn't have a visitor, I still liked to go down and enjoy being around mixed company. I spotted one girl with a guy who was clearly her boyfriend. You're allowed to hug your guests, but they were kissing, his hands were everywhere, and even when the INPE told them to cool things and sit on opposite sides of the table she managed to get her feet onto his lap.

I was happy for her, and glad she had someone special in her life who was considerate enough to bring her expensive-looking clothes and CDs.

That was Saturday. We had another visitor day the following Wednesday and I happened to see her getting ready for her boyfriend again. I wasn't expecting anyone myself, but I was out there anyway when I saw her doing the kissing, cuddling and foot thing – except it was a different guy to Saturday.

I saw the woman when I was with Gonzales soon after, so I asked, with the help of my phrase book, whether the woman was cheating on her boyfriend. Gonzales laughed. The woman in question was married and her husband visited twice a year. In the meantime, she entertained a string of men in exchange for gifts and cash. I must have looked shocked because *La Delegada* said quietly, 'Everyone do – only way.' She rubbed her fingers and thumb together in the universal sign of 'cash'. I nodded like, 'Oh yeah, I totally get it.' But I was actually really shocked. Melissa, typically, saw the funny side.

'Hey Michaella, maybe you should see this Caesar – see what treats you can get out of him. He could be loaded.'

'You're disgusting,' I said, and threw one of my hideous jumpers at her.

She laughed. 'You're thinking about it now, though, aren't you?'

I wasn't. Not now, not ever.

When she came out of work, Rosa put more flesh on the bones of the story. If you registered as having a boyfriend or girlfriend, or husband or wife or whatever, Fatima allowed you one conjugal visit per month. They'd literally let you get a room – a private cell in the *calabozo*, it turned out – and you could be with your loved one in whatever manner you wanted. For a backwards system in a backwards country I thought that was pretty forward-thinking. Of course, it was open to exploitation. The woman I'd seen had a different significant other every month, according to Gonzales' person in charge of the list.

At first I was disgusted. Women selling their bodies is not anything to celebrate. But I'd observed some of these people. They were proud, they were strong, and they were also at their wits' end trying to pay their way through prison. They didn't have caring relatives sending phone cards and cash hidden in books like I was receiving. They had to make do with the hand they were dealt. And if there were men out there willing to pay for a bit of attention, then so be it.

Not everyone was in it for the perks though. With all the chetos around, I shouldn't have been surprised to discover a couple of them going at it on one of the bunks in Rosa's room. I didn't know where to look but they barely acknowledged me. When you're sharing a bedroom with ninety-nine other people any right of privacy is out the window. You see each other shower, you see everyone peeing, what's a bit of sex between you and your most intimate two hundred mates?

I have to admit to being surprised by a couple of the relationships. The chetos signposted their sexuality. Any time they hooked up with one of the more feminine inmates I wasn't surprised, except when they found each other. Others spent so much time showing me pictures of their children and husbands I had to do a double take when I saw them face down in someone else's cleavage. When their bloke visited, they'd be all over him. But for those cold winter nights in between they had alternative sources of comfort. And when they got down to it they were so passionate it was like the world was ending. I was transfixed by their intensity. I'd never seen anything like it.

*

By the end of September, I'd come a long way with my Spanish lessons. There was just one thing: I have a very strong northern Irish accent. Sadly, so did my Spanish. I remember asking one woman a very simple phrase – '*que hora es?*' – and she just stared at me. I repeated it, twice in fact, and she got angrier every time. She was wearing a watch, so I pointed to it and I think she thought I wanted to borrow it because she spat in my face and stormed off.

There was an added urgency to learning the language because our unofficial translator, Rosa, was due for release. I don't know how we would have done as well as we did without her. At least when the day arrived, I could thank her in Spanish.

By coincidence, when she left I got friendly with one of Rosa's friends, a woman called Goudie. Her English was worse than my Spanish, but we managed to get by with the international language of make-up. I would sit on her bed and do her nails and she'd do mine. She was in her late thirties, Peruvian, and had four children. She'd had an affair and the guy's wife found out and framed her for something. Anyway, her brother brought her kids in to visit every few weeks and I'd accompany her. Not only did they always bring fruit for me, but he was extremely easy on the eye, which is useful when you can't understand what's being said.

Melissa had found a friend of sorts as well, a woman called Carmen. They were more like partners in crime, always plotting mischief. I never warmed to her because I suspected she kept getting the guards to search our room. Melissa wouldn't have it. Either way, it had to be healthier for us not to have to rely on each other so much any more.

It wasn't all good news. The bugs under my skin were getting worse and worse. Eventually, after weeks of begging, I was handcuffed and led out via the rotunda to see a doctor. He couldn't find anything. He sent me to see someone called the sociologist, who spoke decent English. She was basically a counsellor for the whole prison.

'You should have come to see me earlier,' she said.

'I would have done if I'd known you existed!'

She had my medical notes and did her own tests as well – not all of them easy with your hands cuffed. At least my legs were free. The upshot was she agreed with the doctor that the bugs under my skin were signs of stress. Which, she said, was understandable. She recommended yoga – 'already doing that' – meditation – 'doing that' – and plenty of sleep – 'you tell that to the bugs. That's why I'm here.' The fact she was a friendly face and I didn't need a book to communicate with her did me more good than her diagnosis. That night, for the first time in Fatima, I slept like a log.

No more stress for me!

The world had other ideas. The next night, after lights out, there was a noise at our door. It was the INPE who'd messed us around. He had a form that he insisted we read. Between his very basic English and our clunky Spanish we worked out it was telling us we were going to court the next morning. He needed our signatures to show we understood.

But we understood nothing.

Going to court? What for? We'd seen everyone we needed to. Fishman said we wouldn't go again until our trial, which, as everyone kept reminding us, was years away.

Or was it?

'I think this is it,' Melissa said. 'What else can it be?'

She was buzzing. I definitely wasn't. I could feel the bugs crawling back under my skin.

'No,' I said, 'it's too soon!'

'What on earth are you talking about, woman? This is a good thing. This is what we wanted.'

'They said four years.'

'I know – and it's taken four months. We win.'

'But I'm not ready.'

'What?'

'I haven't learned enough Spanish!'

She rolled her eyes.

'*Oh, dios mio.*'

CHAPTER SEVENTEEN

WHAT'S YOUR NAME?

The man's leg felt hot against mine – toned, sweaty and definitely pushing against me on purpose. He was rubbing, up and down, slowly, purposefully. I could feel every hair, every scratch, every scar on his flesh. I stared ahead, trying desperately not to react. The face opposite made it hard. The guy's tongue circled his lips slowly, not for one second taking his eyes away from mine. I felt Melissa squeeze up to me. She was obviously getting the same attention on the other side of her. We were caught, cocooned between predators all out for the same thing. I felt the sweat roll down my neck. Not from heat, but from fear. Trepidation. Panic that I was about to be thrown to the wolves.

'Ah, don't worry about these jerks,' a voice said, 'they couldn't get it up with a foot pump. Too much playing with the other boys I reckon, hey lads?'

The accent was broad, clearly South African, but the words were English. This was one woman who had no fucks to give. I couldn't have loved her more.

We were in a rusty transport truck bound for God knows where. Melissa and I and three scabby men in shorts and vests were squeezed onto a bench designed for four people. Opposite was the same scenario. To my far left, the other side of the protection bars, sat two heavily-armed INPE. The guns clearly weren't for my protection. I felt I'd have to be murdered before they took action.

So, thank God for the South African. She was on the bench opposite, sandwiched between four even bigger men than my side. She was tiny but she was older, she had a mouth on her, and she wasn't taking shit from anyone. After all, as she pointed out, 'We're all trussed up like turkeys for Christmas – what are they going to do? Rape you with their knees?' She laughed then pointed to the guy rubbing up against me. 'It's probably the only thing they've got that's hard.'

The men obviously didn't understand her. Not that she cared. You didn't need a shared language to know this was someone who'd been there, done that, bought the T-shirt – and then ripped it up.

The panic had set in just after we signed the forms. Melissa got it into her head that Fishman would know what was going on. I told her she was deluded. The guy had done nothing for his money so far. But she begged and begged the guard to let us call him and amazingly he relented, despite it being out of hours. Even as the call connected, I half expected Gonzales' fat hand to cut the line.

It turned out we needn't have bothered. The lawyer didn't pick up his office phone or his mobile. Whatever was happening to us we were in the dark and staying there.

It wasn't entirely Fishman's fault. We'd all assumed the trial process would take four years minimum. We hadn't exactly asked him to stay on speed dial. Eventually, the INPE lost patience and we were dispatched back upstairs.

It was a tortuous night. I was so wrapped up in what the court appearance could mean that I barely noticed the bugs. I kept playing different scenarios over in my head. Practising what I'd say in this situation or that.

Melissa, as usual, took it in her stride. Come morning and roll call she persuaded the same guard to let her make one more call before we were collected a couple of hours later. Andrea had her ear to the ground. If anyone knew what was going on it would be her.

Sure enough, when Melissa joined me in the patio area she was smiling.

'It's probably just a hearing,' she said. 'Total waste of time apparently – but it's the first step.'

'First step to what?'

'Trial date. Andrea reckons the government's not too happy about the media attention we're getting. They're having the spotlight turned on them so we're getting fast-tracked.'

It made sense. The longer we went without a trial, the sketchier Peru would look in the eyes of the world. They really didn't want to be seen as some Mickey Mouse country. Not if it jeopardised the visits of thousands of European tourists every year.

*

If only there could have been some photographers in that van. We were shackled ankle-to-wrist in the back of an airless metal box with seven potential sex attackers, watched by two gorillas with high-intensity rifles cocked and loaded. If one second of footage of those conditions got out even the most naive gap-year student would have second thoughts about ticking Machu Picchu off their list. It was only the fact the animals caged with me were just as encumbered as I was that gave me hope. That and the mouthy South African sitting opposite.

Ignoring the men's lip-smacking and hand gestures, we got to know a bit of her story. She had come from Santa Monica. It was not, she made it very clear, a place you would want to visit, let alone stay.

'You're not the first person to tell us that,' I said.

'Doesn't matter if I'm the first or thirty-first – you listen. You do whatever you can to stay away from that place.'

I said I would. Even while I was talking, though, I was intrigued by the ventilation holes in the walls at the top of the van. If I could get myself up maybe I could see out and get an idea of where we were going.

When your ankles are connected to your arms it's hard to get any momentum, but I managed to swing my way upright. I regretted it as soon as I did. Hands and a face pawed and nuzzled at my backside quicker than the South African could tell them to fuck off. Through the holes, I saw we'd left the city. The bumps and shunts we'd been taking the last ten minutes were from off-roading it through some kind of shantytown. Some of the people I could see by the roadside were so emaciated they'd be glad of prison food. As for the makeshift houses, it looked like a nightly job to tie the corrugated roof back on each property. I looked at the sturdy, if old, structure of our van. Ventilation aside it looked like it would keep out sun, rain and snow alike.

It wasn't a great view by any means. But it was the first I'd had for a long time. I wished I could have seen more.

'I'm Kate, by the way,' the South African called out. 'What's your name, darling?'

'Michaella. Michaella McCollum.'

'Well, get used to saying that, love, because that's all you'll need today.'

Obviously, my face didn't believe her. She smiled.

'You'll see, darling. You'll see.'

As well as being our guardian angel and peacekeeper on the journey, it transpired Kate knew her way around the Peruvian legal process. From what I told her of our predicament she said we were going for a hearing and it involved nothing more than turning up – just as Andrea had said.

'Why don't they tell us?' Melissa said.

'Darling, the left hand doesn't know what the right hand is doing. That's just the truth. But you're in the game now. You'll get your trial soon enough. You just need to jump through a couple of these stupid hoops first.'

I wondered how she was such an expert.

'Girl, this ain't my first rodeo.'

It turned out Kate had been in Santa Monica for five and a half years. For what, I didn't ask – call it inmate etiquette. Her sentence was six and a half years and she was going to court to try to get an early release.

'Anyone with a sentence under six years and eight months is entitled to apply for early release,' she explained. 'If you're lucky you just serve a third – basically two years and three months. They call it "benefits".'

'I think back home we call that "parole",' I said.

The woman sighed. 'Doesn't matter what it's called if they keep saying no.'

'This isn't your first application?' I said.

'It's my sixth!' she laughed. 'What else am I meant to do with my time and money?'

It was really useful meeting someone who was so clued-up and onside. I asked her what she knew of the sentencing situation. Being in Santa Monica she must have met women from all backgrounds, people who'd committed every crime going.

'If you were on your own, I'd say there's a decent chance of you getting a short enough sentence with benefits,' Kate said. 'The problem is there are two of you. And in Peru they treat that like organised crime.'

'Organised? Seriously? Look at us. We were totally set up.'

She shrugged. 'Then there's the other factor. I've seen your faces on TV. You're celebrities. They're gonna make an example of you, no question about it.'

'What do you mean?'

'I mean, they'll want to show the world that they're serious about dealing with smuggling. They want to send a message to everyone else thinking of doing it.'

It was bleak news. But I had to ask, 'So, how long do you think we'll get?'

'How many kilos was it? Eleven?' She pursed her lips, considering it. 'If they want to say you're dealers, then fifteen years. Each. That's the maximum. But you might be lucky. You might get twelve.'

She saw our shoulders slump. I was speechless with panic. The prickly heat of the van suddenly felt really intense and I didn't know what to do or say at that moment. I would be thirty-five! I'd wanted to have school-age kids by then. What kind of state would I be in if I was incarcerated for fifteen years? I went into a vortex of fear and faintly heard Kate rounding off her analysis.

'Hey, what do I know? Chin up. With a good lawyer, you'll be fine.' Melissa and I looked at each other.

'Well, that's it, then,' said Melissa, gallows humour intact. 'Fifteen years it is.'

After forty-five minutes the van ground to a halt. The guards grabbed their weapons and got ready to disembark. Ignoring the attentions of the vile individual next to me, I threw my weight forward and peeped out the skylight. I expected to see a court building or official-looking establishment. What I saw from the left was a continuation of the poverty-stricken shantytown I'd spotted earlier. To the other side it was a barren desert with just one faceless building blotting the landscape. It looked like an architect's first attempt at something.

'Ah, this shit-hole again,' Kate said, stretching her legs as we got out of the van.

'You know it?'

'Yeah, welcome to Penal Sarita Colonia, home to some of the scuzziest scumbags in the country.' She paused. 'And that's just the lawyers!'

I liked her style. We were outside a men's prison in an area called Callao, on the Pacific and near Jorge Chávez Airport, where this whole nightmare had begun. The area itself had a reputation for being dangerous. But not as dangerous as the people inside the building itself. Or so Kate said, anyway. I'd deal with that when I had to. Right then, I was grateful to be outside. After so many weeks cooped up I realised how good it was to see things like cars or pedestrians and people going about their normal lives. Even if it was in the roughest end of the scariest city I'd ever seen.

There were people everywhere. And sand. It got in my eyes, my mouth, and hair the second we stepped out. I couldn't wipe my face without crouching down. The second I did that I was molested.

But even the ghastliness of the male prisoners didn't compare to the bombshell that Kate had dropped earlier. It kept going round in my head: 'fifteen years'. It would kill my mum; it might even kill me. Life was cheap here. I'd be forgotten and turn into some haggard jailbird like some of the women I'd seen in Fatima. I'd have to speak to my family. Find out if there was a more effective lawyer than the one we had.

There were dozens of inmates wandering this way and that, yelling at us, wolf-whistling and making all manner of provocative gestures. It was intimidating, no question. For every pack of sex-starved men there was one, maybe two guards leading them. But they couldn't have looked less bothered by what their charges got up to. I could have been skinned alive before one of them even noticed.

We went inside one of the low-rise buildings where there was a kind of reception. We got in line with the low-life from our van and waited to be served.

'*Nombre?*' the receptionist eventually said. *Name?*

I looked at Kate, who winked.

'Michaella McCollum,' I said, not for the last time that day.

There was tons of activity in the room. Loads of guys in suits, lawyers I assumed, came and went with their clients. It was busy, busy, busy. The exact opposite to the inertia of Virgen de Fatima.

We were taken back outside and then into another building where we were patted down and searched. For once we were allowed to keep our clothes on. Stepping back outside I got the feeling that might yet change.

Apart from me, Kate and Melissa, everywhere you looked were men. And 90 per cent of those were prisoners. I don't know how frequently they saw women, but these guys could not take their eyes off us. Wolf whistles are one thing from someone on a building site. When they're done a metre from your face it's a different proposition. We were totally exposed. Passers-by swore at us, spat at us, made all manner of crude and lewd gestures in our direction and, if they got close enough, tried to touch us. And the guards carried on like it was the most normal thing in the world. We were fair game in their eyes.

That was just the ones on the outside. We had to walk past what looked like a block of estate flats but was clearly cells. There were no windows, just bars like your classic jail from a movie set. Men were hanging out of every one, banging on the walls, catcalling us, screaming, shouting, miming filth and basically trying to get our attention. I felt like a piece of meat at feeding time in the tiger enclosure at London Zoo. Our guard led us so close to the block one or two hands managed to grab my hair as we went by. Did he actually want us to get hurt? Was he winding up the inmates on purpose? It would just take one of these brutes to get out and I'd be dead. Of that I was sure.

The sand was still whipping in our faces, but I could make out where we were going. There was a door just to the side of the cells. The problem was, to get there we'd have to pass even closer to the animals on the inside. There was literally no way we could get through without being molested. There were at least two guys sticking their genitals through the bars. I was genuinely petrified.

A guy from the van walked in first and got a couple of hearty slaps on the back. Then it was my turn. I backed up as close as I could to the opposite wall but there was nowhere to hide. I couldn't run. I couldn't even raise my arms in defence. They got my hair, they got my face, they got my breasts. I was petrified.

A second later two guards burst out the door with truncheons raised and started cracking down on anything they could reach. Faces, fingers, elbows, they didn't care, they smashed anything they could reach. The guys with their dicks out disappeared pretty sharpish.

It was the same story inside the building. Worse even, as a riot was going on. Four guards were standing back to back among a crowd of inmates, thrashing out with their batons, basically trying to clear an area near the door just so we could get in and away from the groping monkeys outside. I didn't fancy our chances. People were crushed in shoulder to shoulder – all colours and nationalities. But only one gender.

Which explained why we were getting all the attention.

The second we got through it was a full-on petting zoo. Handcuffed hands reached out from everywhere. I hate to think how much worse it would have been if they weren't bound.

Some were prisoners waiting for their day in court, like us; some were just enjoying a bit of a walk, making a nuisance of themselves among the tourists before going back to their cell. It didn't matter. They were all vile. For every wandering hand and finger the guards cracked, another pair found their way to me. It was like living inside a game of Whack-a-Mole.

For the first time, Kate seemed rattled. That's how I knew it was serious. A foot shorter than me, she was even more vulnerable. I instinctively put myself between her and some of the nastier-looking men until the guards got us through.

It took a while, and cost some of them broken bones, but we made it to a door and were shoved inside. It was like being back in the van. There were two benches facing each other with a divider midway separating the two like a tennis net. Both were full of people. A female guard pointed her gun at one and told everyone to shove over for us to squeeze in. I'd had enough of being felt up by strangers. I preferred to stand. Funny how you change your mind when the gun is turned on you. I slumped down next to a teenager who was hunched over, head in his hands. To my right were Melissa and Kate. Face forward I saw a table with a Peruvian flag on it and half a dozen plastic chairs.

The harassment and abuse en route really took its toll. I didn't think once about why we were there. I just wanted to change my clothes and wash the filth of all those hands off my body.

After a while, I became aware of the man on my right laughing. Kate said something to him in Spanish and he stopped. Whatever he said after that caught Kate out.

'Apparently, the one on your left is a child abuser,' she said, pointing at a guy a couple of years younger than us. 'He raped a six-year-old.'

It explained why he had his head in his hands.

'So why is your man laughing?'

'Because he's going to kill the son-of-a-bitch the first chance he gets.'

They both looked so normal. How the hell were we in the same building, let alone the same room as these scum? I looked at the cuffs biting into my wrists. As far as the authorities were concerned, we were no different.

The would-be murderer hadn't finished. He nodded towards another guy and made a circular volcano shape with his hands.

'That's code for "robber",' Kate translated. 'He's virtually a saint compared to this lot.' Another he described by putting a closed fist in the palm of his other hand.

'That's the sign for someone wanting sex. I'm guessing he doesn't ask too nicely.'

It was atrocious. Terrifying. But, as Melissa pointed out, we had no idea what Gonzales was doing time for. Or anyone else for that matter.

After an hour or so Melissa and I were taken into another room on the other side of the corridor. The second we emerged into the crowd there was cheering. The amount of fingers that found me in just that short walk was sickening.

The new room was identical to the previous one except, instead of murderers and rapists, it housed men and women in suits. One of them, against all expectation, was Mr Fishman.

'How did you know about this?' I said.

'They told me.'

'And you didn't think to pass that information on?'

He looked genuinely confused. 'Well, you're here now. Let's get ready.'

He ran through the other people in the room: a judge, the prosecutor, a translator, an admin woman and a typist. Crucially, there wasn't a single journalist there. The horrors of the last court still haunted me.

We entered the room at 1.30. By 1.37 it was over. In those seven minutes the prosecutor had done a lot of chatting in Spanish, which the translator didn't bother to repeat. The only time he did intervene was to ask us to say our names. About six times. Kate had been right. Our only other involvement was putting a fingerprint on a couple of documents to prove we'd attended.

'Is that it?' I asked Fishman, as we were bundled towards the door. 'No verdict?'

'It's just a hearing,' he explained. 'And it won't be the last.'

Was he serious? We left Fatima at 8.30. It was only a forty-five-minute drive. The other four hours had been spent queuing, waiting and fighting our way through the swamp of gropers. 'Do you know what we had to go through just to get in here? Just to tell them my name, which they already knew?'

'It's just how they do things,' the lawyer said. 'But the good news is we're on the books. The trial itself won't be far behind.'

*

The walk back to that tin can of a bus was just as harrowing as before. We made it relatively unscathed out of the building, then the chimpanzees hanging off the walls got their chance again. The only way I got through it was focusing on the main gate up ahead. It was only a five-minute walk, if that. We'd soon be back in the safety of the van.

But that's not where we went.

To the left of the building was a basketball court. A game of twenty-a-side seemed to be going on. The second we got close they all ran to the edge of the court and started screaming obscenities. I felt sick. All that separated us was ten metres and one guard. It would just take one of those animals to make a break and the pack would follow and there'd be nothing we, the guard or anyone could do.

It was the longest walk of my life. When we got to another building, I didn't ask questions. It turned out to be another holding room. It was mostly brick apart from windows either side. I say windows. There was no glass, just metal bars, exactly like the ones the men had been hanging through. The room was empty apart from a filthy shelf that doubled as a bench, and two broken toilets at the back. Someone must have taken a hammer to them. If you sat on them, you'd cut yourself on the jagged edges. Except no one would ever sit on them because not only were they disgusting but they faced directly outside. Every single person walking by would get a faceful. As if that mob needed any more encouragement.

For five hours we sat there in that stinking, fetid chamber. Every two minutes there'd be a bang on the doors and some ugly face pressed against the bars. Now we were the ones in the cage.

Everyone who walked by stopped to have a look or worse. An Italian guy who was meant to be gardening knew a few words of English, but he had only vile obscenities for us. We were a captive audience. At least he couldn't get in.

Or could he?

His face disappeared from the window and moments later the door flung open. I literally screamed. We both did. But it was only Kate. I don't think I'd ever been more grateful to see anyone.

When I got my breath back, I said, 'Do you know what's going on? Why are we stuck here?'

'The bus won't leave till everyone's back.'

'So, we've got to wait? In here? For them? They're as rapey as everyone else.'

The conveyor belt of seduction never stopped. Some people offered us food, which I refused to accept even though I was starving. One guy even tried to sell us some weed. I smelled him before I saw him. He reeked of the stuff. The guards didn't seem to care.

We were eventually put back on the bus but for another hour it just sat there. The men were going crazy. They started banging on the walls, yelling, screaming. Despite the temperature outside, it was a furnace in there. And the stench. If it weren't for the ventilation holes, you'd die of it.

I desperately needed the toilet. I wasn't the only one. The difference was I didn't act on it. A guy on the bench opposite shuffled his way to the corner of the van and just pissed against the wall. Soon they were all doing it. A river of putrid urine edged closer and closer to my feet. I don't know what was in their prison diet, but it didn't smell good coming out. Kate was going crazy, screaming in Spanish for the guards. The men just laughed. They had no shame. No sense of decency. To my eyes, they were barely recognisable as human. I wondered if they'd arrived like that or whether prison had done it to them.

And would it do it to me?

Ask me again in fifteen years…

CHAPTER EIGHTEEN

YOU'RE NOT
THE JUDGE

I never thought I'd be so relieved to see Fatima. We finally got back at 10.30, fourteen hours after we'd set off. Fourteen hours of hell. Fourteen hours of physical and mental abuse – just to tell a stranger my name. *Six times.* I fell into bed and not all the bugs and cockroaches in the world were going to stop me sleeping.

The next morning my first thought was of my mum. I'd promised to call her the day before and obviously I hadn't been able to. This had really brought me down. My second thought did even worse.

'Mel, are you awake?'

'I am now,' the voice from the bunk below said. 'What is it?'

'Fifteen years,' I said. 'We're going to get fifteen years.'

'Shit,' she said. 'I thought it was a nightmare.'

'Me too. I just remembered. And what was all that about "benefits"?'

'We need to get some help, pronto.'

'Let's call Fishman first thing.'

'No, I mean *serious* help. I think we should talk to Andrea.'

It said a lot for our situation – and about the Peruvian legal system – that the only two people who seemed to know what was going on were a stranger in a van and a tabloid journalist. Our lawyer wasn't incompetent; he was just out of the loop. Which made him no use to us. For my own peace of mind, I needed answers. I needed a strategy. More than anything, I needed to know what the hell was going on. If only I'd had more time to learn Spanish . . .

Andrea came the next available visiting day. She was horrified by our experience at court but not surprised.

'That was your initial hearing,' she said. 'You'll have another session, called a "declaration", where you tell your story. Then you'll get your trial.'

'And they'll all be at that place?'

'Usually, yes.'

We told her Kate's analysis of our situation. She concurred.

'If they choose to prosecute you as a team, and if you continue to plead not guilty, then fifteen years is the maximum they can give.'

'And what about these "benefits"?'

'That only applies for shorter sentences. Basically, anything under seven years.'

'So we're screwed?'

'Only if you get fifteen years. But that might not happen. It all depends how they want to play it.' She paused. 'And who you get for a judge.'

*

The next few days were a blur. If it weren't for having to do our chores and classes, I'd have gone mad thinking about the sentence. It was killing me. I'd only recently come to terms with waiting four years for a trial. The idea of more than triple that was churning my stomach for real.

Andrea could only do so much. So, Fishman admitted, could he. When he next visited he brought his mother, who had more experience of the process. Between the four of us we tried to thrash out the best way forward, starting with these so-called benefits. They really were a thing. According to 'Law 261' you could see your sentence reduced by two-thirds if you behaved, paid your fines on time and generally didn't cause a fuss. But, he pointed out, it only applied to sentences under seven years.

The problem was, we didn't yet know what law we were being tried under. Law 261, Fishman explained, saw you charged as a '*burro*' – a drugs trafficker – literally a 'donkey'. That carried the maximum sentence of six years and eight months. Law 273, on the other hand, was applied against mobsters or organised crime or cartels. It carried a fifteen-year sentence with zero chance of benefits.

'We have to hope for 261 but prepare for 273,' Mrs Fishman said. I nodded, but no way was I preparing for that. If I thought there was a chance of fifteen years I'd go mad.

Next topic of discussion was our plea. Fishman felt we should stick to our 'not guilty' pleas, otherwise it could reflect badly in court and paint us as liars. His mother thought the court might go easier on us if we came clean. They were both valid arguments. I just had one question: 'Which plea will get us the shorter sentence?'

They agreed that not fighting the charges was most likely to get the judge on our side. It would also speed proceedings up. 'But,' Fishman pointed out, 'you'd have a criminal record.'

'If "guilty" gets me out of here even a day earlier then I'm fine with that.'

But there were no guarantees of anything. As Andrea had pointed out, it depended on the judge and the prosecutor as much as the law. Two weeks later we were due to meet both.

The day started exactly the same way as before. We got a form to sign late one night and the following morning endured a load more thigh rubbing and deep discomfort in the back of a rusty death trap that reeked of stale urine.

The groping chimps hanging from their cells at Penal Sarita Colonia were just as active as last time, although there seemed fewer of them inside the building. The guards looked at me like I should be grateful.

We had to squeeze onto the same packed bench in the waiting room. Last time we'd been the first to be called out. This time we watched as every single person was called out and their space on the bench taken by someone else. After an hour I asked the guard when we'd be seen.

'*Pronto, pronto*' – soon, soon.

Another hour passed and I asked again.

'*Pronto, pronto.*'

Another hour and the same reply.

'What is it with these people and time?' I said. 'Everything's either *pronto* or *mañana*. No one does anything *now*.'

We'd been there five hours before someone paid us attention. And that someone was Fishman. I couldn't tell if he was angry or worried. Turned out he was both. The declaration had been postponed because the translator was ill.

'They've kept us here all day for nothing?' I wailed. He nodded. 'Okay, what are you waiting for?' I said. 'Let's get out of here.'

'You can't do that,' he said. 'You still have to wait for everyone else from your van.'

*

When the next form for us to sign arrived one night in October I nearly didn't bother. What was the point? But it wasn't as though we had a choice. The same van, the same violations, the same waiting room. This time the wait was just an hour. It was show time.

The prosecutor was the guy who'd originally taken our stories and had tried to convince us to plead guilty. I remembered him as being okay. The judge was a skinny guy in a crumpled suit who sat with his feet up on the table, much to the annoyance of the typist who had to sit next to them. He seemed more interested in stuffing his face with crackers than paying attention to our story, which obviously had me very worried. We'd just endured the same monstrous journey, been violated every which way physically, and this prick was acting like it was all a big joke.

This is my life we're discussing here. Not some damn football match.

Andrea had come with Fishman. She could see I was fuming.

'You need to cool it,' she hissed. 'You need these guys onside.'

'But look at him,' I said. 'He's a pig.'

'But he's the only pig we've got – so play nice.'

The prosecutor was straight up. He knew our story back to front but he let us tell it again. The judge may or may not have been paying attention. At the end he dusted the crumbs off his tie and said, via the translator: 'The charges against you are very serious. My job is to decide whether to try you under Law 261 or 273.'

Six years or fifteen years. My life hung in the balance.

'If it were up to me, then I would say Law 261. But it is not up to me. It is up to justice.' He paused and flicked again at his tie. 'You will be tried under Law 273. Maximum sentence fifteen years.'

He stood up. 'Thank you. Next case please.'

And that was it. No asking if I was guilty or not guilty. No talk of benefits. No mention of six years and eight months. No hope whatsoever.

*

I spent half the next day crying. Melissa was just as bad. I rang my mum and could barely speak for tears. I hated dumping my problems on her when she was too far away to help and in fragile health. I couldn't help it. I was broken.

For the rest of the month and the next I prayed for a miracle. In early November, one arrived in the shape of Andrea. She had brilliant news.

'I've spoken to the prosecutor,' she said. 'He's prepared to cut a deal.'

'Is that allowed?'

'Not exactly. But . . . well, these are unusual circumstances. And he's a friend. He likes you. He wants to help you out.'

The deal was, we would plead guilty in exchange for sentences of six years and eight months – in other words, the exact amount needed to qualify for early release. He didn't know we'd already decided to drop our 'not guilty' defence anyway.

'Why would he do that?' I asked. 'What's in it for him?'

The answer was simple. The prosecutor loved his country. Our case was bringing a load of negative attention to Peru's legal system – a system he believed in – so he felt if he could do anything to change that, especially if it got us out of the country quicker, then it had to be worth it.

There was only one condition. We had to keep the deal secret. All our other court appearances had made it into the newspapers – even the one where we didn't need to go in. Someone was tipping off the media and the prosecutor was afraid it was us.

'That's impossible,' I said. 'We only get told the night before.'

'That's what I told him. But seriously, if one word of this deal leaks out then he'll get in trouble and the whole thing is off.'

'No one will hear anything from me.'

'Me neither,' Melissa said.

'Then roll on court time.'

*

There was only one thing I wanted more than the trial. And in November it happened. My sister Stephanie, brother Glenn and cousin Astrid came to visit.

My mum had told me a fortnight earlier. She would love to have come herself but none of us would let her. She was terrified of flying and it was a long journey to Peru from Northern Ireland. I couldn't wait to see the others, although when Mum told me the flight details I winced. Visitor days were Wednesday, Saturday and Sunday. They'd be here Thursday. The only way you could get an extra day was if you got your embassy involved – not because of any law but because prisons hate the bad press that embassies can whip up internationally.

Which meant I was screwed. I called the British Embassy in Peru, who told me to contact the Irish lot in Mexico, and they said the earliest they could help was when they next visited – in the New Year. I was still regretting getting that Irish passport.

My only other option was the director. I begged her. I pleaded.

'You've got to help. They're travelling sixteen hours.'

Maybe it was the tears but she agreed – sort of. Instead of a whole day she'd give me two hours. Ten till twelve. I could have kissed her.

I woke up at four in the morning and I pretty much just stood there until six waiting for them to open the door for roll call. I just wanted to get the day started. At breakfast I sat there watching the door like a lunatic, even though I knew they were hours away. The excitement was building and building. I couldn't remember ever feeling anything like it.

The constant chatter from the street behind our cell had never given me anything but bad nerves. Today was different. I stood at the window hoovering up every sound, every sight. And then it happened. I heard them.

I'd know my family's voices anywhere, but in a sea of Spanish three Irish accents stand out. I flew out to the stairs. Any minute now that door would open. Any minute . . . any minute . . . I forgot how long the security checks took. It was more than an hour before the INPE's radio crackled and I was summoned to the rotunda. I was already crying before I got to the gate. That didn't stop for ages after we all hugged.

Glenn was just as upset as Keith had been about my conditions but no one had travelled all that way to tell me off. They got a rude awakening to how unpleasant a process it was getting through Peruvian prison security, in stifling heat. They'd been interrogated, subjected to degrading searches and kept hanging around for ages. But it wasn't so long ago they were worried I was missing and possibly dead. Anything else was a bonus. They didn't come empty-handed. Their cases were full of gifts from Mum: microwave meals, chocolates, books, bedding, toiletries and, most importantly, clothes. I was still wearing the men's XL stuff that Keith had brought me in August. I'd been borrowing off Melissa for court. Not any more.

Of course, as soon as they arrived, I told them about the deal we'd been offered, and everyone was in good spirits when they found out. Stephanie and Astrid brought a lovely, calming presence with them.

They are both spiritually-minded women and being with them made me so homesick for the things I used to take for granted. It reminded me to try and take the best care I could of myself, so I could survive the ordeal of it all.

All your belongings in prison are kept in tall plastic bags. The second the other inmates saw me lugging two full ones in – on a non-visit day – they were all around me. I'd never worried about thieves in Fatima – because I had nothing to steal. That situation had now changed.

I would have given it all up for another minute with my family but the fact they had come all this way to be with me was amazing. I vowed to make it up to them in future, whenever I got out, which hopefully would be sooner than I'd thought only a couple of weeks ago. I didn't think we could have cried more than when they left but we managed it.

Yet again it was only the distraction of working and doing classes that prevented me going mad. That and the daily phone calls back home – twice daily if I could persuade someone to sell me their timeslot. We were all so excited about the prospect of the shorter sentence. I couldn't wait to get the trial over with. What's more, we'd even got a date for it now. 17 December. Things were definitely looking more positive.

At the end of November, three weeks before our trial, we had an emergency visit from Fishman, which I assumed was to talk about strategy in court. He wasn't a particularly imposing man – slightly built, receding hairline and monotone voice. But then I'd never seen him angry.

'Which of you did it?' he said, almost shaking with rage.

'Did what?'

'Talked to the press! Your deal is all over the papers. They're calling the prosecutor a crook. He's got to think about his career and the only way he can prove he didn't do it is by not doing it.'

'What do you mean?'

'He's not going for it. He's resigning from your case. The deal's off. You're getting Law 273.'

'Fifteen years?'

'Fifteen years.'

I felt like I'd been run over by a truck. I was too shaken to speak. I could barely move. The last time I'd felt so disoriented I was on ketamine. It must have been half an hour after Fishman left that I found the energy to talk.

'You know I didn't tell anyone, Mel,' I said.

'I know. Neither did I.'

'I know.'

'What about your family?' she asked.

That got me sitting up. I'd told them about the lifeline we'd been thrown – as had Melissa to her family – but I knew my lot were watertight.

'What the fuck? My family would never do that. They never speak to the press. They hate them. You know that. What about your dad?'

'He'd never do that.'

Yeah, I thought, *apart from the time he did.*

It was really getting to me. Over the next two days I dwelt on the treachery, trying to work out who was the snake in the grass. The obvious person was Andrea but that made no sense. Yes, she was a journalist, yes, she helped us, but this was her deal. She'd told us that she was always careful with her stories, filtering out anything that could have a detrimental effect on our case. The prosecutor was her friend. It had to be someone either at the courts or the prison. I wouldn't have put it past the head of security. The woman resented us. And it made sense for her to sabotage our case. We were a cash cow for her. Of course she'd want us to be around for longer.

It was driving me crazy. But weirdly, whoever the press had been talking to, whoever had ruined my life – and that of the prosecutor, by the sound of it – had stopped talking. The TV news was filled with pictures of British photographers and reporters and camera crews pitching up their stalls outside the court. No one had told them we weren't appearing. It was ironic, but there was no comfort to be found in their wasted time.

After nearly a week of reflection and self-doubt and paranoia, I was told Andrea was coming for a visit. I needed to see her friendly face. If I couldn't see my family, she was the next best thing.

Come Sunday, I realised she was as down as we were. She'd worked so hard to get the deal on the table. For a couple of minutes after the initial hellos no one spoke. Then she turned to Melissa and said quietly, 'Why did you do it? What did Beverley promise you?'

I couldn't follow. 'Beverley who?' I said.

'The Beverley that Melissa spoke to. The one who ratted you both out for her story.' I couldn't believe what I was hearing. I turned to Melissa, suddenly hysterical with panic and anger.

'Is this true?'

She slowly nodded. 'My dad said I had to do it. He said it would help.'

'Help who? Did yous get paid for this?' She didn't reply.

'Oh my God, you traitor. You stupid fucking idiot!'

I wanted to kill her. Thanks to that woman I was looking at an extra ten or so years in prison. And not just me. So was Melissa. How could she have been so naive – and selfish?

Beverley was the original journalist who had taken the photos of Melissa with her birthday cake, back in Dirandro. Although the *Daily Mail* had taken her off the story – and replaced her with Andrea – she was still snooping around for exclusives. And Billy Reid had her phone number. The information was being passed to her out of my sight and earshot. Eventually, Melissa confessed that she'd called the woman on the prison phones.

'I hope whatever you got was worth a decade of your life,' I said. 'Because it sure as hell ain't worth a decade of mine.'

I said goodbye to Andrea and ran back to the cell. If I could have shut the door myself I would have. What I could do was switch beds. I packed all my gear and moved as far away from Melissa's bunk as possible. For days she'd watched me crumble. Had even suggested I was responsible for the leak. And all along it was her. I never wanted to see her face again.

My mum had always said not to trust the tabloid press, and she was right. If only Melissa's father could have followed the same principle. Everything had seemed hopeful and now those hopes were dashed utterly. When I called my family and told them what had happened, they were naturally devastated. I had tried to be really strong for so long – to protect my family from how awfully low I felt much of the time, and to put my emotions to one side. Now they were looking at me getting this longer sentence it was a sickening blow. And all because of the greedy motivation of others.

There was a lot of fallout from this turn of events. I had a kind of breakdown, rendered unable to keep up the pretence of positivity to my family. It also made sharing the cell with Melissa unbearably stressful.

I didn't speak to her for days. I didn't just ignore her; I pretended she didn't exist. Wisely, at first, she kept her distance. When she did try to speak I turned on the TV. When she shouted, I turned it up. I turned in on myself and bottled everything up. The person who had been a confidante – with whom I'd shared this whole crazy rollercoaster of events – had betrayed me. And that hurt really bad.

On Day 3 she tried again. Still I ignored her. She moved to a different bunk, to get closer. I stayed firm, unreachable. She moved again and again. It didn't make any difference. I closed my eyes and tuned her out. When I opened them again, she was inches from my face.

'My dad made me do it,' she cried. 'He said it was for the best.'

I totally lost it. I screamed right in her face. 'If he told you to stick your head in an oven, you'd do that, would you?'

'I didn't realise . . . I was just doing what my dad asked me to do. I didn't think . . . I . . .'

'It's not just me you've screwed here,' I shouted. 'You've ruined it for yourself as well. You've just doubled your own sentence for the sake of your dad getting paid by a tabloid newspaper. Why didn't you listen to Andrea? You are so stupid!'

The shouting went on for some time until the pair of us were exhausted. She knew she had messed up really badly. Her face betrayed her anger with herself. I wondered if she'd agreed to go behind our backs out of the guilt she felt for dragging her own family into the whole shitshow of our arrest. That if they could earn a decent pay-out for the stories it was some kind of compensation. Whatever, I was in no mood to forgive.

*

To get out of the atmosphere of our room I decided the next visitors' day I'd accept everyone and anyone who put their names down to see only me – apart from Caesar, of course. I had a nice hour or so with a young missionary called Kelly who lived about ten minutes up the road from my mum's house. She was only twenty-three and was travelling over to visit an Irish girl in Ancón, so she thought she'd call in on me – being a tourist attraction and all. And she brought chocolates, so win-win.

I very rarely open up to people who aren't close friends, so the majority of things she asked me I dismissed with a joke or changed the subject. She hit a nerve, though, once. She said: 'For a couple of weeks last summer, your mum and your family were worried you were dead because you hadn't been in touch. How did that make you feel?'

I don't know what came over me. The tears poured out. I'd already apologised to my family but it hadn't assuaged the guilt. I was so, so sorry.

Maybe it was Kelly getting me thinking, but I couldn't be at war with Melissa forever. I'm not that type of person. She was also my only roommate, so it just wasn't practical. That didn't mean I'd ever forget the betrayal – and I certainly wouldn't trust her with anything to do with my future again. But we couldn't carry on having screaming matches every day.

A fortnight after the British media packed up again, Andrea called in with an update from her contacts at the courts. The prosecutor had ridden out the storm and was back on the case. What's more, there was a new deal on the table: if we named names, gave sources and basically shopped everyone we'd had contact with, then his original proposal could still happen. This time above board.

There was only one problem. I didn't want to tell him anything. It was five months since we'd started out on this adventure but I remembered the people who'd got me into it like it was yesterday. Just like I knew they would remember me. I had no doubt Paulo or the Brummie, or Mateo could get to me in any Peruvian prison. More importantly, I knew they'd find my family – and what they'd do when they did.

What's more, if we did give names and descriptions, wouldn't that make it look like we were working for a cartel? Wasn't that the opposite of what we were trying to say? Melissa took a bit more convincing.

'Haven't you done enough to your family?' I said. 'Do you really want Mateo or one of his friends turning up in Scotland? You know what these people are capable of.'

It was enough to frighten her. 'When you put it like that . . .'

Andrea left disappointed and empty-handed but she promised to keep up the good fight.

Everything was up in the air from that point on. We got a new court date of 12 December and I didn't tell a soul. Melissa pledged the same for whatever that was worth. Fishman prepped us as best he could, as did Andrea. But even as I went through the ordeal by groping to get into the building, I still didn't know which law we were being charged under. Or what the hell Melissa was going to say.

We were used to being kept in the dark but when the guards arrived to collect us that morning, and we both stood there with wrists out ready for the cuffs, the INPE told Melissa to go back to the cell. I had enough Spanish by then to ask why.

'One at a time,' was the reply. 'She's coming later.'

Melissa looked as shocked as I was.

Travelling in the sin bus was horrible at the best of times. Without Melissa I was the only target for the male prisoners.

I expected to go back into the same room with the two benches but the trial court was something different. The area for us and the prosecution was the same but there were a hundred or more seats for spectators. Every one of them was full. It was terrifying. And even though Fishman was in my corner, without Melissa by my side I felt exposed.

The prosecutor asked me what happened and I told them I was in Ibiza working and I met a guy who offered me €3,000 – the less money I was earning made me look more naive and gullible and less like a criminal. They asked for the guy's name and I said I didn't know. I met him in a bar and he just gave me tickets and then I met Melissa and we stayed in a hotel. I told them the whole story. Sort of. There were no real details. When he'd sent me texts he didn't go by a name – he was just an initial – 'C'.

'Did you know what you were doing?'

I sensed the courtroom go quiet. Everyone was straining to catch my answer.

'Yes,' I said. 'I knew the drugs were in my case. I knew I was being paid to break the law. But,' I added, 'I was scared.' I chose not to repeat the lie that we'd been kidnapped but I made it clear I felt I'd had no choice but continue once the ball started rolling.

I said, 'I'm really, really sorry for lying but once I had drunkenly agreed I couldn't get out of it.' That much at least was true. 'I accept full responsibility and I would never do it again.'

I had to say everything three or four times with plenty of pauses for the typist to get down what the translator repeated. Each minute of testimony took another ten to process.

The prosecutor was in no hurry. I knew that *he* knew I was leaving out a lot of detail. I also knew he'd pinned his entire case on me and Melissa contradicting each other. Guilty pleas or not, he still wanted to make examples of us.

I was shown loads of pictures, some of locations, some of people. When I saw the faces of Mateo and the Spaniard staring back at me, I nearly froze. No one noticed and I denied recognising any of them.

Just like I was careful not to mention anything else that put me in too much contact with the real criminals in the case.

I said again, 'Look, I only met one person at a bar and it snowballed from there. I wasn't privy to any places or people or information. Why don't you believe me?'

I really hoped I'd done enough but it wouldn't matter if Melissa's version didn't back me up. She just had to contradict me on one photo or one location and the prosecutor would have cause to hang us both out. I knew she was smart enough to guess what I'd have said. But would she? What if her dad had told her not to? What if the prosecutor had given her a deal if she shopped me? I could drive myself crazy worrying about 'what ifs'. I had to believe that Melissa would do the right thing. For both of us.

When they'd heard enough, I was sent back out to the holding room. Before I left, I hissed at Fishman, 'Whatever you do make sure she gives the same answers.'

He looked up nervously. 'Will do.'

My part of the proceedings had lasted ninety minutes. I don't know what Melissa was saying but three hours after she went in I was still waiting for some conclusion. The logical part of my brain said it was mind games from the prosecutor. He wanted me to sweat. The really logical part of my brain said that he was struggling to break Melissa's story down.

The longer it went on, the less logic got a say. By the time I was called back I'd convinced myself we'd be facing the firing squad. For all my fears and mistrust of Melissa, the second I saw her in the dock I broke into a large smile. She did the same and said, 'Thank God you're here.'

The judge had sat through the entire proceedings with no comment – and no crackers either. Now it was his time in the spotlight. He stood up and, via the translator, asked how I pleaded to the count of smuggling eleven kilograms of cocaine.

'Guilty.'

He asked Melissa the same question.

'Guilty.'

He looked at us both, then down at his notes. He was truly milking it.

'I sentence you to . . .' I heard the gasp from the Spanish-speaking members of the audience. It took a few seconds longer for the translator to get the message to us '. . . eight years in prison.'

It's so weird how the brain works. I'd gone into court that day knowing there was a very high chance I'd not see daylight again for fifteen years. Yet when I'd heard the words 'eight years' I flew into a fury. No one had mentioned that result. You couldn't get benefits from eight years. It may as well have been twenty! I was freaking out and Fishman was closest. I dropped down onto the chair next to him.

'What's this? You lied. You said we'd get six years eight months.' He looked genuinely terrified. Not of the result but of my reaction.

'Calm down. What do I keep telling you? This is just how they do things.'

'Yeah, so you say. But I don't know whether to accept this or not.'

He stared at me blankly. 'Michaella, look where you are. You don't have a choice.'

Hesitantly, we accepted the judge's verdict. As soon as we did his face changed. He said, 'In accordance with Peruvian law I'm reducing the sentence to six years and eight months. Now, I just need your signatures to prove you accept.'

It took a few minutes for the paperwork to reach us. As we signed we must have looked like cats who'd got the cream. With benefits, six years and eight months was shorthand for two years and three months – and we had already served five months. In the space of a few hours we'd gone from looking at fifteen years behind bars to less than two. I wanted to hug someone. I wanted to hug *everyone*.

Just when I thought the day couldn't get any better, we got back to our cell and discovered a parcel freshly delivered. It was from Andrea – and judging by the smell it was Chinese food. I couldn't wait to tuck in.

I wasn't the only one. I ripped open the packaging, screamed and quickly shut it again.

'What's wrong?' Melissa asked.

'Cockroaches,' I gasped. 'Hundreds of them.'

I don't know how they got inside the package but they weren't coming out. Not alive. I threw the carton on the floor and for the next minute we were stomping and stamping and shouting and smashing at anything that escaped. More than one voice from the other cells told us to shut up but we didn't care. We were in a party mood, we had Chinese food, and not even some bugs were going to stop that.

We tossed a coin for who would open the package the next time and I lost. Gingerly, I pulled back the wrapper. There was no movement. I pulled it further – still nothing. I yanked the whole bag off and squealed as dozens of baby cockroaches had been released by the squashing of the mothers. It was horrific. But the boxes were sealed tight and none of the foul insects had made contact with the actual food.

Five months earlier I'd have chucked the lot in the bin – bugs and food combined. It says a lot for how we'd adjusted that we didn't even sweep the carcasses up. Neither of us had had Chinese food since Europe. We just flicked the bugs off the boxes and filled our faces.

Best day ever.

*

Head count and breakfast the next day went like a dream. Plenty of the inmates knew we'd been to court. No one expected the result we got. Everyone was happy for us. To our faces, at least. I wouldn't have put it past one or two to be annoyed, especially the ones whose benefits applications had been rejected.

A couple of days later, Fishman arrived with a bunch of paperwork for us to sign. This was just a formality. There was no hurry. He said he'd collect everything the following day when we'd had a chance to go through it all.

It was a visit from Andrea the following day that once again threw me back into purgatory. She had devastating news about the terms of the benefits. Unbeknown to us, just a month before we had been arrested, a new law had been passed saying that drug traffickers were no longer entitled to the scheme.

It had been passed but not yet published. Andrea knew the score because she was close to the prosecutor. But there was someone else who should've known what was going on in the legal system as it applied to his clients:

'Fishmannnnnnn!'

CHAPTER NINETEEN

YOU'RE MY BABY

'*Ustedes dos vienen conmigo.*'

'You two are coming with me.' The delegate, Gonzales, had appeared between our bunks.

'*A donde?*' I said. 'Where?' Half-a-dozen women came in and started getting busy with my clothes bags and food stash.

'What the hell?' I jumped up to grab everything back but they seized me. This giant woman had me round the waist. I was screaming for Melissa to help but they got her too. I called out for the INPE, top of my voice. All that happened was twenty or thirty more inmates came to see what the fuss was about. A few of them looked shocked, but the majority smiled, cheered even, as I was carted kicking and hollering towards them.

I managed to lurch over and grab one of the beds. For once I was grateful they were secured to the floor. As long as I didn't let go, no one was taking me anywhere. Gonzales was losing her rag. She ordered two people to sort out my hands. I've never felt so strong but December's the height of summer in Peru so my hands were sweaty and I had a giant pulling me and two bitches with very sharp nails digging into my fingers. At least when I did let go the woman holding me was thrown back into the crowd.

They managed to get me to the doorway. I saw my last chance and flung my arms and feet across the frame. I lasted seconds. I was a leaf compared to some of those women. If I hadn't let go I'd have been snapped in two. We were halfway across the hall when I saw two INPE coming to investigate the commotion.

'Hey,' I yelled, 'help. They're going to kill me.'

One of them laughed. She nodded to Gonzales and said, '*Elle esta a cargo. Elle es la delegada.*'

'What did she say?' Melissa called from behind.

'She said, "Gonzales is in charge – she is the delegate."'

The INPE then stood aside for us to be carted I knew not where.

Everything changed after we were sentenced. We went from being filed under 'going through the system' to 'processed'. It was official. We were in the system, fully fledged criminals. And now fully Gonzales' property.

We were dragged into the cell shared by nearly a hundred women, including *La Delegada* herself. There were a couple of spare bunks at the back near the toilet. The second I was released I dived onto one of the lower beds and hugged my knees, reeling with the shock. Seconds later my possessions rained down on me.

I had grown to hate our cell. The noise from the window was a constant reminder of life outside. It was frustrating beyond belief knowing that freedom lay about eight inches away. Freedom that – thanks to a new ruling we'd known nothing about – we would not taste for many, many years.

But that didn't mean I wanted to give it up. And I certainly didn't want to be thrown to the company of wolves. I could already see various eyes staring at my possessions. I decided to throw them onto the top bunk so at least the shorter women couldn't touch them. None of the bunks had ladders. You had to be tall and strong enough to climb up unaided, which ruled out more than half of this lot.

Obviously, everything I did was wrong. When Gonzales came over to check on us she was livid I was using two bunks. In any case, she said, the lower ones were for the old and infirm.

'But they're both empty!' Didn't matter. She didn't care. Her cell, her rules. I honestly thought I was going to get punched.

As English speakers, at least Mel and I could communicate in some privacy even in a crowded room. It wasn't her I wanted to talk to though. My poor sister Stephanie got the brunt of my emotions. I'd worked so hard at putting on a brave face for my family, forcing those smiles, pretending I was strong enough to cope, that they never saw a meltdown coming. Well, they saw it now.

'I can't do it, Steph, I can't!' I sobbed down the phone. 'I can't spend six more years here. It will kill me.' I was wailing, swearing, totally losing it. Everything I had bottled up came pouring out: how I hated being in the new cell, how I was being bullied, how it was claustrophobic, how I was stuck on a top bunk even though no one was underneath and it was next to the toilets, and there was no privacy to get undressed or pee or shower. On and on and on.

I didn't care who heard. At that stage I didn't even care if I survived. Six-and-a-half years to a twenty-year-old sounds like a death sentence. At that moment I wasn't sure which option I'd prefer.

I didn't know where to turn. Goudie tried to calm me, but for once the language barrier wound me up. Andrea couldn't change anything. My embassy – being based in Mexico – was out of reach and, worst of all, when we'd harangued Fishman about the law, asking why he hadn't known about it, he just sat there looking gormless. Since then we hadn't heard a word from him. I was in a dark, dark place.

'Look,' Steph said, 'do you want me to come back over? I can be there within the week.'

'Oh Steph,' I said, 'I just want Mum.'

It didn't matter how hard I tried to protect my mother from my pain, the damage was already done. The run-up to Christmas was the lowest point of all.

I'd look through the bars and hear normal life going on outside, punctuated by the fiesta of the Nativity, fireworks and the sound of laughter. It gave me cause to reflect on everything I was missing, and what life could be like and currently wasn't. When would I be able to spend Christmas with my family again? My misery was all but absolute when I next spoke to my mum.

'I'm not doing Christmas this year,' she said.

'What? Why not? You love having the family over.'

'What kind of mother would I be if I celebrated with you stuck over there? You're my baby.' That cut me.

Unfortunately, the hurt kept coming. One day she told me there'd been a big exclusive in the *Sunday World*, an Irish paper, which had really upset her with some of the things I was quoted as saying.

'Mum, I haven't given any interviews since I was first arrested. I swear.'

'Well, it says here you have. It's the "Drug Mule's Full Story". And there's going to be more. They're putting one out every Sunday till New Year's. And there's a TV documentary as well.' She paused, too choked to continue. 'There's adverts everywhere.'

I was spinning. It made no sense. I hadn't seen a soul with a tape recorder or a notebook. Had someone crept into the trial? Nothing I said in there was new to anyone.

It was a week before a copy arrived in the post for me. I didn't recognise the name of the writer but I recognised her photo. It was 'Kelly', the so-called missionary who had come to see me in November. The lying, conniving little bitch! She'd got nothing from me but a few tears yet had spun it into this. It was a real cut-'n'-paste job from bits and pieces I'd told other people. I guess she needed to justify her flight, but it was exploitation pure and simple. It wasn't just my life she was messing with; she was ripping holes in my family too. They were the ones in the media's sights back home.

The only bright side was that the story never made the Peruvian press. The director of Fatima, as nice as she appeared, had made it clear that any publicity was bad publicity. Bring her prison into disrepute and it was *calabozo* for us.

Against all this misery, *La Delegada*, Gonzales, had plans for a Christmas party. Peruvians do their big celebration on 24 December, so Gonzales's helpers got everyone to chip in twenty soles each and then around 150 of us squeezed into the hall on plastic chairs and ate chicken and rice – the national dish – and panettone, and drank non-alcoholic fizz and played pass the parcel and other games. They'd put a nativity scene on a table and at midnight everyone gathered round the little figures of Mary, Joseph and the baby Jesus. There was no mention of Santa Claus or presents – they kept to the religious meaning. One by one even the most hardened, tattooed inmates went up and made a prayer. All I was praying for was that no one had nicked the Christmas gifts my family had sent over.

Christmas Day happened to be a Saturday, so that meant visitors. You'd think it would be Maureen's big day in her line of work but she rolled up first thing with a beautiful ham and turkey that she'd been up all night preparing. I didn't mind sharing a few prayers with her, although I'd never done it in ninety-degree heat before.

I'm not normally one for resolutions but, a week later, I decided that just because 2013 had been a shitstorm, that didn't mean 2014 had to be the same. The almost-seven-year sentence could only hurt me if I let it. Time to think positive, time to stop letting outside forces influence my life. Time to get a grip.

I got a chance early on. I'd been pestering Gonzales for work for so long and finally she relented. There was a vacancy for an assistant in the salon that everyone went to when they could afford it. If I wanted I could help out there.

The woman in charge was called Amy. Like Goudie, ours was a relationship based more on make-up and treatments than deep conversation but I now had enough Spanish to get by. I really enjoyed the work. We offered facials and massages. It worked just like the kiosk. Amy bought all the stock then charged the girls what she liked and kept the profits. She'd do it for six months then someone else would get a chance if they could afford the upfront collateral. Melissa was stuck working in the kitchen, but Carmen was there as well so she wasn't bothered.

I liked spending time with Amy. Her brother Mearang was in Ancón prison, wrongly accused, she was convinced, of drug dealing with gangs. Her dream was to be transferred to Ancón to look after him. He was an innocent. He could never survive on his own, she said. Luckily, she had a good friend there called Jackie.

I realised something about myself at this point. Every second I'd been in Fatima I was scratching at the walls, thinking I didn't belong there. Well, now was the time to get used to it. When I looked at the other prisoners, it was the ones serving their sentences who were most chilled. Those awaiting a trial were edgy, bitchy, clinging on to the hope they'd get out. Well, that didn't apply to me any longer. I was there for a good while. While I worked on finding a way through the new ruling, I was determined to turn things around.

The Christmas sun made our cell reek, but being on the patio offered some respite. After so many months of shivering and discomfort, I could actually step out in my flip-flops and feel over-dressed. I took it further. One Monday Mel and I put our towels down to soak up the rays. When I closed my eyes, I could believe it was Ibiza all over again.

And then the rain started. Except it wasn't rain. It was Diosa. She'd got the groundsman's hose and was soaking us, screaming as she did: *'Putas! Putas sucias!'* 'Whores. Filthy whores!'

It was quite frightening, especially the pressure of the water on my face, which was brutal. I'd have bruises for days. I thought the Goddess was just being her usual psycho self, but it turned out that displays of the flesh weren't encouraged. God knows why not. They turned a blind eye to sex in public.

*

February brought a huge surprise – something that part of me hoped would never happen, but yet I craved with every fibre of my being. My mum was coming to Peru with Samantha and Astrid. She was literally going to the ends of the earth to see me. Part of me didn't want her to see how I was living. None of me wanted to consciously register that she was seeing her youngest daughter behind bars.

But I now had something to look forward to and, when you are incarcerated, that can make all the difference to getting through your day without despair. I got up really early on the appointed day, which was Valentine's Day, so I could be ready for them. I sat at the rotunda, waiting and waiting for them to be let in at 9 a.m.

When they announced, 'McCollum, McCollum', the tears poured down my face. When we saw each other it was as if time had been turned back to my infancy. I was her baby, and she was there for me unconditionally. The feeling of love was all-consuming. When she asked me to sit close to her, it still wasn't enough. She pulled me onto her lap and hugged me, crying. I didn't care that I was reverting to a form of childhood. I stayed there – all five foot eight inches of me landed on this poor woman who had been through so much.

The stress had taken its toll on her. She looked unwell. Her arthritis was bad and she could not adjust to the climate or the food, which was unsurprising as she had been out of Ireland just once – and that was only to England. Added to that, getting through security had been a degrading and awful experience for her. Security had been so rude to her and I was furious. No concessions had been made for an older woman. Families of drug traffickers were not shown even a fragment of decency.

But there were no questions, no recriminations, no accusations or bitterness. It was all forgiveness and love. And then we got down to talking about things back home, and happier times and memories and daily life in jail. I told her about the salon and what the women were like, and we even managed a few laughs.

They were only able to stay for five days. I got to see them on the Wednesday and the Saturday and I begged for one more day from the director. There were restrictions on my visiting days. Consequently, my family ended up spending more time in the air travelling than with me.

When they left I was crushed. But I'd been reunited with my mum for the first time since I'd breezily jetted off for Ibiza the previous summer. Her love would stay in my heart and carry me through the coming months.

*

We had the occasional visit from Andrea, and my visitor log was as busy as ever. In April, I got a message that a local guy had contacted Mum and said he'd be in Peru for work and could he pop in? He offered to carry any presents and essentials. He wasn't just any old random guy – he was involved with a massively famous boy band – One Direction – on tour in South America. What young girl didn't love that band? I wanted to know *everything*. But I was also very careful to keep his arrival secret.

In May he arrived and, with Melissa working in the kitchens, I went down to meet him on my own. His name was Terry and he was packed to the gills with food and toiletries and the usual from my folks. That's not all. He'd also brought a DVD player and a small TV, but the guards made him leave those in the car. There were forms to fill in.

He was so lovely and happy to talk about anything but he did say, 'You have to keep this between ourselves. No offence, but this is a private visit. I can't be getting the band's name in the papers for a visit to a prison.'

I totally got it. There'd been a story not so long before about one of the band using drugs. The last thing they needed was being linked to a cocaine smuggler.

'Your secret's safe with me,' I told him. 'I'm just so grateful you bothered coming to see me.'

'You know what . . .' he paused as an inmate from the kitchen offered him a coffee. I waited for him to continue, then looked up. It was Melissa. And she had no intention of going anywhere. She plonked herself down and said, 'So, what's your story, then?'

Terry did his best to talk without being rude but she was an interrogation machine. We must have been there another three hours and all of it was spent with him answering her questions.

Still, Terry said the same thing to her as he said to me: 'No one can know about this visit. The band can't be associated with a prison. Is that cool?'

'No worries,' she said. And that was that.

Terry's final act of generosity was a dozen tickets to the Lima

One Direction gig. I couldn't use them, obviously. But he thought, rightly, that other people might want them. Gonzales promised me a fortnight's unlimited phone access in exchange for a pair.

The tickets certainly bought me some freedom from bullying. A couple wound up in the head of security's possession, so even she was onside, which meant that work, sleep, meet visitors – *repeat* – was our lives for a while. And we were grateful.

One day, the director called me to her office. As usual I was handcuffed. Unusually, she didn't invite me to sit down. She had an article on her desk that she pushed across to me.

'What is this?' she said.

I scanned the newspaper story. It said how I was having a great time in prison because the staff were so corrupt I could bribe them to do anything with tickets for One Direction. The director was furious. So was I. I hadn't told anyone about Terry's visit – and I knew he wasn't the one who had leaked the story. The fact there was a picture of him with One Direction in the article would have driven him mad as well. I told the director I had nothing to do with it. She wasn't having it.

'If it wasn't you then who was it?'

The answer was obvious. At the top of the story was the name 'Billy Reid' – Melissa's dad.

The director was yelling: 'The more you lie to me the worse your punishment. You want one week in *calabozo* or one month?' I had no choice. I pointed out in no uncertain terms who Billy Reid was: 'Melissa papa, Melissa papa.' The director summoned her. She arrived all carefree and giggly as usual. That didn't last long. Before the director could get her say I started shouting. Accusing her of selling me out yet again. Of feeding her dad titbits so he could make yet more money from my misery. Of stabbing me in the back yet again.

She denied everything, as usual. Eventually the director sent her away. Me, on the other hand, she had banged to rights. I was the one who Terry had come to see – she had it in black and white in the visitors' log. Stupidly, I'd lied at the time of the visit and said he was family as an attempt to hide who he really was. That was a rule break in itself. It also gave the director an idea. I was spared *calabozo* but instead she said, 'You are banned visitors. For ever.'

*

Melissa and I didn't speak for two weeks. I was getting punished, yet again, for Melissa's mistakes, for her sneaking around. Yet again I was carrying the can for her mess. The rest of the cell found that hilarious. The repercussions rumbled on even longer. My family was exasperated with me because, yet again, Melissa had leaked information via her father, who was saying in the media that Terry had come out to visit her, not me! I was also told that various missionaries and travellers had been sent away from the gates when they'd asked to see me. It didn't really make much difference to my life until one day in late May. I was talking to my mum and she said, 'Guess what.'

'What?'

'I'm coming to see you again. We're flying out in a few weeks. The hotel's booked and everything.' Normally I'd have hit the ceiling with joy. But not this time. My mum could sense it.

'What's wrong?' she said. 'Don't you want to see me?'

'Oh Mum, you know I want to see you, more than anything. But your timing's terrible.'

'Why? What do you mean?'

'I mean I won't be here. I've just been told . . . they're sending me away.'

CHAPTER TWENTY

FEEDING THE 5,000

The director cried when she told me we were being transferred to Ancón. She'd enjoyed the novelty of us not being Peruvian. Shame her feelings didn't filter down. I had four bags of possessions by then. Should have had five. I never got the DVD player and the TV in the end. They never made it past security.

Which was the problem I was now facing.

My books filled up a whole bag by themselves. I also had a parcel from Amy to give to her beloved brother Mearang, which wasn't small. The second she'd heard we were going to Ancón she'd started writing letters and notes and spending every penny on treats for him. Cereals and milk sachets and cake and biscuit treats from my family took up a load of space as well, then I had clothes, a little radio, jewellery my family had given me, all of it neatly packed. But not for long. About 500 yards from the exit we were stopped and strip-searched. I was still pulling my gear back on when they started on my bags. A Stanley knife ripped through each one, spilling the contents onto a table.

Two INPE I'd never seen before came in. One of them, a woman, started going through my stuff. She picked up my radio – which had been such a comfort to me during the times I'd been miserable – and said, '*Que bonita*.'

I had to agree – it was nice. I loved listening to music on the radio stations it picked up. The songs they played helped me with my Spanish. She put it in her pocket.

'Hey,' I shouted, 'that's mine. Radios are allowed.'

She grimaced at me. 'Yes, but I like it.'

I yelled the place down so much the Fatima guards had to drag me away. All the while the woman was trying on my rings and necklaces and everything else that caught her eye.

After about fifteen minutes we were let back in and told to tidy up the mess. There were a dozen shitty carrier bags to replace our luggage. I only needed a couple. Anything of any value had gone.

We were cuffed again and taken outside to a van with blacked-out windows parked in the inner yard. It was about ten o'clock at night. Standard antisocial tactics. Not a soul to be seen except, waiting for us by the door, the woman wearing my jewellery.

'You're a thief,' I said. 'You're the one who should be in jail.'

Big mistake. She reached down to my cuffs and squeezed them tighter. I winced as the metal cut into my wrists. She smiled and pushed again. This time it drew blood. Only then did she let me and Melissa board.

For the next four hours I sat gloomily in the dark as we trundled along. I'd dreamed of leaving Fatima every day since December but not like this. I was hurting and lonely, gutted at leaving Goudie and Amy and dreading having to make friends all over again with new people. I still hadn't forgiven Melissa for her last betrayal. Worst of all, my family was coming soon and I'd heard such awful things about where we were going. They'd just got used to Fatima.

About 4 a.m. we turned down a big driveway and came to a halt.

I waited to be summoned but the call never came. An hour we sat there, then another, then another. The director of Ancón hadn't been told we were arriving, so they had to go through all their admin procedures – in their own sweet time – before we were allowed entry.

Having had the handcuffs on for so long my wrists were swollen and painful. Sleep was impossible given the positions we were sat in. Luckily, I hadn't needed to go to the toilet, but if I had, I would have had to do it in the van. The conditions were inhumane. By early morning, the temperature in there was brutal.

The crackle of the INPEs' radio startled me about 9 a.m.

'Get your stuff!'

'How can I get anything in these handcuffs?'

'Okay. Leave it.'

I staggered out into the blinding light. It was already 28ºC. I wasn't the only one struggling. Dozens of other women were emerging from other buses parked neatly in line behind us. I thought we had it bad. Some of these buses had twenty or more women in and I knew for a fact there were only eight seats.

Twenty-five men in black uniforms with yellow piping marched out to greet us, combat weapons at the ready. Proper military and, judging by the fear etched on the faces of the other prisoners, not people to be trifled with. When a man loaded all our bags onto a trolley and pushed them off to God knows where, I bit my lip like everyone else.

I could make out a block on our right. They looked like offices but they had balconies. Actual balconies. Unfortunately, they weren't for us. We were led along a walkway surrounded by a huge grey wall, about twenty feet high in places. Along the top were more guards, heavily armed, their assault rifles aimed in our direction.

We stopped at the door to an imposing grey structure, as anonymous as it was threatening. Melissa and I were put on one side, everyone from the other vans on the other. It was the first chance I got to have a look at them. At a guess I'd say they were all South American, certainly Hispanic. A few of them were miming blowjobs at the guards and laughing. I must have stared too long. I was aware of one girl giving me evils. Then another. I dropped my eyes immediately.

I was actually relieved when one of the men started doing a

roll call and the women began disappearing one by one through the door. Then it was my turn. In one room a doctor got me to strip and searched me top to toe. Again. Next door a psychologist asked a few questions in Spanish that I could just about follow. Then it was the fingerprint room, then the photograph room, then we had to sign various documents, then finally I ended up in a large hall with two tiers of eight cells down one side. At one end was a heap of bags. I found mine and took them to a table for a guard to search. It didn't take long; all that was left were toiletries and clothes. My little radio and jewellery had been robbed from me by thieves in uniform. When that was done he told me to go to my room.

The second I left the guards there was whooping and hollering from the other side of the gate. A sea of male faces pressed against the bars of the cells. I couldn't make out their words but their gestures and expressions left nothing to the imagination.

The first cell was empty, so I took that one. It was about six foot wide and had two stone bunk beds coming out of the wall, and a small window at the rear. It was snug. And about to get snugger. When Melissa came in I quickly threw my stuff on the lower bunk furthest from the loo and said, 'I was upstairs at Dirandro. It's your turn now – unless you want your face next to the bog.'

The toilet was basically a wide plastic pipe that you either stood or crouched over, depending upon your business. We were back to vile conditions.

The appearance of a man in the doorway got her moving. I assumed he was one of the officials, maybe the director, come to check on his celebrity inmates.

'Where are we?' I asked. 'And how long are we going to be here?'

He didn't reply. Didn't even answer. He just walked over to the other bunk and climbed to the top! I could hear Melissa giggling. Damned chetos had me fooled again.

The final bed was taken by a petrified-looking European woman in her late forties. She sighed when she saw her bed. Once you put your stuff on it the only way to sleep was in the foetal position. That is, if you could sleep on the concrete base.

It says a lot for what we'd gone through that I was just grateful there wouldn't be cockroaches inside it. As it turned out a guard came by ten minutes later and threw some mattresses in. As usual, they were the thin, scratchy fibre-glass issue that made my skin burn.

I asked him what I'd asked the cheto. 'Where are we? Is this Ancón? Is this where we're staying now?'

He laughed.

'Well, at least tell me when I'll be moved from here.'

'*Mañana*,' he said. 'First: processing.'

Tomorrow, I thought. *I can handle that.* It's not like I had anything to unpack.

*

The cheto turned out to be a Mexican called Marcel, incarcerated on drugs charges. Sweet enough, but clearly not to be messed with. The European was a German called Bettina and had been living in Lima. She'd been done for tax fraud. She looked even more out of place than I did. No wonder she seemed terrified. They'd been in another part of Fatima towards the end of our time there.

Once all the other cells filled up, the women started mingling outside. Most of them were from Santa Monica and obviously knew each other. After all the evil eyes I'd got outside I didn't want to get involved but Melissa was out there like a shot. I didn't venture out at all until I heard such a commotion I couldn't resist seeing what the fuss was. What I found was three guys delivering lunch pots to a horde of hungry women. Except it wasn't the rice, potatoes and meat the girls were starved of. From the way some of them were reacting, I don't think they'd see men for months, maybe years.

There was a Colombian girl called Vanessa – tiny, but with massive fake breasts and, from the look of it, implants in her bum. She was going from guard to guard trying to get a kiss or run her fingers down the front of their shirts and trousers. They didn't seem too fussed either way, but when she saw the delivery lads she was straight over to one in particular. He was handsome, well-built and familiar-looking.

'Hey, Mel,' I said, 'do you think he looks like Amy from Fatima? Do you think that's her brother?'

'Come on, what are the odds of you finding him in your first ten minutes?'

I agreed. Then I heard one of the guards calling out 'Mearang' and I said, 'Shit, it *is* him.'

The guys put down the lunches and I assumed they'd leave but they didn't. In fact, a few new faces arrived, and they too were swamped by the girls. I think it was just me and the German, Bettina who even looked at the food. We each grabbed a bowl and darted back to our cells before any men could get near us. Clearly, Mearang was a regular visitor – I'd hand over Amy's stuff later.

It sounded like a party was going on in the hall. You didn't need to speak the language to understand what flirting sounds like. And it wasn't just the prisoners. I became aware of someone standing in my doorway. It was one of the guards.

'What's your name?' he said.

'When am I being moved?'

'Hey, I'm just being friendly.'

And he was. What the hell was going on? We'd only been there two hours and it was like a knocking shop on a Saturday night: men hitting on women, women hitting on men. Crazy. Absolutely surreal. I was totally shocked. Having been in Fatima's all-female environment, the behaviour seemed massively over the top. And I certainly didn't trust a guard who was capable of chatting up one of his inmates.

'I like you,' he said. 'I will come back tonight. Wait for me.'

For the next few hours I was really anxious. The last thing I wanted was some armed guard on my case. I just wanted to be left alone. I was clearly in the minority. It wasn't just Vanessa working the men; an Italian woman called Simona was going crazy. She took herself over to the gate and performed a lewd dance in full view of the men caged up on the other side. She was a striking and fearsome presence. She was probably in her early forties but she acted like a teenager. She had long dark hair, a symbol of femininity, but this was compromised by the fact that she was built like a pit bull – muscly and strong, and covered in tattoos. The men didn't mind. She was writhing, stripping down, shoving her fingers inside herself then licking them. It was grotesque. Her audience lapped it up while the guards just stood around smirking. It was like a Quentin Tarantino movie version of a South American jail.

I thought things couldn't get worse. At six o'clock there was a roll call. We all lined up and then I assumed there'd be TV time or some kind of entertainment. How naive. The second the guy with the clipboard left, the gates to the outside patio were unlocked – and so were the doors on the men's cells.

It had been bad enough before when people couldn't touch. Now there was kissing and groping and all sorts going on. Outside was even worse. There were two cubicle toilets on the patio. Both of them were engaged – and totally rocking. By the sound of it, Simona was in one of them. When a guy did eventually emerge, she stayed in – waiting for visitor number two.

It was like car crash TV – so gross you couldn't take your eyes off it. The only worry was the guards turning a blind eye. If that guy threatening to see me later was expecting anything like Simona then I was in big trouble. I didn't dare go back to my cell in case he was there.

At nine o'clock the choice was made for me. Two guards wandering around the patio got their assault rifles out and starting firing into the air. All the women were screaming, the men were yelling, swearing at the guards who just laughed and told everyone to get inside for roll call. I was just going in when I saw – and heard – Simona emerge virtually naked from the cubicle. One of the guards tried to nudge her with his rifle but she just slapped it away. She really wasn't the full ticket.

With the men and women separated once again, and the gates locked, I nervously got myself ready for bed. Melissa came in buzzing a few minutes later.

'This place is wild,' she said.

'Tell me about it. Simona was shagging strangers in the toilets.'

'Well, Patricia's got a night of it.'

'Who's she?'

'Spanish woman. Short, fat, covered in make-up and desperate to get laid.'

Apparently, Patricia had connected with one of the male inmates, so she'd paid a guard twenty soles to get into his cell after hours. She'd waited for roll call, then this corrupt INPE had sneaked her out and into the male block.

'What? Tonight? Jeez, these women don't hang around.'

'Well, if you're only here one night better make the most of it.'

*

Mearang and his two mates were back in the hall serving breakfast the next morning. There wasn't quite the same level of groping and flirting as the day before. Clearly, a lot of people had worked off some steam overnight. I was heading back to my room to sort out Amy's letter and gifts for her brother when the pneumatic Colombian, Vanessa, ran past screaming, 'I've got it! I've got it!' Ten minutes later, I saw her again, surrounded by other women, high as kites as they passed a crack pipe between them.

'Where'd you get that?' I asked.

Vanessa smiled, completely chilled.

'Mearang, the delivery boy,' she laughed. 'He can deliver anything.'

Can he now? I thought. *Well, he can deliver these himself.* And I flung Amy's bag back onto my bed. So much for Mearang being innocent. The guy was a dealer, exploiting some very vulnerable women. Crack cocaine affects users in different ways and very rarely for the good. Some people just need to take it once and they're psychotic for ever. It was the last thing we needed in that powder keg of a place and Mearang should damn well know it. I didn't want anything to do with him.

Vanessa and friends were barely upright at roll call but at least they were there. When the guy got to Patricia's name there was no reply. He called it again and again, really angrily. Suddenly, one of the guards by the wall leapt into life. You could see it on her face as it dawned on her: *Shit, that's the woman I let sleep in the men's block.*

Even if she did know Patricia's name, the roll call is done by surname, which she definitely wouldn't have known. She bolted out of the hall to the sound of murmuring. When she returned five minutes later the murmurs turned to cheers. Patricia was small, with blond hair, outrageous make-up and quite overweight. But she had a smile on her face.

The guy with the clipboard was not impressed. And he definitely didn't believe the guard's story that Patricia had slipped, so had been taken to see the doctor. But what could he do? For all I knew he was the one decent man in a cesspit of corruption.

All the girls wanted to hear Patricia's story. I couldn't help myself – so did I. I wish I hadn't. Her guy shared a room with seven others and his was a top bunk, but she was so hefty that she couldn't get up there, so they'd bribed his mate to switch.

'What did you give him?' someone asked.

'What do you think?' Patricia laughed and slapped her own ass.

It became clear that he wasn't the only one to benefit. By daybreak she'd gone round the entire cell.

I was numb with shock. How could you go to some random guy's cell and do that? He might be a murderer or a serial killer. It was so full on. These women were crazy to put themselves in such danger, but no one was forcing them. I was witnessing human behaviour at its most degraded level, like watching animals at a zoo. But being disgusted with nature is like being angry at rain. They'll carry on doing what they do whether you like it or not.

I'd been there twenty-four hours and the nicest thing about it was not being visited by the male guard. I was very pleased to see that the female guards slept on little beds in our hall. You could hear them snoring from inside our locked doors. The truth is, though, as Patricia had proven, you could get anything with the right incentive. I would use only money. Luckily for most of the guards that was enough.

I hadn't been allowed to make a phone call on Day 1. I hadn't even seen a phone. I'd hoped to find one down near the patio but even then, you wouldn't want to make a call to your mum with the sound of Simona's sweet loving in the background. I asked every guard and eventually I found one who said it was possible. The fact it would take place after hours and would require me pretending to be ill should have put me off but it didn't.

I was ready at 10.30 p.m. when the guard knocked on my door.

'Are you ready to see the doctor?' she said.

'Yes.'

'Good,' she said, and held out her hand. I gave her twenty soles and she nodded. 'Follow me.'

Melissa decided to come as well and, by the time we reached the hall gate, there were two other women waiting, just as 'ill' as us. We were led down one passage then another. At various points there were locked gates and guards that needed to be persuaded into opening them. At one point we went outside and passed next to a men's block. Eager hands stretched out from the windows. The guard hit a few knuckles with her rifle butt, although more for fun, it seemed, than as a deterrent. Eventually we reached a block marked 'Tópico' – clinic. And inside there was a payphone.

Plus about thirty men and women, some patients, some staff, all wandering around chatting like they were at a party, a lot of them clearly high as kites. You'd never guess it was a hospital, let alone a prison. Drug-taking seemed rife. It was a world away from Fatima.

We were no sooner in the door than half the men were all over us, sniffing around, bombarding us with questions. It wasn't that they'd never seen a woman before. They'd just never seen us before. We were fresh meat. A new challenge. I half expected to see cameras pointing at us like we were on some cheap reality show: *Love Prison* or something. The only aroma stronger than the testosterone in the air was the reek of weed. And that's saying something. A lot of them spoke English, but only to spew out a load of filth. All the while our guard stood there, arms folded, not bothered one jot.

Finally, it was my turn for the phone, and for seven or eight blissful minutes all was right in the world. All the while I was talking I was slapping roving hands away from my bottom. Still the guard did nothing.

I was pleased to get out of there. Without the phone call as a distraction I realised how grim the walk back to the cell actually was. There was no shortage of baying noises coming from the dark. It was like a maze. Then there were the guards. At the first checkpoint one of them tried to hold my hand. At the next I was propositioned: if I gave them something, they'd give me something. And we weren't talking money – more Patricia's currency. It was sickening but again our guard eventually put a stop to it.

I was very relieved indeed to get back to our cell.

*

Usually when me and Melissa were a bit down, a chocolate bar or cake from my secret supplies was a little fillip. I wish I hadn't bothered this time. Melissa couldn't make up her mind till the whole lot was spread out on my bunk. Which other people saw, of course. I didn't mind Marcel or Bettina having something but I drew the line at the strangers outside who came in with their hands out like begging bowls.

'No,' I told them, 'come back when you've got something to trade.'

Apart from maybe a cigarette there was nothing I needed, so I didn't expect to see them again any time soon.

Vanessa the Colombian stayed away, as did her aunt, who by coincidence was in at the same time. Another girl, Diane, hadn't got involved either. Of the rest, there were a handful of Asian girls, some from the Philippines, some from Indonesia, who also hadn't got involved – but more because they were too off their heads on crack to notice. They were all so slightly built, like young girls really, but you'd be sitting there talking to them and then the next minute they'd be standing up shouting in your face like the scariest bitches ever.

Of course, some people didn't need crack to get crazy.

On Day 3 one of the Asians called Nancy went to the patio to hang up some clothes she'd just washed. There was a little washing line there, a rope hung between two walls. There were already some clothes on the line but they'd dried, so Nancy folded them and put them on the wall and hung hers up. End of story.

Problem was, the other clothes belonged to Simona – the pit-bull dancer.

She was watching the patio from her cell's little window and when she saw her clothes being touched she went apeshit. She was down there, screaming in the other woman's face, completely raging. Nancy didn't speak a word of Italian, so she was chattering back in her native tongue, which didn't help. Simona wrenched the washing from the wall and, before Nancy could move, she wrapped it around the Asian girl's neck and started strangling her.

Everyone was stunned. The other Asians reacted first. En masse they piled into Simona but she was double their size. They were climbing on her and she was shaking them off, all the while with her hands on this rope by which she was dragging Nancy around the yard.

Vanessa got herself in the middle but Simona knocked her out the way, so then Melissa had a go. I thought she was mad. You don't want to be making an enemy of a nutcase like Simona.

But she got somewhere. A guard came and started firing his rifle close to Simona's head. It was the only way to shut her down. Nancy was taken to the hospital and Simona was left to collect her laundry like nothing had happened. As she went back in, she shouldered Melissa out the way.

'That was brave,' I said, 'but really stupid. You'll be needing to watch your back now.'

It was the same day when Melissa noticed her towel was missing. Within an hour I'd spotted it in Simona's cell. I was tempted not to say anything but I had to. Melissa went marching in there, grabbed it and stormed out. It took her a while to get off her bed. By the time she did a load of other women were separating her from Melissa.

Better them than me. At this rate we wouldn't make the end of the week, let alone six more years.

*

I had no idea what had happened to the 'mañana'. We'd now been held in our waiting zone – called 'Prevention' – for seven days and we'd still not been allocated to the wing of the prison that would be our home for next God knows how many years. Seven days of not knowing who was going to explode next, what sex game was going to be played out in full view, or what drugs were coming in via food deliveries.

During this time there was a visit from Andrea who, on this occasion, turned up with her husband, a presenter for a well-known TV news programme. I hadn't known about it in advance, but I assumed it had been cleared by the prison, as they were on the premises with a film crew.

They wanted an interview but I didn't want to know. I had no faith in the media, whether they were from the UK or Peru. Melissa complied, but she looked a fright. She'd chopped her hair off and looked quite crazy. I hung around watching them, but I didn't give an interview.

Sure enough, there was a backlash. A couple of days later a big meeting was held. The director of the prison came storming in to express his anger. Ancón 2 was supposed to be the showpiece of modern Peruvian prisons, yet the news piece had shown it to be a lawless melting pot.

We were supposed to be processed quickly but now there would be a delay for us. And as another punishment we were not allowed phone calls. Even though I hadn't contributed to the interview, yet again I was being punished. The authorities saw Melissa and I as one entity, so we would both suffer, regardless of the fact that I did nothing to encourage this latest media attention.

Eventually, we got the call. We all did. Before we could be allocated a permanent cell, we had to undergo a process of categorisation, where the prison board would decide which wing we would be housed in. One by one we were all summoned to meet with the powers that be. The guards erected trestle tables outside the cells and six men and women in suits sat down. When our name was called we were passed along the line. I was fine with it. But Vanessa and the ones who had been on the crack pipe, mostly the Asian girls, were bricking it.

The first person to grill us was the prison director. The building, he explained, had five wings: one for terrorists, three for Peruvians and one for foreigners. The foreign section was split into two blocks: maximum security – *maxima* – and minimum security – *minima*. The maximum wing was obviously for people considered a risk to the public. The minimum one was for people like us and our German cellmate.

The next person asked about my crime, how long I'd been there, and when I last took drugs. Then came a barrage of invasive personal questions. He took my hands and examined them closely, including my palms. His colleague asked if I was a heavy drinker, a smoker, even what my sexual history was. Most of it I answered honestly. What the hell they could tell from my hands I did not know. The whole process took about thirty minutes. By the time I got to the end, other people were already on the conveyor belt.

The decision as to where we would be housed was obvious – we weren't terrorists; we were young women with no history of violent crime. It had to be *minima* – although we weren't told their decision there and then.

I'd just got out of bed the next day when a guard called for me and Melissa with the familiar cry of '*Translado*'.

'Pack your things, you're leaving.'

I was actually excited. I got dressed and threw my stuff together. I had a quick hug with Marcel and Bettina and presented myself to the guard.

'Mattress,' he said. 'You'll need it.'

Slight as it was, it was still hard to drag out with all my other bags. But we made it to the gate. As usual, the caterwauling from the male cell started the second the door opened. The guard on the other side just looked at us.

'Where are you going?' he said.

'We're leaving.'

'I don't think so.' I spun round to our guards for help but they were just laughing. It took a moment for the sola to drop.

'I make a mistake,' the guard said patronisingly. 'Maybe *mañana.*'

The walk of shame back to our cell was so humiliating. I wanted to scream but I didn't want to give the guards the satisfaction of knowing they'd got to us. But they had. I was fuming. Wasn't it enough for them that we were locked up in this atrocious environment?

Two days later they pulled the same stunt. I wanted to shout and swear at these unfunny jokers. The problem was that even though we knew they were taking the piss, if we didn't do what we were told they could come into our cell and literally drag us out without our stuff if the call for '*Translado*' turned out to be genuine. The thought of those jackals going through my bags the second I was taken out did my head in, so every time I was told to leave I did. Even though we all knew it was one big fucking joke.

No one else was targeted. Each time the joke was on the '*gringas, stupidas*'. Maybe word had got round that we were the ones from the TV. Maybe it was because we hadn't slept with the guards. Whatever the reason, it was humiliating torture.

Three weeks after we arrived – and two weeks after our interview with the panel – we were dragged out yet again. Half the block was outside their cells pointing, laughing, as we made the familiar journey. I wasn't even surprised when we got to the gate and the guard said, 'It was a joke. You can go back now.'

I'd done the anger, I'd done the resentment. They'd won, I was conditioned. If this is what the next six years had in store then I was ready for it. I wasn't going to give them the satisfaction of getting my hopes up. We were halfway back to our cell when the other guard from the gate called out, 'Where do you think you're going?'

I ignored him and kept walking. It was the distinctive cocking of a gun that made me stop.

'Get back here!'

'*Por que?*' I shouted, tears in my eyes at yet more humiliation. '*Este una broma mas* – another joke.'

We were virtually shoved through the gate, mattresses and all. For the next ten minutes we dragged our gear along the grimmest corridors. Some of the time we ran the gauntlet of men trying to touch us. Sometimes we could see football pitches and buildings from the small windows. After nearly half an hour of walking we eventually came to a halt in a large waiting room with doors coming off it every which way. No one was in any hurry, so I plonked myself down on the mattress and waited to be shouted at. No one bothered. In fact, over the next couple of hours we were joined by everyone else from the block.

I saw people come and go through different doors. There were two next to each other. Through one I could make out a flower garden, all colourful and welcoming. Through the other it was like a scene from a horror film. What looked like dog kennels stretched back as far as I could see.

'Get a look at this, Mel,' I said. 'Don't tell me they put humans in there?'

'Lucky we're going to *minima* then, isn't it?'

Much as I was wary of most of my recent block mates, I pitied any poor soul who ended up in there. It didn't look fit for animals.

With everyone there we got going. A guard started reading from a list of names and one by one the women around us picked up their belongings and passed through the door leading to the flower garden. When Nancy and the other Asians went through, I knew I could relax. Their drug smuggling had been far worse than mine. But, crucially, she wasn't considered a threat to anyone. None of them were, any more than Melissa and me.

Which is why what came next was like a bullet to the heart when the guard said, 'McCollum, Michaella: *Maxima!*'

CHAPTER TWENTY-ONE

YOU'RE JUST LIKE EVERYONE ELSE

'*D os quatro seis.*'

I stared at the guard. I didn't know what else to do. No matter how many times he repeated it, it didn't make any more sense.

'*Dos quatro seis.*'

I knew what the numbers were – 246. I just didn't know what they meant.

Or why they had been written onto our arms in black marker pen. I was standing with Melissa at the bottom of a flight of stairs looking up at two levels of cells with prisoners hanging out between the bars seeing what fresh meat was being delivered. It was about half eight in the evening. We'd been queuing all day. I just wanted to lie down. But I didn't have a clue where.

I'd been trying to tell the guards there must have been a mistake. I was for *minima*, surely. They ignored me completely, of course. I was too far down the line now for anyone to be coming to my rescue.

I smelt *maxima* before I got a good look at it. The putrid odour of bad drains and the sewage system assaulted my nostrils, at the same time as the noise of the inmates assaulted my ears.

Suddenly, we were mobbed – rushed at by a bunch of women I

assumed to be established residents. They set about twisting our arms this way and that to see our numbers, while simultaneously pulling at our bags.

'No, you're not taking that!' shouted Melissa, clutching on to her meagre belongings.

'Oh my God, Melissa – we're in maximum security. They are bound to steal our stuff,' I called to her, terrified of what was happening to us. I was overwhelmed by it all – the noise, the smell and the sheer number of inmates. We'd come from a prison that housed some six hundred women. And now we were in a pressure cooker of ten thousand. I felt sick and dizzy. And the women took full advantage of our disorientation. We were surrounded as we walked through the corridor, the shouts of the multi-national inmates echoing off the walls. The cells looked chaotic.

'Floor two, cell four, bunk six,' said one of the English-speaking women, ushering me along. So that was what the numbers meant . . .

Bunk 6 was at the top by the window, which is where the good news ended. It was another concrete slab affair but this time it came with a small shelf, not that I'd trust putting my belongings on show. No sooner was I in the cell than my new neighbours were poring over my bags. One of them, Charlene, a really large black woman from Chicago, said, 'I'm going to help you with this,' and all I was thinking was how to protect my own space. I knew how important first impressions were in prison.

There were seven of us in this tiny square room and Charlene seemed to be taking up most of the space. It was so claustrophobic, and she was so big, and my head was still spinning from being categorised as maximum security. I wanted to scream. I was on the verge of passing out. Only the thought of being unconscious in this company kept my eyes open.

Who were these people? Why were they maximum security? And where the hell was Melissa? I didn't even know which door she'd gone through. What if this was it? What if we'd been separated for good like they'd always threatened?

I managed to fob Charlene off, saying I needed to rest. I couldn't have done it if she spoke a different language. I wouldn't have dared. She shrugged and said, 'Whatever, honey, you let me know when you're ready,' and waddled back to her bed. I examined my surroundings. The toilet was a hole in the ground with a flimsy screen around it. Literally, a shit hole, right there in the middle of the room. It obviously served as the shower area as well. Not that anyone in the room looked like they used it.

There was a Brazilian girl in her underwear and some sort of crop top, half naked, sort of dancing to nothing. In Fatima, it was considered disrespectful to show too much skin, but I quickly learned this Danielle wouldn't be bothered by a rule like that. While I was fighting off Charlene, she fired question after question in broken English. It was relentless. It made me miss the days of no one understanding a word I said – until I remembered *La Diosa* and how mad it had made her.

Another woman was from Ecuador, one from Mexico and another from Nigeria via London. We were like the United Nations of prisoners. In fact, with World Cup 2014 in full swing in Brazil, the entire cell was represented. I knew very little about football but an awful lot about allegiances.

Nationality is what defined us. But apart from Rose, a Nigerian so crippled with arthritis she could barely walk, each inmate was progressively bigger than the last, none more so than a woman from Texas called Corinne, who was built like a ranch house. She was really tall, as well as hefty, with short hair. She was wearing cut-off denim jeans and a checked shirt, like a typical Texan. She seemed pretty easy-going, but I didn't want to see her in a bad mood.

Bang on nine o'clock there was a commotion outside and all the women got up.

'Roll call,' the Texan drawled. 'You need to be coming down.'

I got to the door and I nearly cried when I saw Melissa standing there. 'Please tell me you're in here,' I said.

She nodded. 'Two four eight.'

'Oh, thank God.' Although it did mean there was one nation – Scotland – that hadn't made the World Cup finals.

As far as I could make out we were the talk of the yard. There were eight cells, eight beds in each, which meant sixty-two pairs of eyes staring at us during the register. I was relieved to get back to the cell. With Melissa there I ventured a little conversation with our new cellmates. I wanted to get the lay of the land as soon as possible. Mainly, though, I was desperate to learn where the nearest phone was. My family were coming to visit soon and they didn't even know where I was! The Texan was happy to answer everything if you had the patience to wait for her to finish speaking. More often than not Charlene interrupted with shorter, sharper replies. Net result: the phones were downstairs and you had to write your name down to book a slot.

Okay, I thought, *I just need to get downstairs before anyone else.*

The air was stifling and sticky but I was so exhausted that I was able to sleep. The next morning I was awake early, anxious to find those phones. Bang on schedule I heard the doors opening up downstairs. I climbed down my ladder – at least we had one of those in these bunk beds – and waited by the door for the key to turn. Because it was so early, six o'clock, I thought I would be the only one down there. I was wrong. I could hear the chatter before I was halfway down the stairs. Loads of women were already stretching their legs. When I fought my way through the crowd to the phone list my heart sank. The whole first page was already full. There were even a few names already written on the back. They were all from downstairs. How the hell was that fair? Of course they were going to get to the list first.

I didn't see any guards, but a woman was monitoring the phone. I pleaded with her, saying, '*Familia, familia*' enough times for her to insert my name on the list.

'Okay,' she said in English. 'But if you are not down here when I call your name, you lose your place.'

I worked out that if everyone used their ten minutes, I had at least a four-hour wait, so I went back upstairs. After only an hour I heard 'Michaella, Michaella', so I hightailed it back downstairs. I ran up to the phone but as soon as I got there the monitor said, 'Where were you? If you're not here when I call your name you have to go to the back of the list. You're not famous in here,' she said. 'You're just like everyone else.'

Back in the cell I was in tears. Charlene was all for marching down there but I knew she wouldn't. She was all talk. Corinne was more helpful. She said I could always complain to the delegate.

'Don't tell me they have that stupid system here too?' I said. Come on, then, where will I find this *delegada*?'

'Oh, you can't miss her,' Corinne said. 'She's got star quality.'

She was right. *La Delegada* of Ancón 2 was a woman called Monica, a voluptuous middle-aged Colombian with long, glossy dark hair. Unlike the majority of inmates, Monica clearly had money. She was dressed nicely and, more importantly, she was clean. How she managed it in that sewer I didn't know, but she smelled as good as she looked. She had real presence and commanded a lot of respect.

I introduced myself in Spanish and fortunately she was friendly – even when I said precisely what I thought of the person monitoring the phones.

'Oh,' she said, 'she's my friend. My good friend.'

Oh shit.

She said, 'Come with me', and led me downstairs. There was a girl already on the phone talking and she just went over to her, grabbed the handset, placed it in the cradle and said to her, 'Your time is up.' The girl was about to kick off when she realised it was Monica, so she backed right down and turned her attention to me. She got right in my face and told me to watch my back.

Great. I'd only been there five minutes and I'd already made a new enemy.

Even I could see how bad it must've looked that I was getting preferential treatment. 'Oh, the girl from all the news thinks she's better than us . . .' I could imagine everyone in the queue saying already. But, you know what? I didn't care. I just wanted to speak to my mum.

When I got through, I told her where we were and to research everything. But, the more I thought about it, the more I was convinced she shouldn't come.

She wouldn't be told. 'I missed your Christmas,' she said. 'I will not miss my baby girl's twenty-first birthday.'

With everything going on I'd virtually forgotten. But there it was. On 27 June I'd be turning twenty-one in the company of some of South America's worst criminals.

It was enough to make any mother proud.

*

The security at Ancón was very visible. The rotunda was teeming with guards, although they left the cells to be ruled by *La Delegada* and her monitors. And whereas you might have one or even none at various points in the corridor inside at Fatima, here there were no fewer than four, five sometimes more. There were routine checks around the clock. In the short space of time I'd been there I'd seen several searches of cells or individuals. I couldn't get over how busy it all was. Everywhere you looked there were so many people, so many things going on. There was nowhere to sit, nowhere to stand. It was horrible. And trying to find someone was a nightmare.

Before I left Fatima my friend in the beauty salon, Amy, had told me to look out for someone called Jackie. She was at Ancón and apparently she'd look after me.

I hadn't forgotten, but considering Amy had no idea what her brother Mearang was really like I didn't hold out much hope for this Jackie. Still, one afternoon Charlene was doing my head in, as usual, so I went outside and decided to track her down. I started asking people, 'Do you know Jackie, do you know Jackie?' and got nowhere. It was weird, because while everyone there was really interested to know as much about the newcomers as they could, none of them actually wanted to talk to me. It was like I was speaking to a brick wall, like I wasn't even there. They just blanked me. And I know it wasn't the language problem because this was a prison for foreigners and virtually everyone in my own cell spoke English, so why wouldn't these others?

A few months earlier I would have just given up and gone away, but hey, I'd learned a lot, and what did I have to lose? I kept persevering, working my way up the whole block until eventually someone took pity on me and actually answered.

'Jackie?' she said. '*La chinita?*' And she pointed to a cell I hadn't yet visited.

I was really grateful, especially to be tipped off about what Jackie looked like because that made it a whole lot easier when I arrived at the cell and there was only one Filipina in there.

'Oh, I was waiting for you to come,' Jackie said. 'I saw you on the news. I was wondering when you would end up here.'

Grateful that she wasn't as crazy as everyone else, I ran off and grabbed Melissa. Then we sat on Jackie's bed for the next hour getting the lowdown on how the prison worked. Jackie ran the salon for our block, so she knew everyone. She was really sweet. She had some make-up remover and used it to clean my arms of the inked numbers. She introduced us to a Dutch-Moroccan girl called Kaouthar. I couldn't believe how good-looking she was, and her personality was just as nice. Not everyone was a fan. We went down to the patio to chat and there was obvious hostility towards her from various inmates. In fact, one woman named Rochelle, the self-proclaimed 'number two' to Monica, beckoned me over. She made it clear that Kaouthar was no good, that I should avoid her if I knew what was good for me. She was basically trying to recruit me to her own imaginary little gang. I made my excuses and left.

'They're just jealous of Kaouthar's looks,' Jackie explained. 'And the fact she gets more attention than they do.' Apparently, complete strangers would send her money just because they'd seen a picture of her. It was amazing.

Melissa laughed. 'And to think you only get letters from nutjobs like Caesar.'

I'd almost forgotten my weird admirer. An upside of leaving Fatima was that he could no longer pester me. He probably couldn't even find me.

Kaouthar was only a year older than me. In fact, her birthday was just two days after mine. We planned to celebrate together with my family. If they ever arrived.

*

On the morning of the visit I was beside myself. The place was chaotic and I couldn't get access to anyone organising visits and didn't know how things worked. I patched together information from some of the friendlier inmates. Visitors were allowed in from ten, although I didn't expect to see anyone before eleven. The prison got so many visitors that inmates were not allowed onto the patio on visitor days unless called. However, we were allowed access to the little kiosks nearby, so I told the guard I needed to buy some toiletries and went out. Even that early the patio was filling up. By the time a guard told me to go back inside there must have been a thousand people chatting away excitedly.

It should have been me.

Inside I sat by the phone for ages, waiting and waiting. Midday came and went, then one o'clock.

'You won't see them for at least another hour,' Jackie said, joining me. 'The guards have their lunch at one.'

Two o'clock came and went, then three. I was exhausted from crying. But then my name was called and the floodgates opened again. I sprinted out to the gate at the back of the patio and flung myself at the tiny woman standing there. I'd never been happier to see anyone in my life.

I have to say, the jubilation was short-lived. I was sobbing out of relief. My mum was crying from distress. She was broken, so horrified to see me in that place and, as I was soon to learn, still suffering the trauma of even getting in.

Mum wasn't alone. She'd come with Astrid, and thank God for that. They were staying this time with Maureen, the nun, who knew Ancón and had accompanied them all the way, even queueing with them to make sure they got in okay. Visitors started queuing at the crack of dawn, so if you weren't outside by 5 a.m. you wouldn't get in. The prison was a three-hour drive from Lima, so that had meant leaving their hotel at 1 a.m.

The horrors hadn't stopped there. Taxi drivers don't like the desert roads, so the last few miles had been done in a tuk-tuk – a kind of prehistoric golf cart – so they were covered in sand by the time they arrived. Then they'd had to endure several very invasive searches. I hated picturing my mum going through all that. No sixty-year-old should have to lift her skirt up so strangers could check her pants for concealed weapons. The more I learned the more awful I felt. They'd been shouted at in Spanish, not understanding the process, and were left utterly distressed by their treatment. The guards had blatantly stolen the magazines and sweets they'd brought for me – just like they'd stolen my radio – and they were even ordered to leave their shoes outside, not knowing if they'd still be there on the way out.

They'd only been there an hour when they had to start the journey back.

'You shouldn't have come,' I said. 'You shouldn't have to put up with this. Please don't come back tomorrow.'

Mum's eyes agreed with me but her heart had different plans.

'Listen to me, darling. I'd rather die than miss your birthday.'

The problem was: there was a real chance she might.

*

I don't know what time Melissa woke up, but she'd been busy. When I opened my eyes for the first time as a twenty-one-year-old

I saw balloons tied to the edge of my bed. For a few minutes I was happy. Then I remembered all my friends back home reaching the same milestone. They'd had parties in civilised bars and houses. I was dragging my family across the world to a hellhole prison.

I had a nice morning with Mel, Jackie and Kaouthar. They all tried to keep my spirits up but knowing what my mother was subjecting herself to at that exact moment made it hard.

When they eventually got to the visiting area, I couldn't believe it – my sweet, dear mother had brought my favourite food as a treat for my birthday – steak. South America is noted for its beef, and they'd got a whole bunch of steak cooked the night before by one of the best restaurants in the area. They'd even brought enough for me to share with my three friends, along with the whole works – chips and vegetables.

After the visit, I rushed into Jackie's cell to tell her and Kaouthar the good news that we'd be dining well that evening. We put our names down to use the microwave and I positioned our food in the queue, calculating there would be about twelve minutes before it was our turn. It was only when I returned after the time had passed that I realised my stupidity. The friendships I'd made with Jackie and Kaouthar had made me forget I was in the maximum-security wing of a women's prison. Logic dictated that a good number of people in there were thieves. Placing that juicy steak on the counter had been a temptation too far for a robbing, hungry inmate. There wasn't a trace of it left. I'd rarely felt so sorry for myself.

I'd been dealt a crushing blow and learned a bitter lesson. I consoled myself with the fact I'd at least been able to spend my twenty-first birthday with Mum, though. No one could take that away from me.

My mum couldn't believe it when I told her what had happened on the next visit. I felt so hopeless. It still smarted to think her special treat had been whisked away from under me because I was too trusting.

My family were in the country for six days and managed to see me four times in all. For a while, I managed to forget my troubles. Then I'd see the fear and worry etched in my mum's face and the guilt would pour back. When they waved goodbye for the last time, I was actually glad they wouldn't be returning the following day. I couldn't watch my mother drag herself through that ordeal again. Even so, knowing I wouldn't set eyes on her again for possibly six more years was a dagger in the heart.

Luckily, then, I had no shortage of other people desperate to take her place.

CHAPTER TWENTY-TWO

ANY FRIEND OF YOURS

I hadn't seen our friend Andrea since she'd filmed the documentary. She always used the same driver – a lovely guy called Jaime, who studied languages. He started visiting me on Sundays, often bearing gifts from Andrea. Kaouthar was seeing a friend called Dell, so me, Jackie and Melissa all went up and sat in the sun together with them. The weather was closer to winter than summer but there was still a good few hours of heat every day. It was nice, sitting around in a group, chatting, taking time out from our situations. The next Sunday the six of us did it again, only this time we'd all just sat down when I heard shouting.

'I think they're calling your name,' said Kaouthar.

It did sound like it, so I got up and everyone who'd been yelling cheered. I saw the woman in charge of visitors waving at me from the gate. I made my way over, through the tables and chairs, and she said, 'Your visitor is here.'

'No, my visitor is already here,' I replied, pointing towards the crowd where Jaime was sitting.

'No,' she insisted, 'he's waiting there. You must take him.'

She gestured to a door where eight men were waiting to be

admitted. I scanned their faces. None of them meant anything to me. The guard wasn't having it. She grabbed my arm and marched me over.

'Him,' she said. 'Your husband.'

I stared at this really dishevelled-looking guy, dressed a bit like a mechanic, big work boots on and hands black with dirt.

I went to turn away and he walked forwards.

'Michaella,' he said. 'It's me, Caesar.'

Oh, my good God! I was so stunned I barely had time to move as he leant in for a kiss. I panicked.

'Look, I have to go back to my guests now,' I blurted out. It had taken me only a second to realise this wasn't someone I was going to find any common ground with, let alone start a friendship with.

The simple reason that I'd spoken even a few words to him was all the proof that stupid guard needed to let him in. He followed me past the tables, through the throng, until we reached the group. I didn't get a chance to introduce him. Melissa was laughing like a drain. She already knew.

'It's only fucking Caesar,' she said. 'Sit down, my friend! Sit down!' I scowled at her but she just winked.

'Everybody, this is Caesar . . . Michaella's husband.'

Everyone was gobsmacked, no one more so than me, but it didn't matter what Mel or the others said or asked Caesar, because he only had eyes and ears for me. It was freaky. If I wasn't surrounded by friends – including two men – I would have been intimidated, which to be fair was not Caesar's intention, but I knew I couldn't do anything to encourage him. In this country, with its bizarre rules of prison etiquette, the simplest gesture was seized upon as a token of love. He had a gift of fresh fruit for me, and a love letter. He was clearly borderline poverty stricken. I told him he should save his money.

He shook his head and just stared.

It stopped being funny after a while. I wasn't getting any sense out of the guy, so I turned back to my friends, but it's impossible to have a conversation when you have a pair of eyes burning into you.

For two hours he sat there in silence. When it was time to leave, I needed to make sure he actually did. The last thing I wanted was him bribing one of the guards for a nocturnal visit.

I made one last attempt at conversation and asked where he was from. He said a place I didn't know, about five hours away. Horrified, I told him never to come again but he said he would never leave me.

Okay, I thought, that's enough. I looked at Jaime, who hadn't left my side. He moved round in front of Caesar and said, 'Look, I'm sure you're a lovely guy but Michaella is my girlfriend and I don't want you seeing her any more. Do you understand?'

Caesar looked like he was going to cry. He said goodbye to me and ran out.

'Probably to slash my tyres,' said Jaime. 'But at least you won't be seeing him again.'

'Thank the Lord for that.'

*

The following week passed in a flurry of arguments between Charlene and Corinne, Charlene and Melissa, Charlene and Danielle and Charlene and everyone else. The biggest topic of contention, weirdly, was the World Cup. Maybe because it was in the same continent it felt more important. I wasn't too fussed but Danielle, the Brazilian, didn't miss a minute in the TV area when her team were playing. She liked nothing better than coming back and insulting the Ecuadorian, the Mexican and everyone else. When they lost to Germany though, by 7–1, that was another story. She went apeshit. There weren't any Germans in the block so she had a go at the next best thing, which was Kaouthar. When fighting her didn't work she ran into my friend's cell and started ripping her clothes out and throwing them at the toilet. It was full-on psycho, and I prayed I'd never be on the receiving end.

The only cellmate who didn't want to start a war was Nigerian Rose, who was gentle and fragile because of her arthritis. I don't know what she did before I arrived at Ancón, because every day I had to help her over to the bathroom and down the stairs for roll call and mealtimes. I said to Monica one day, 'What does it take to move rooms here?'

She explained that the head of logistics, a man called the OTC, was responsible for rooms. In Monica's three years at Ancón not one soul had ever got a transfer. Unless it was to *calabozo*.

'What about Rose, though? She needs a room downstairs.'

'And I need a four-poster bed. But we can't always get what we want.'

I hated that attitude. If she didn't want to do it for herself then do it for the people she was meant to represent. Do it for Rose.

Call yourself a delegate.

I'd heard from the other inmates that Monica had been associated with the notorious Cali Cartel, who took over Colombia's cocaine empire after Pablo Escobar had been taken down. There's no room for empathy in that world, and Monica was as hard as she was glamorous.

Come Sunday, I was looking forward to a bit of me time, reading a new book while the others had their visitors. I was on the patio, barely a chapter in when a guard angrily called me, 'Your visitor is here.'

'What visitor? What's his name?'

'I'll find out – for a sola.'

Paying him was less painful than going out myself. He returned fifteen minutes later.

'It's your husband,' he said. 'Caesar.'

'Oh shit.'

He laughed. 'What's wrong? Are you divorced? Did he cheat on you?'

'No. He is not my husband. He's just some fruit loop who saw me on the TV.'

'Well, he's travelled five hours so you better say hello.'

'Absolutely not. Can you tell him I'm ill?'

'For another sola I can. For ten I'll tell him you're dead.'

I wish I'd taken him up on the offer. For the next two months Caesar made the ten-hour round trip to Ancón. Having people create fantasy lives goes beyond creepy when they get other people believing it. When you're a captive audience it's terrifying. My only consolation was that as long as Caesar was on the outside, I was safe. He wasn't getting past security. Unfortunately, some other people didn't have to.

They were already inside.

At Virgen de Fatima we were only permitted to receive mail from the national postal service. Despite being a maximum-security prison, things were a bit more lax at Ancón. A woman called 'Maria the package lady' used to come and go between all the different parts of the prison, dropping off parcels and letters, as well as taking orders for shopping. Anything from the outside world she could get for a price. Obviously she had to pay off security for their discretion, so that wasn't always cheap. But it was a useful service.

One of Maria's little sidelines – which I didn't discover till later – was to keep the male prisoners up to speed on any new blood arriving. She'd get asked who was new and she'd describe them, which started the game of Twenty Questions.

'What colour's her hair?'

'Is she pretty?'

'Is she young?'

Funnily enough, they never asked if the women were married.

Obviously, one day she described these two European girls out of their depth, because Melissa and I were soon being bombarded with love letters from men in the other wings. I was horrified.

I admit I read the odd letter. It passed the time of day sometimes. But I stopped whenever they got weird. And I never, ever, replied. I didn't want to give a single one of them the wrong idea.

It must have been frustrating. Usually, the writers gave up and a new correspondent took his place. One fella was more persistent. He signed his letters 'Diogo' and I quickly learned to recognise the handwriting and not bother opening them. But Diogo was made of more entrepreneurial stuff.

I rarely turned down visits from strangers on female day. Usually it was a nun or a friend of a friend of an Irish person. On one Saturday it was a young Peruvian girl. We sat down and I waited to hear her story. I'd heard them all by then – or so I thought. She said, 'I'm a friend of Diogo. He wants you to have these.' And she handed over a load of letters and a painting of flowers with my name on.

I thought that was weird. I said, 'I don't want this stuff. I don't want anything from Diogo. Please take it all back.'

'I can't. He won't pay me.'

'Pay you? So, you're not a friend?'

I didn't know what was going on. Somehow this guy I'd never met was hiring women to deliver his post. It made my skin crawl. I didn't care this woman wasn't getting her piece of silver. I didn't want anything to do with it.

That wasn't the end of it. Over the next four months I encountered half a dozen different women who turned out to be go-betweens for this nutter. The last woman who visited me was carrying a box. Of kittens.

We had access to a 'sociologist', so I complained about Diogo to her. She said she'd get his delivery girls stopped at source. In hindsight, that probably just meant asking Maria not to bother me any more. I thought it was the end of the matter. Then one day the social worker asked to see me.

The social worker handles all sorts of paperwork. She's the one I had to see to apply for a special visiting day on my birthday. I enjoyed our chats, even though I was handcuffed for the duration. On this occasion it made signing the forms a bit tricky but it wasn't anything I hadn't done before.

Maybe if I'd had two free hands I'd have signed more quickly. As it was I was able to read most of one of the documents before I even picked up the pen.

'Does this say what I think it says?' I asked.

'Yes,' she smiled. 'It's permission for your conjugal visit. With Diogo, your husband.'

'Okay, this is scary now. Listen to me: I don't have a husband. Are you farming me out to strangers now? Is that what you do here?'

She was shocked, offended even, but so was I. Still she went on, though, telling me about how my husband had booked the marital room for one night as per our human rights. She still thought I was joking.

'Seriously,' I said, 'I have no idea who this person is.'

'You don't want to see your *coppolino*?'

'No, I do not!'

She was obviously confused. She said, 'I've been over to see him. He has a photograph of you in his wallet and pictures of you on his walls. Where would he get these from if you weren't a couple?'

'The internet?'

'Why would there be pictures of you on the internet?'

'Because I'm in here. Don't you read the news?'

Amazingly, she'd not heard about us. She had no idea we'd been all over the news and that you could Google me and find pictures. She skipped over that, getting annoyed now.

'He says you have been together for eight years. Are you telling me he's lying?'

'Damn right I am. Listen to what you're saying. I'm twenty-one years old. How could I have been with anyone for eight years? I only arrived in this country a year ago!'

In the end I had to call Melissa, who burst out laughing.

'Okay,' the social worker said. 'I've heard enough.'

But she hadn't. The next day I was called back. This time she was with her boss and there was a ton more paperwork.

'We have letters sent to you going back four months. Are you saying they are not written to you?'

'I don't know,' I said. 'I never opened them. *Because I don't know him!*'

The boss read out one of the letters. 'I've applied for the conjugal visit. Soon we will be together again, my love.'

'Why would he say such things? Why would he write to you so many times?'

'Because he's mad! Do you have any letters I sent him?'

Finally they looked embarrassed.

'No.'

'There's your answer. You won't find any because I never wrote any. Because *I've never met him*.'

Ultimately the boss had to agree I was telling the truth, which was good for me but bad for them. The next time I saw the social worker she said Diogo's lawyer had started filing complaints against the prison for violating his human rights and keeping a married couple apart. The law was on his side. But only if he was married. It didn't matter what I said, he said the opposite and enough people believed him to keep it alive. It's possible that he was actually insane rather than just making trouble but still the officials treated his claims with due process.

It was so stressful. For everyone. The social worker was under pressure from her boss to sort it. She was under pressure from her boss and he was under pressure from the Ancón director. In the end they forced me to take out a restraining order on Diogo just to keep him from suing the prison. I really should have asked for something in return.

At least they kept up their side of the law. There was a social event one afternoon – a play put on by and for male and female inmates. I went along but as soon as I stepped inside the hall a guard stopped me.

'You can't come in.'

'Why not?'

'Because you have a restraining order on Diogo. You're not allowed to break it any more than he is.'

My heart froze. Quickly I scanned the room.

'Which one is he?' I asked. I was keen to see the cause of all this stress.

'Over there. By the window.'

A skinny, balding scruffy man waved back. He looked exactly like the sort of person who'd do what he'd done. I felt the bile rising in my throat. I could barely stutter out the words to Melissa – 'Look, that's him! Can you believe it?'

I was banned from entering, but she wasn't, and the minute she got in, she was right in his face, with an audience gathered around her.

'Why are you saying you're married to my friend?'

'Because we are. We're in love. We've been together for eight years.'

'Eight years you say? Well, I've got news for you and all your friends. Eight years ago she was *thirteen*, which makes you a fucking paedo! What do you think of that, boys?'

I never heard from him again.

CHAPTER TWENTY-THREE

JUST GO WITH IT

Some people you just know to steer clear of. The Brazilian in my cell, Danielle, was this tiny, pretty little thing. On the outside, you'd probably say 'butter wouldn't melt'. Inside, she could be like that too. She liked to hang around me and Mel, practise her English, do things together like paint each other's toes. She always supplied the nail polish. Money no object.

But my God, could she change!

I was on the phone one day and I must have gone a second over my ten minutes. She'd been waiting in line with me for an hour, happy as Larry. Not any more. She ripped the handset from me and started swiping it at my head, screaming like a banshee. I don't know what she was saying but if it wasn't for the fact the phone was attached to the wall, my face would have been paste. I ran up those stairs like greased lightning, absolutely terrified. I'd be sleeping with one eye open from now on.

An hour later I was with Jackie, still traumatised, when Danielle came in, laughing and joking like nothing had happened. I instinctively backed away but Jackie mouthed, 'Just go with it. She's forgotten.' Weirdly, I think she was right. Danielle never mentioned it again.

It wasn't long before she found another victim. Once again, the phone appeared to be the trigger. Gouda was Paraguayan and they were screaming at each other in a combination of each other's languages, so fast I couldn't keep up. Then Danielle had enough of dialogue and started smashing Gouda's head on the table next to the phone. She had her by the hair and was swinging her like a rag doll. I don't know how she did it. Gouda's my size, a good head and shoulders taller than Danielle. She should have been more than a match for the Brazilian.

A crowd formed. I was watching open-mouthed, shocked and appalled at the violence. Some of the others were cheering; I guessed they'd seen it all before. Gouda was getting pulverised. I was really hoping someone would stop it. Suddenly, there was a shout and Monica stepped in.

Thank God, I thought. And I went to rush to Gouda's aid.

But no. I quickly realised Monica wasn't there to stop the fight. She was there to relocate it.

'What are you idiots thinking doing this in here?' she shouted. 'The INPE will be back any minute. You'll get us all punished.'

She was particularly furious that there was blood on the guard's table.

'Someone clean that up!' she said, and two Asian women ran over and started wiping it with their own tops.

I couldn't believe it. What the hell is a *delegada* for if not to look after her subjects? I swore that in the next election I'd be voting for anyone but her.

I thought Gouda would take Monica's intervention as a chance to escape but Danielle didn't let go of the Paraguayan's hair and dragged her into the large hall where, once the crowd had formed in a semi-circle, she started pummelling her again.

The old me would have intervened. But fourteen months in the Peruvian penal system changes you. Sickened as I was by these two women taking chunks out of each other I couldn't take my eyes off them, and I certainly wasn't going to interfere.

All I could think was, *I'm just glad that's not me.*

Of course, my time was soon to come. I made the mistake of wanting to watch *The Wolf of Wall Street* while Danielle wanted to watch some soap opera. It didn't matter to her that it was my time in the schedule, or that she was already banned from the TV room for her craziness during the World Cup. Or that she was a foot shorter than me. She went for my throat with a knife, and if it wasn't for a Spanish girl called Lyra intervening with some crazy ninja moves I wouldn't be around to write this book.

Looking back, I don't know why I didn't just back down immediately. I knew what Danielle was like. I'd seen it a dozen times before. And as much as I wanted to watch that movie, it wasn't worth dying for.

But the biggest disappointment I had afterwards was how I was treated by the delegate. We'd had an election and, sure enough, I'd voted ABM – Anyone But Monica – which is how we ended up with Colombian Vanessa. Her reaction to my being attacked by Danielle was to have us settle it with our fists in private. Which of course was absurd. I wasn't some prison-hardened female thug. I didn't want to fight anyone.

'Look,' Lyra said, 'if you don't go in there and fight Danielle, everyone will know you're a soft target. They'll all come after you.'

'I'm a soft target where knives are concerned.'

And that was it, decision made. I just screamed and screamed and screamed and, despite Vanessa and everyone trying to shut me up, the doors opened and four heavily-armed guards came running in. You've never seen two hundred people disappear so quickly. It's only because Danielle was so crazy that she stayed, desperate to finish the job. I quickly told the INPE what had gone on and they carted her away, spitting and threatening. It took all four of them, one limb each. She really was a powerhouse.

And not someone you wanted as an enemy.

Vanessa was no better as a delegate than Monica. I was naive thinking she would be. But every delegate had a cabinet of helpers like a little government. One would be in charge of security, another in charge of cooking, another looking after cleaning. I volunteered for – and got – the job as phone monitor. Anyone who didn't turn up for their ten-minute slot donated it to me. If Ancón was going to endorse such a stupid system, I was going to make the most of it. Just like everyone else.

It's one thing playing the rules, another to let the environment change you so much you don't know right from wrong. It was so easy to be pulled down into the moral cesspit with everyone else. You needed to be strong to resist. With the right help, I hoped I could.

I connected with Jackie for the same reason I'd connected with Amy back at Fatima. They both were nice people in a poisonous world who would help others without judgement. And they both ran their prison's beauty salon. I hadn't been in Ancón long when I asked Jackie what I needed to do to get a foot in the door. Unfortunately, it wasn't up to her. Every prisoner needed to do a basic six-month stint in one of the manufacturing workshops to prove you could be trusted. They made plates and handbags and touristy stuff they could sell to the outside world. Working also earned you credits, which went towards your benefits.

Although I wasn't eligible for benefits, I had started making enquiries about the paperwork I needed to amass if the ruling changed, or someone took an interest in my case. I'd been told it could take a year to get this together, and involved all kinds of assessments and certificates and good character reports.

'If you turn up sixteen days in a row you get a docket,' Jackie explained, 'which you can show in court as proof of good behaviour.'

Just the incentive I needed. I was determined to get a good work record. I wanted to prove I was trustworthy. I officially had four and a half more years to serve, but I had this strong personal belief that I would be out before then. I don't know why, but I felt positive I could turn my situation around, and working would be the kick-starter of amassing all the forms I needed.

Jackie, on the other hand, was up for parole in less than a year. 'If you're working with me by then I'll put a word in so you can take over the lease.'

I didn't *need* to work. Not for money anyway. My embassy had finally got its act in gear and was sending me 600 soles – about £200 – a month and my family came up with about £200 a month, all of which soon got soaked up by the various bribes going out. But if you sit around too long in jail you go spare. You start seeing things that aren't there. And you can't avoid the arguments. I thought it would be a quieter life in the workshop.

Wrong.

The first thing you notice is the heat. The workshops were giant aircraft hangars with corrugated tin roofs that may as well have been magnifying glasses for the sun they channelled. Heading towards January the weather was evil. If it was 35ºC outside, it was 45 inside. Which put absolutely nobody in a good mood.

And there were a lot of people to annoy.

Each workshop had rows and rows of tables with enough benches to seat 1,000 bums comfortably or 1,200 bums really uncomfortably. It was sweaty, nasty, claustrophobic work. And, I soon realised, never going to be the oasis of calm I'd hoped for.

On my first day I was sitting there sewing – or trying to; I'd never held a needle before – when a girl sitting three down from me suddenly stood on her bench and dived across at the woman opposite. It came out of nowhere. She just flew at her, screaming, punching, biting. It wasn't my first sight of this sort of thing, but I was still shocked at the randomness of the attack. What if I was next?

A cheto called Eddie read my mind.

'Don't worry,' she laughed, 'it won't happen to you – unless you steal someone else's girlfriend like that bitch did.'

'I should be okay, then,' I said. 'I'm not like that.'

'Are you sure?' she winked. 'Everyone is eventually.'

Eddie was a good sort. Clued up, funny, in with the right people. Then I found out she ran one of the largest drugs rings in Ancón. She was loaded. People respected her. They needed her. Or, more accurately, they needed her product. And woe-betide anyone who tried to step on her turf.

We sat next to each other for months and no two days were the same. We bonded enough for her to say one day, 'You might want to go to the bathroom now.'

'Why?'

'You'll see.'

I wanted to finish my little project, so I hung on – too long, as it turned out. Eddie tapped me on the arm, and I watched as she picked up her huge casting needle and dived across the table at a large tattooed Colombian the other side. There was no punching, no hair pulling. She just plunged the needle into the woman's neck then stood on the table and yelled at her girls to attack.

The Colombian ran her own drugs empire and she'd been moving into Eddie's territory. It hadn't gone unnoticed. Eddie's attack was the cue for her army to move in on the Colombian's. It was a bloodbath, a full-on riot. No wonder she'd told me to leave.

I had to fight my way out. Even the girls not involved were scrapping with each other. Sewing machines usually screwed to the benches were being ripped out and flung in any direction. I was halfway up the corridor before dozens of INPE filed past in the other direction. I heard a cheer, then gunfire, then silence.

The next time I saw Eddie she was bloodied but proud despite fifteen days in *calabozo*. Not only had she beaten off the competition, she'd stolen the Colombian's market as well. As for the Colombian, dead or alive nobody saw her again.

Not all the disturbances in the workshops were the result of violence but they were just as mesmerising. I was there one day, middle of the bench as usual, women to my right and left. I was chatting when I got a nudge from the girl on the other side of me. I turned around.

The girl on the other side of her was off the bench, her trousers and pants round her ankles, and my neighbour was giving her oral. Just like that, right next to me, in front of hundreds of prying eyes. It was a weird situation. Every single person around the table carried on sewing and chatting or watching as if it was the most normal thing in the world. Honestly, I think we were just grateful for something to break up the day.

There was so much moaning, so much noise, it was mad. After they finished, they kissed, pulled up her pants and then got on with their sewing.

Maybe it was normal. Like scratching an itch. A couple of times a day you'd see two or three couples or triples at it. You'd get one girl perched on the bench and someone else's face or fingers between her legs. Often it was between chetos and others but sometimes two very feminine-looking women would go at it as well. And then the next Sunday I'd see them with their boyfriends or husbands in the visitors' patio. As Kaouthar put it, 'You don't have to be gay to have gay sex. Everyone has needs.'

*

I was approaching my second anniversary of being incarcerated. My second anniversary since the worst decision of my life. I'd put myself through hell and my family through worse. But I never saw quitting as an option. That's just the way I was. But not everyone was so lucky.

And it was often the people you least expected.

We went to bed about 9 p.m. The lights went out then. There wasn't much to do otherwise. Then we'd have to rise around six the following morning. This particular night we didn't make six. We didn't make midnight. At about eleven o'clock I was woken by screaming. I turned over, ready to yell at the Ecuadorean. It was definitely her. But I didn't yell. I didn't swear.

I screamed. Danielle's face was three feet from mine. And it was swinging.

The noise was incredible. Everyone was on their feet, rushing, yelling, doing something. *Anything*. I couldn't move. I was transfixed by the dead eyes staring back at me.

Corinne was first to act. She hoiked Danielle's body up while

Charlene untied the knotted bedsheet. The Ecuadorean was screaming for the guard. Everyone was screaming. It was chaos.

A minute later four INPE burst in and carted Danielle's limp frame out. I didn't like her, but the last thing I wanted was her taking her own life. The others all stood at the door while CPR and mouth-to-mouth were administered outside. When we heard coughing and spluttering, we breathed a sigh of relief. She was alive.

But for how long? And, being selfish, why should we have to put up with it? I was definitely seeing Vanessa about moving cell first chance I got.

Danielle was obviously troubled. She wasn't alone. My cell window opened out over the patio towards the *calabozo*. From time to time you'd hear screaming and fighting as someone was dumped in solitary. Not everyone who went in came from our wing. It catered for the entire prison. Potential inhabitants: ten thousand people.

One night I overheard a real party going on down there. Three distinct voices were shouting at the guards. I could picture them in their cells – yelling into oblivion, nothing to look at, nothing to touch, nowhere to go.

It was late, and for a while even the less shouty conversations travelled. Then it was all mumbled nonsense. The three women were grouching but not so much as to be audible. I felt myself begin to drift off.

And then came the scream.

After Danielle it shouldn't have been a surprise. One of the *calabozo* inmates was yelling the place down, trying to get guards to check on her friend. She'd gone silent and, from what I could make out, that was very, very suspicious.

I pressed my face against the bars and waited. Then it came. Genuine howls of distress. The silent woman was dead. Found hanged in her cell. A cell where you shouldn't be able to do that.

Danielle was luckier. A fortnight after finding her swinging she walked back into our cell. Once again, just as if nothing had happened. Even when Charlene asked to see her neck, and reached out to touch the burns, she didn't rise. It was like it happened to another person.

I'd like to say that was the end of it. That she learned her lesson. But no. A month later I found her crawling around on the cell floor, blood gushing from her wrists. She'd cut herself and was holding up her arms, staring at the red fountain like she was watching fireworks. I got a guard and she was hospitalised again but it was really disturbing. And not something you can un-see.

Of all the people happy to see Danielle dig her own grave, you'd think Gouda would have celebrated. She didn't. She couldn't. She had her own troubles. And once again I was first on the scene.

It was a Sunday. She'd had a male visitor: her husband, a boyfriend, I don't know. But I did see her on the way down to the patio smelling of perfume and looking a million soles. So when I heard screaming from her cell a wee bit later I didn't imagine it would be her. I ran in just in time to see her mouthing something through her window to a woman in another block. Then she lifted her glass perfume bottle up, smashed it on the ledge, and drove the largest, sharpest shard into her arm. It was ridiculous. She never once stopped looking at the woman the other side. She was screaming, 'Trash! Whore!' and worse, all the while slashing at her arms and then her chest and then her throat and her stomach. She was on fire with blood. It was gushing from everywhere. I grabbed her head and shouted at her, 'Come on! Stop it!' but it was like looking into the face of the girl in *The Exorcist*. Gouda wasn't there. She was possessed.

I couldn't stop her. I couldn't even get the glass off her to slow her down, so I ran into the hall and screamed for help. By the time the INPE arrived she'd slashed every square inch of her own skin. Blood was spurting from three separate points. She was a mess. At serious risk of dying, without a doubt. And nobody could understand why.

Jackie had a theory. Crack cocaine was everywhere. There was weed and heroin as well. But the biggest culprit was the antidepressants. We're not talking Prozac – these were old-school downers. The psychologist and the doctors in Ancón were dishing them out like

Smarties. I'm sure they had the right reasons but the results spoke for themselves. Danielle was dynamite waiting to be ignited; Gouda was a lovely girl whose moods were on a knife-edge. Almost certainly they were bipolar – that's what everyone in prison said, even the doctors and guards – and almost certainly they weren't getting the right meds. And that was affecting us all.

It was shameful. It was scary. It was so prevalent. But two years into my sentence all I was bothered about was keeping my head down. Surviving. Speaking to my family whenever I could. Amassing my good behaviour record. And getting out. There was no way I was going through four more years of this hell. And I certainly wasn't doing it in that cell.

CHAPTER TWENTY-FOUR

THE ONE BOOK YOU NEVER FINISH

I finally got my chance to work with Jackie. As her release date got closer, we were both counting down the days till the place was mine, albeit for different reasons. In the middle of 2015, she was finally released. It was sad to see her go but she left me with some good memories and, more importantly, her shop.

The woman in charge of the businesses took thirty-five soles a month for the space, but I also had to rent chairs, treatment tables and everything. As for my stock, I asked the package woman, Maria, to buy things like hair-straighteners, make-up, oils, and all the electronic equipment I needed to run a salon. It was a huge initial outlay but I knew I would make the money back quickly. If I'd learned one thing about the women in Peruvian prisons, whatever their culture, whatever their sexuality, they were all obsessed with their appearance. It's just what you do in there. It keeps you busy. It's the one book you never finish.

I was wary of handing over too much money but I gave Maria three hundred soles – everything I had – and a list, and said anything extra I'd settle afterwards.

When I saw her again I said, 'How much did it come to?'

'Just over five hundred.'

'Okay, I'll give you the rest as soon as I get my first customers.'

'It's fine,' she said, 'it's already been taken care of.'

'Taken care of? By who?'

'Your admirer.'

I rolled my eyes. 'I'm not being funny, Maria, but who is this? If it's Diogo I'm burning the lot of this.'

She laughed. 'No, not Diogo. Alfonso.'

'Alfonso? I don't think I know him.'

'Well, he knows you, and he wanted to do something nice. He says you never reply to his letters.'

'I never reply to anyone's letters. They creep me out.'

'Well, he's not a creep. He's in a prison in Lima. He's a nice young man. Do me a favour, reply to his messages. It's the least you can do after he's bought you this.'

Maria was useful, but there was always an agenda. With so many people using her service, she was in a position to make connections and have influence – and take commissions.

'You tell Alfonso I'll be paying him back within the week. I'll not be owing anyone in here. I don't like the kind of interest they charge.'

My first week as the salon manager went well and I had more than enough to reimburse this Alfonso. A few days later Maria returned with the money.

'He won't take it,' she said. 'It's a gift.'

I got really annoyed, but not only did he not take the cash, it wasn't his last gift to me either. I got flowers, a teddy bear, groceries, milk, all these stupid little things. And still I couldn't get him to take what I owed. One day Maria said that Alfonso had mentioned he wanted some £150 Nike trainers.

'So?'

'So, I'm thinking if you buy them then you'll be paying him back.'

I agreed, and instantly regretted it. The next week she came with a special package from Alfonso – a Swarovski diamond bracelet as a 'thank you'. It was ridiculous.

I could only assume Alfonso was paying Maria heavily because she would not let the subject drop. 'Have you replied to him yet?' 'Have you thanked him yet?' 'Have you sent him a photo yet?' It was relentless. Eventually she said, 'I think you're rude not talking to him. If you don't write back I won't buy you anything else for your salon.'

No matter what I did, and how hard I tried to stay away from getting involved with random people with their own agendas, I kept encountering the codes of prison life. Everything was based on favours and bartering and backhanders. So I forced myself to read some of Alfonso's letters. There was quite a backlog but I was relieved that he wasn't like my other penpals. I'd seen photos of him, courtesy of Maria, and he looked nice – he was young and tanned with dark hair. I never sent him a picture of me but it was clear he knew exactly what I looked like. He was arrested six months after me, so he'd had plenty of opportunity to see me on TV and in the press. I replied to a couple of his letters. But while he poured out his life story and put his soul on every page, I was non-committal and vague. Anonymous almost. But over time I started opening up a bit more and I got to like him. I even began to look forward to his letters.

*

Jealousy was a massive thing in Ancón. If you were lucky, people would just bitch about you if you had something they didn't. The next step was to physically assault you. The final stage was a lot, lot worse.

I was in the salon one day. I had blonde hair by then – I'd been one of my own first customers. I was treating Carmen, the Venezuelan friend of Melissa, who was in particularly high spirits.

'You seem happy,' I said.

'Best day of my life.'

'Why? Is it your birthday?'

'Even better. You know that bitch Camilla?'

'The Mexican?'

'*Si*. She was applying for benefits. She got really close. And I fucked it up for her.'

'What? How?'

It turned out the pair of them had been moving around from prison to prison together for the last ten years. They'd been friends, enemies, everything in between. For whatever reason, right there, right then, Carmen despised Camilla. When the Mexican had got near the finishing line with her benefits claim, Carmen had paid a lawyer to literally lose the woman's file. No file equals no case. You could have a pardon from the king in your folder one day and the next you're not going anywhere.

Carmen was so proud of herself. She had no concept that she'd ruined someone's life. Two years of hard work and hope dashed in one selfish second. And Carmen could not have been happier.

'I sorted it,' she said. 'Camilla's not leaving here any time soon.'

And she wasn't the only one. It was barely days later when another inmate was boasting to the other customers about screwing up a woman's chance at early release. The salon seemed to bring out the confessional in my clients.

'Why?' I said.

'She's always using all the water.'

'You ruined her benefits for that?'

'Bitch was lucky I didn't kill her.'

Everyone found it hysterical apart from me. I still wasn't eligible for benefits but I filed away the information for future reference. To think someone would sabotage another woman's release over a petty argument. They were all as bad as each other. I certainly learned something from it, though – I wasn't telling a soul a single thing that was going on in my world.

But prison life is prison life – and opportunities would crop up for ways to bypass the rules for those who could afford it, or who had connections. Vanessa, *La Delegada* herself, sidled up to me one day as I was closing the salon. We'd been getting on okay in recent weeks. She was seeing a Colombian guy, Juan, in the men's part of the prison, who could supply a cellphone – at a price. She didn't have the money to buy one, but she thought I might. Was I interested? You bet.

I knew they were strictly off-limits, for obvious reasons. Phones could be used to intimidate people on the outside. But they were very useful for staying in touch with family and loved ones, which is all these women wanted it for.

I thought about it overnight. It wasn't the cost that bothered me – I was putting in the hours in the salon and it was going very well. But I was a model prisoner; I could scupper all my good work with this one purchase. Then I thought about the stressful and demeaning phone monitor system; perhaps more than the awful food, it was the thing that really got to me. But how would we use the cellphone without being caught? And how would we get it delivered?

The next day, I had a few questions for Vanessa. And a proposition. I was still determined to move cells and, if I had my choice, it would be to the one she shared with Monica. They were the two most powerful women in *maxima*. But just because there were two empty beds, that didn't mean they wanted them filled. For all I knew, Monica and her confidantes used them for something else. I decided to be upfront with Vanessa from the off. I asked how I'd get the money to Juan in the first place.

Her plan was to use a different package lady from Maria. She had already been proven trustworthy with some other deal. I then went for the killer line.

'How about me moving into your cell?'

She laughed. 'Yeah, come over whenever you like. We'll be in.'

'No, I'm serious. I want a transfer into your place. Melissa as well.'

'Why would you want to come in with us?' she asked.

'Number one, you're the delegate. You're the powerhouse in this place.'

'And?'

'And, number two,' I whispered, 'If I shell out for this phone, I want to be able to use it in peace. Look who I'm with – Charlene and Corinne, two of the loudest and most argumentative characters on the wing. If I use it in my cell they'll rat me out to the guards. I figure you run your place. Monica will keep quiet. She's got bigger fish to fry. No one's going to say a word if you tell them not to. And if I'm in your cell, my phone is your phone. How does that sound?'

Now she was smiling.

'I'm in charge of alot around here, but I'm not in charge of moves.'

'Don't worry, I'm going to see the OTC about that,' I said.

'Good luck with that.'

*

I'd already had previous conversations with the OTC. He was in charge of logistics. He was the one who designated beds and cells and floors. He was the one who'd had to sign off on me working in the factory, then getting the salon. His whole life was moving chess pieces around the board. Plenty of officials in Ancón saw it as a dereliction of their duties if they didn't make sexual advances on the inmates. Others, like the OTC, would take a genuine interest in how the prison was run. He was approachable. He wasn't pervy. He was almost human.

I arranged to see him on the pretence of talking about my salon. It took a day or two but the appointment came and I was escorted to his room. I considered every which way of approaching the conversation, but in the end decided on being direct.

As soon as his door was shut, I said, 'How do I get me and Melissa moved to a different cell?'

There was a pause – surprise probably – then he laughed.

'You don't,' he said eventually. 'Your cells are your home, your life.'

'Says who?' I said.

He laughed again, to himself this time. 'You're looking at him. And "he" says nobody moves.'

But I could tell he was intrigued. He knew I wasn't a troublemaker, or a drug addict or displaying serious mental health issues. Was there room for negotiation? I'd prepared an answer: 'Here's the thing. We really want to move in with Vanessa. There are two spare bunks in her cell and I think that because she's the delegate she could be really useful for helping us fit in here even more.'

He nodded. 'I'm sure all of that is true, but I'm also sure it's not the reason you want to move. If you're not going to tell me the real reason, you may as well leave.'

Now I had a problem. On the one hand this guy could do me the biggest favour ever. On the other he could get me locked up in solitary.

What to do, what to do? A hundred versions of the same story flashed through my mind, all with different endings – most of them bad for my health. All the while the OTC was looking at me, waiting, hoping I wasn't going to let him down.

What choice do I have? I needed to bite the bullet. I needed to tell the truth.

'Okay,' I said, staring straight into his eyes, 'someone is getting me a phone, and if my current cellmates see it they'll blab to the guards. I want to move in with Vanessa. She's the delegate, and she can protect me.'

He puffed out his cheeks.

'You put me in a very difficult position.'

'I know.'

'Not only is what you are telling me against the laws of this prison, but you're asking me, the OTC, to aid your crime.'

My mind was racing. I was desperate to get him onside. He knew a lot of the guards were meatheads. And he knew I wouldn't be using the phone to bully people. 'Listen,' I said, 'I've not told anyone before, but I'm telling you now – I want to run for delegate as soon as possible.'

I had no idea what good it would do, but I blurted it out to show him I could be trusted with responsibility. So that was now something I'd have to follow through on. God knows what Vanessa would think when she found out.

The OTC looked me square in the eyes and clasped his fingers together.

'I'll see what can be done,' he said. 'It would be highly irregular. But . . . your work so far has been very good. Let me think about it.'

I left his office in good spirits and with high hopes.

*

Three days later he came good on his word. An INPE arrived in the morning with some forms to sign, as me and Melissa gathered our stuff together.

'So, what's with all this?' said Corinne, following us around the cell as we packed up. 'Who we gonna get instead?'

'I don't know,' I replied. 'They're just moving some folks around, I think.' I didn't dare let on that I'd requested the move or there would be far too much explaining to do, and a barrage of questions. We exited swiftly, shifting just a couple of cells to the left on the same floor, to Number Two – the powerhouse. I was desperately trying not to show any emotion, but I couldn't stop it coming through. I had a stupid, wonky grin the whole way.

My new cellmates were a concentration of the most powerful women in the block. Monica was in there, plus her sidekick Carmen – Melissa's friend from Venezuela who'd destroyed Camilla's hopes of benefits. Another crazy Venezuelan called Veronica was the loosest cannon. Then Vanessa, plus her aunt. I'm sure if I'd met any of them on the outside I'd have crossed the street, but they were the movers and shakers of *maxima*, and by having access to them, I had access to all the news.

The second Melissa and I moved the tongues started wagging. Nobody had been moved before unless it was to *calabozo* or hospital. Every customer in the salon asked the same thing: 'Who are you having sex with to get moved?'

That was standard. Some of them were quite spiteful. I had to throw a couple of girls out mid-treatment. They were nasty. Threatening. Danielle obviously was one of the worst.

'I don't know what you did but I will find out and I will expose you.'

I shrugged. Then she added, 'Show me your nail paints. I'm feeling like a change.'

Unbelievable. But no way was I picking a fight with that psycho.

*

In prison, it pays not to be too judgemental too early. Someone who might seem unnerving or predatory on first meeting could turn out to be easily flattered and harmless. And useful. The savvier inmates got to know which of the guards would help you and who wouldn't. The male INPE who had taken a shine to me during my first hours in Ancón, before allocation, was now someone I regularly spoke to during my visits back and forth to the dentist, where he was in charge of escorting me from Point A to Point B. His interest in me followed predictable lines, but it didn't hurt to have someone in authority on my side. The simple fact that I smiled rather than scowled at him made all the difference.

From time to time, we were required to attend prison social events – 'friends' days' with participation and music and speeches. Pretty boring, but there were snacks and soft drinks and it passed the time. A couple of days after sending the money to Juan for the phone, I spotted my INPE friend at one of these events. He already knew about the phone! He had access to Juan, and said he would help get the phone to me via the head of security. I thought I'd misheard him, but a couple of days later I was called to the rotunda at a time when there were no visitors.

Every inch of the way I was shaking. Had I been dobbed in? When I eventually saw the head of security standing by the gate, I was so wound up I thought for a moment I was going straight to *calabozo*.

The whole patio area was empty and the guards up on the terraces were busy chatting and looking elsewhere. I didn't know for certain if that was a coincidence or not but I suspected the latter. If anyone could arrange a blind eye to be turned it was him.

'Here it is,' he said, and handed me a plastic bag.

'Thanks,' I said, more out of instinct than comprehension. But I continued the charade, just in case. I needed him to spell out exactly what he was doing. 'What is it?'

'Your phone,' he said. 'You paid for a phone and here it is.'

I couldn't believe he'd actually delivered. It was too good to be true. He didn't seem fazed by my surprise.

'We are clear,' he said. 'This stays our secret?'

'Er, yeah,' I spluttered, my mind racing. This guy was second only to the director of the prison. But nothing about the prison system in Peru made any sense.

If this was a set-up, what's the worst that could happen? My benefits were already screwed. I may as well take the phone and deal with the consequences of it being a trap later. But there was still one thing bothering me – impromptu cell searches.

I thanked him, and said, 'I won't have this phone very long if the guards keep searching my room without any warning. I need warning if my cell is going to get turned over. Can you help with that?'

'Maybe,' he said. 'For a price.'

Everyone was on the take. But at least I knew where I stood.

'What is the price?'

'Three hundred soles.'

'Great,' I said. 'Done.'

'Every time,' he added. 'You pay every time guards come.'

The buzz of taking that bag back to my cell got me walking ten feet tall. The whole plan had come together. A few words in the right ears and a few hundred soles in the right hands could make a world of difference in Ancón.

It took about fifteen minutes to get back from the rotunda – by armed escort, of course. I couldn't say a word until the guard had gone. As soon as he shut the door to our floor I pulled out the phone from down the front of my jeans. A second later I knew I'd made friends for life.

The mobile wasn't a make I was familiar with. It was a black

Chinese touch phone, that's all I knew. But Vanessa knew how to use it. We took pictures, lots of selfies. Everyone was messing around, excited, screaming and dancing. We straightaway plugged it into charge, doing role play with it, or pretending to talk to loved ones. It was funny and sad at the same time.

You cannot imagine the joy of having your own phone after two years without. Putting in calls any time you liked to your family was magical. And it wasn't just me doing it. Vanessa used it to run her business on the outside. Another woman, Miguelina, a fifty-year-old from the Dominican Republic, had her life turned around when I let her have a go. She hadn't seen her children in the thirteen years she'd been at Ancón. One had been only two years old when she went in, and she was serving a fifteen-year stretch. Now she was able to receive photos and message them on WhatsApp, and it transformed her world. If I never achieved anything else in that place, I'd always know I'd touched her life for the good.

We were a motley bunch – but sharing that secret, that phone, brought us all together. It was us against the rest. It wasn't just an advantage for me. I was sharing my lottery win with seven other women, and it was good to have back-up. I'd share it with more if I could trust them. As it was, we had our work cut out keeping our little secret secret. The head of security had been as good as his word. At least once a day the mobile would buzz with a text: 'Search at 12.' 'Search at 4.'

He was totally on it but it was also worth his while. On the occasions he was in a meeting or out, or at home and couldn't let us know, the OTC was a decent back-up. He didn't text. Nothing so crass. He'd either wander down himself, summon me for a meeting or get one of the guards to pass on a message and then one of us would scoop up the phone and charger and go and visit someone else until the danger had passed. But that system only needed to break down once for our world to go up in smoke.

We had a close call on one occasion, when Vanessa took the phone to the patio toilets after hours. She had an arrangement with the guards so they turned a blind eye. It should have been fine but she must have knocked the phone off silent because it was the dead of night and suddenly it started ringing.

We weren't the only block that backed onto the patio. Within a couple of seconds two hundred strangers were shouting at guards that someone with an illegal mobile was out there.

Luckily, Vanessa was quick off the mark. She buried the phone deep in a flowerpot and legged it back to the cell. When the inevitable search came the guards were disappointed. We were clean. Whatever they thought they knew was wrong, and Carmen made sure they knew that.

But as the weeks passed, I was aware that more people were learning about the phone than I was comfortable with. It could only end one way.

It just so happened one day we were all in the cell. It was between last roll call and lights out. The noise from further along the block was unmistakable. The INPE were on the march doing one of their impromptu searches. And they weren't going cell by cell. Monica was closest to the door.

'They're not going in order,' she hissed. 'They're coming straight for us.'

By my calculations we had about a minute to lose the phone. But where the hell were we going to put it? When the searches happened they really happened. Every bag was gone through, all toiletries were examined, even the mattresses were patted down. No stone was left unturned.

What were we going to do? There was nowhere in the room to hide it that a child couldn't find.

La Delegada stood up. 'Michaella,' she said, 'you need to put it inside you.'

'*What*? I'm not doing that!'

She rolled her eyes, sucked her teeth, basically did every physical gesture she could to denote her derision of me. Then she put out her hand and beckoned with her fingers.

'Give it to me,' she said. 'They won't find it here.'

'You have got to be joking.'

'Hurry. You might not have a man on the outside to talk to but I do. I need this phone to survive. Give it to me now.'

I handed it over and stared transfixed as she pulled down her pants. I spun my head away but not quickly enough. The sight of that phone disappearing inside Vanessa will haunt me forever.

A couple of the other girls high-fived her. But then Melissa said, 'What about the charger? Even Vanessa can't have space for that.'

I was straight up. 'I'm not hiding that thing anywhere on me. You all know the deal. You don't pay for phone calls, you don't pay for anything. In return I expect you to guard that phone with your life.'

A big old argument kicked off. The things they said to each other would get a man arrested if he said them. Just about the nicest thing Carmen said to Vanessa was, 'You must have room for this, you've had three children. Where did they come from?'

In the end it was Vanessa's aunt who stepped up. I knew what was coming this time so I didn't watch. But I couldn't avoid hearing her wince as the two-pin plug made its way inside.

*

The things you do to keep a level of home comforts in your life. But it got me thinking. Why weren't we allowed to make phone calls when we wanted to? Why did we have to pay for everything, either legally or not? There should have been a system in place. Vanessa was fun, but she was rubbish as a delegate. Look at Rose – that poor woman was stuck upstairs when she needed to be on the ground floor and probably in a wheelchair. Why wasn't anyone doing anything about it? Sadly, people like Rose didn't make enough fuss to be worth taking notice of, so they got ignored. It was the troublemakers like Simona or Danielle who'd slash their bodies at the drop of a hat and – hey presto – get what they wanted. Obviously, I felt sorry for them. But not more than I felt sorry for the innocents among us.

Surely there had to be a different way. Or at least a different *person*. It was time for me to step up and try for the thing I'd mentioned to the OTC.

'Mel,' I said. 'I know how to fix everything.'

'What's that then?'

'I'm going to run for delegate.'

CHAPTER TWENTY-FIVE

NO GOOD DEED GOES UNPUNISHED

Anyone interested in being a delegate had to be nominated. If seconded you had to make a presentation to the entire block and key staff. I wasn't looking forward to any of it. But I'd put it out there that I wanted the position – not only to Mel and the OTC, but also to my new cellmates. Initially, I was terrified that Vanessa would kick off, but she'd grown tired of all the work it involved and was ready to throw it in.

Monica was delighted, saying she would second me. She knew Vanessa was fed up with it but to have another *delegada* in her cell was power by proxy. It was a win–win for all three of us.

When the initial rounds were done it came down to a contest between two middle-aged Mexican women and me.

Monica was loving her perceived role as kingmaker. But right up to the final minute Melissa was saying, 'You don't have to go through with this. Do you have any idea the level of shit you'll bring on yourself if you win?'

Whether I did or didn't, what really mattered was I had a mobile phone and I wanted to firm up my position to ensure I kept it for as long as possible – although obviously I couldn't tell the electorate anything of the kind. I also genuinely wanted to improve conditions for everyone. Even the more aggressive, fractious ones would improve their behaviour if they had a regular supply of clean water and an extra microwave.

Normally I wouldn't have stood a chance, but from early on I heard people saying that the Mexicans only wanted to win so they could guard their drugs empire. On Election Day I had to stand up in front of two hundred of my peers, plus the psychologist, sociologist, sub-director, OTC and various others from the main staff. I'd made these boards with drawings and headers to prove where I hoped to be taking the block. What I wanted to do. What rules I wanted to impose or adapt or remove. All done with my own brand of stuttering Spanish. Obviously, the language counted against me. But I hoped there were enough non-Spanish speakers to identify with what I could bring. I was determined to make things better. I suggested we do some fundraising activities to buy new stuff to make things that bit more liveable for everyone. When I promised new microwaves and televisions, they could believe me. I ran the salon. I was trustworthy with money. I wouldn't steal. I could be relied upon to deliver.

Speaking in front of so many people was daunting. I was staring out at a sea of faces, some of whom were friends, many more I'd had run-ins with. Why did I think I could represent this bunch? Why would they listen to me? Somehow, the nerves held and I got through it. By the time I sat back down I had no recollection of anything I'd said.

Everyone was given a piece of paper to write down the name of their preferred candidate and asked to put it in a box. It was a secret ballot. Just like the elections back home. Unlike back home candidates weren't allowed to vote for themselves.

After everybody had written their 'X' next to the appropriate name the psychologist came to the top of the room and started sifting through the votes, putting them into three separate piles. I had no trouble watching. There was no anxiety for me at this stage. The South American vote was much bigger than the European bloc, plus the Mexicans were far more established in the prison community than me. The odds of my victory were practically nil.

And yet . . .

After a slow start I realised my pile of white slips was getting bigger and bigger. Barely ten minutes later it was the biggest of them all.

I'd won.

The psychologist, the sociologist, the sub-director and the OTC all offered their congratulations. They stayed around for the block party afterwards. We had music and some party food, all paid for by the block fund – now my responsibility. Every inmate contributes a weekly fee to cover cleaning, payphone maintenance, kitchen appliances, bedding. Basically everything. If I thought balancing the books would be arduous, the second the authorities left, my job began in earnest. Of the two hundred women present, at least a quarter of them came rushing at me with some complaint or request or demand. It was all I could do to not be crushed. It took Monica to wade in with Carmen by her side to whip everyone into order. When there was silence, I said, desperately trying to keep my voice from shaking, 'I'll be putting up my rules tomorrow. I'll deal with everything then.'

Then I thanked everyone for coming and fled back to my cell.

My heart rate was through the roof. What the hell had I got myself into? Melissa was right. It was a fool's errand. You couldn't please these people. They were all too selfish.

But that was tomorrow's problem. Right then I had more pressing matters in the shape of what Vanessa was holding behind her back.

'Congratulations, darling!' she screamed, and presented me with a bottle of rum that one of the doctors had given her in exchange for God knows what. There was only me, her and Mel in the room, so the three of us had a merry old time for the next hour. The perfect end to a surreal day. And the effect it had on me was extraordinary. After two years of sobriety, the high-proof alcohol went to my head big time. It was like being on drugs – although that part of my life was over.

Day 1 of my reign as *La Delegada* was a baptism of fire, but I had the help of Melissa, Vanessa and Monica – all strong women with strong opinions. I drafted a bunch of new rules and posted them in the hall. New phone times, looser limits for TV time and music playing, and more flexible work arrangements. I tried to be as generous as I could. To make it all work I needed a team. Monica was angling for second in command, so it made sense not to rile her. She was already furious that I wanted to dismantle the oppressive time limits on entertainment that she and then Vanessa had maintained. I had eight posts to fill but I found jobs for twelve people. My plan was to have as little to do as possible. I was going to be the first delegate who really lived up to the name.

My most controversial appointment was making Simona my head of security. Carmen wanted the gig but she was all mouth. The 'Italian pit bull', I knew from experience, could crack the whip if necessary. And because everyone knew she was prepared to, meant people stayed in line.

My changes pleased most of the people most of the time. The real influence I had, however, was achieved behind the scenes. Now I was a delegate I was expected to have regular meetings with the prison authorities. The only one I really wanted to see was the OTC. On the second day as *delegada* I presented him with a list of names.

'Who are these?'

'They are people living in the wrong cells. I want them moved.'

'I can't do that.'

'You did it for me.'

He laughed. He was good at that. He was also a reasonable man at heart.

I don't think he had ever seen anything like it before from a delegate, but I'd drawn up a list of people I thought should be moved and why – and my plan was based solely on humanitarian reasoning. I'd worked it all out for him. He didn't have to do a thing other than agree to it.

'Okay, we'll try your system. But there's no going back if it doesn't work out.'

The atmosphere in the whole block changed almost overnight. Guards appeared with letters for eight inmates. I witnessed only one open hers. It was Rose. There was a moment when she couldn't believe what she was reading. Then she smiled, then she cried.

'What is it, Rose?'

'I'm being moved downstairs. Next to the patio. I won't have to go up these stairs ever again!'

One by one the screams of delight punctuated the general chatter. Some people like Rose were being moved for their own health. Another woman was a cancer sufferer. She went off for regular bouts of chemo and would return drained and lifeless. That's bad enough but she was sharing with three junkies who wanted to party 24/7. So I asked for all the junkies to be moved in together. And that gave me the idea to move the suicidal ones together, too, which in hindsight wasn't the best idea, as they started winding each other up.

Typically, it took only a short period of time before the good thing I'd instigated became the focal point of a near revolution. Suddenly, everyone wanted to be moved and the queue to see me on the patio stretched back for ever. I told everyone the same thing. 'It had nothing to do with me. Take it up with the OTC.'

*

There were practical improvements, too. By my second week in charge I'd got a new microwave on each floor. There'd only been one previously and that was so knackered you'd wait half an hour for water to boil. I bought a load of mattresses via Maria the package lady and sold them cheaply to those with money and gave them away to the Asians who mostly slept without even blankets on the concrete bunks. I really wanted to get the showers fixed and some proper toilets but that cost money I didn't have, so I started arranging social events where everyone paid a few soles to attend. We made fruit juice to sell to visitors and I even persuaded Monica to let us use her secret cooker to make a better quality meal that we could sell to the male prison, rather than them keep selling their boring rice, chicken and potatoes to us. I did as much as I could and most people appreciated the effort.

I bought water filters in bulk, too. They were only forty soles each but you couldn't buy them in Ancón. People who couldn't afford to buy bottled water were getting sick from drinking the tap water. Sean Walsh had visited recently and had bought me and Melissa a water filter. So I made sure the whole block had access to drinking water by getting a few brought in. It wasn't as good as the bottled stuff, but at least people stopped getting ill.

But there was always someone who wasn't quite as appreciative as they might be.

It was summer and the weather was so intense everyone was a spark away from having a meltdown. The day after I got the new microwaves installed, there were fights kicking off between the women queuing to heat their little ready meals. Simona dealt with the majority of them in her own inimitable fashion, but two women would not be silenced.

Monica was in my ear like a gnat. 'You have to make a stand otherwise the others will run over you.'

Easy to say if you'd grown up among the Cali Cartel; not as natural to a girl from a small town in Ireland. I knew what she wanted, and it was the last thing I felt comfortable with. In my twenty-one years, I'd had no experience of human beings en masse physically fighting over the basics of life, such as water and access to a cooker. To now be in charge of sorting out their squabbles felt surreal and terrifying. I wasn't a gang master or a mafia boss, but I found myself having to act like one now I was *delegada*. Ultimately, I was left with no choice. Everyone was screaming, demanding resolution. It was no good. I had to do it.

'Simona,' I instructed, 'take these women to a cell and let them settle it their own way.'

The next time it happened I decided to try something different. I couldn't bear the thought of these women tearing strips out of each other, so I called in two of the INPE who were hovering on the patio. I thought my words as *delegada* would carry some weight. Maybe the words got lost in translation. The guards took one look at the two women scrapping and started laying into them with their metal truncheons. It was grotesque. They did more damage in ten seconds than the women could have achieved in an hour. But it taught us all one lesson: we were on our own. And the justice the INPE would mete out was worse than anything the women would do to each other.

I guess I wasn't the first delegate to suffer. Part of the deal of becoming new block leader is that you agree to see the psychologist twice a week so they could monitor how you were handling the pressure. After the brutality of the guards I was ready for it. The guy was quite nice, really sympathetic to the situation. I suppose he had a handle on my mental state but what I remember most about the visits is chatting about life in the UK and Ibiza.

But I was soon going to need all the help I could get. Circumstances beyond my control were about to blow up to the point of mutiny.

Running water was probably the number one bone of contention in Ancón 2. Or, rather, the lack of it, as it was turned on for only about an hour each day. It was so hot, we were so dirty, and not being able to wash ourselves when we wanted was the worst part of the punishment. There would be many, many hours where we couldn't flush the toilets. For the one hour it was on each day, everyone would go crazy trying to get access to the tap. Add the heat to that and it was a recipe for serious discomfort.

The INPE at the main gate determined how much we got, and if you had someone on duty who was manipulative, or a dick, they played around with the supply. This applied to the electricity too. Without it there were no phones, no microwaves, no way to make food. We had TVs, which kept some of the rowdier prisoners occupied, but without electricity they couldn't watch it – which added to the simmering tensions.

As we counted down towards Christmas 2015, the hottest part of the year, disaster struck. I'd got enough soles in the kitty to mount a reasonable celebration like we'd had at Fatima. On Christmas Eve, though, the water went off – and never returned. Even worse, it took the electricity with it. Christmas Day, Boxing Day, New Year's Day and beyond, we had nothing.

The kiosk ran out of bottled water. People usually kept the plastic bottles and refilled them with filtered stuff, but even that was now scarce. People started going crazy. The INPE stopped doing roll call because they didn't want to face the mayhem when they entered our block. Think about it – a maximum-security jail in the middle of a sweltering South American summer. With no water or electricity. We were desperate. How people didn't die was a miracle. The only water in circulation was what visitors brought.

The whole block was in literal meltdown. Nothing I or my committee did could calm them down. I demanded an audience with the sub-director to sort it out. It transpired the cut-off wasn't due to someone being a dick this time. Apparently, work was being done outside the prison and they'd cut through a pipe. Something that would be fixed in a couple of days in Europe was going to take the Peruvian water and electricity companies weeks. No one cared about prisoners' rights.

And a lot of the prisoners turned on me. They weren't used to the more reserved European manner of expressing discontent. They wanted to see me shouting and screaming at those in authority, banging my fist on tables and threatening them with all sorts of things. In their eyes, I was too meek. I wasn't putting up enough of a fight.

Some people stuck up for me – lovely Miguelina, the woman I'd been allowing access to my phone to keep in touch with her kids. She always rallied round. She was a calm and solid presence in the block when all else was falling apart. Also, a lovely girl called Sharda, who was now sharing a cell with Kaouthar. She was Dutch-Indian and quite spiritual. We connected on a level that was slightly more thoughtful; we'd have chats about the universe and the meaning of life. It was important not to absorb all the negative energy that was flying around the prison at this time. And there was plenty of it.

To make it a perfect storm, at the same time as we had no running water and electricity, a new intake of about ten inmates, mostly Eastern Europeans, arrived from Santa Monica – every one of them in for trafficking. They were proper bitches! From the get-go you could tell they were trouble in their attitude and their disregard for everything. They had no respect for the delegate system. When they heard about the phone list, they smashed the phone. Told to queue for the microwave, they dragged it from the wall and used it for kicking practice. They caused absolute mayhem.

It took almost a civil war to bring the Lithuanians, Bulgarians and Romanians into line. A war I didn't want to fight but could not afford to lose. They were planning to destroy our TV room. I wasn't going to let that happen if the guards were invisible as usual. At least I had numbers on my side.

Everyone was so angry at the system. The INPE even stopped coming inside. I wish I could have waited outside with them. The last thing I wanted was any controversy attached to my name. Because there was another reason I'd run for office. It was to show that I took my rehabilitation seriously. And something else.

I was applying for benefits.

CHAPTER TWENTY-SIX

CARLOS THE JACKAL

I'd been determined to continue investigating the ruling that convicted traffickers weren't eligible for benefits. I kept saying to myself that there must be a loophole somewhere. We were first-timers, young women, not hardened criminals or part of some murderous cartel. I'd been wishing and praying for a long time that some opportunity would present itself. Maybe I was being stupid. It was a pipe dream at best. But a window of opportunity *did* present itself and, when it did, I was determined to seize any crumb of hope that fate threw my way. Twenty months in Ancón had changed me. Made me focus on what was important. And what was important to me was getting out of there. If I could achieve that a single day before the end of my six years and eight months sentence, it would all have been worthwhile.

As delegate, people came to me for all sorts of things. One day it was the psychologist. He was working on the benefits papers for two Thai prisoners who spoke not a word of Spanish. They did, however, have a smattering of English, so he asked me to translate. Like everything I did, it was a way to break up the monotony of the heat and oppression of life in maximum security.

Naturally, I was curious about their claim, especially when I realised they too were in prison for drug offences. Listening to their case I realised something very, very important. If these foreign nationals were eligible for benefits, then so was I.

The whole problem Melissa and I had faced with the new law that had come in during 2013 still stood. But while the law had been passed in summer, it had not made its way onto the statute books by the time we'd been sentenced. As far as I could fathom, that meant we'd still be eligible for the prior standing benefits. So was it possible? Could I get early release? Fishman had disappeared soon after I was sentenced, and everyone else kept saying it was impossible. There was only one way to find out the truth.

I told Melissa of my discovery. Like me, she'd suffered these past two years. She didn't want to get her hopes up for no reason.

'We just need to keep our noses clean and serve our time,' she insisted.

I was put in touch with a lawyer called Alberto. He seemed proficient as far as the new law was concerned. He certainly thought I stood a chance.

'There's a lot to be done before you go in front of a judge, though,' he advised.

'Like what? Talk me through it.'

'You'll need to provide proof of a job and a Peruvian address on your release and get your reports in order first.'

There were a dozen or so people I needed to get affirmations from: the prison psychologist, the sociologist, the doctor, the sub-director, etc. etc. All of these would need to be collated alongside my work dockets.

'How long will that take?' I said.

'If they put their minds to it, about a year.'

What?

'I can't wait a year!'

'Michaella, the very earliest you can even submit a plea for benefits is after you've served two years and three months. You're still six months away from that.'

The way the Peruvian system worked, if you were granted benefits, and released early as a foreigner, you had to remain in the country for a further two years. They wouldn't grant parole unless you could give an address and a letter of employment to prove you had work lined up.

'How the hell am I going to do that?' I asked. They only person I knew was Andrea. She was very well connected, which got me thinking . . .

Alberto shrugged. 'Like I said, these things take time.'

Logically speaking, I'd been ready to serve nearly seven years. Now that I had a sniff at getting out early, even another few months seemed unbearable. I saw a light at the end of the tunnel and I was sprinting towards it, with or without Alberto's help.

'I don't care about the rules,' I said. 'I want it started. I'll do anything it takes.'

I contacted Andrea. I wasn't seeing her quite as often as I did when we were in Fatima, but she remained interested in our case and was always receptive to my questions. On my private phone, I called her from the cell one day when no one else was around. I told her about the benefits loophole – and the restrictions.

'You can always say you'll be working for me,' she said. 'You can be a live-in housekeeper, and you could use my address.'

'Really?'

'Well, obviously it wouldn't be a real job, but it would get you sorted for your parole.'

This was proving easier than I could have possibly imagined. But then something happened which meant sorting out paperwork was the last thing I cared about.

Uncle Gene was the father I never had. He'd looked out for me, loved me and had shown me a childhood my own dad hadn't. In my darkest hours he'd been there for me. I'd been at his bedside when he was ill. We were tight. We were a team.

Getting the news from my mother that his cancer was back, and aggressively so, was a kick in the teeth. I kept trying to speak to him but it was never the right time. Eventually he had a heart attack and fell into a coma. I was beside myself. It lasted for weeks. I must have rung a dozen times some days for updates. Different members of the family took the calls. I was passed around like a hot potato. Then one day Mum said, 'If you call tomorrow at six in the morning your time you can speak to him and tell him how you feel.'

I woke up at three and couldn't get back to sleep. Bang on six, the guards unlocked the door and I flew down to dial my mother from the main phone. I couldn't wait to hear Uncle Gene's voice.

Mum answered.

'Is he there? Is he awake?'

'Is he awake? No, Michaella, love, he's gone.'

'Gone where? You told me to call at six. You promised I could speak to him. Why'd you let him go before I rang?'

'Michaella, he hasn't gone anywhere. He's passed. He died. He never woke up from the coma.'

I stared at the phone for ages. My mum's voice barely registered. I couldn't work out how he could have died when I was told he'd speak to me.

Mum tried to explain. She said he was gone when I'd called the day before. She thought she'd made that clear. When she said I could call at six it was so I could tell him I loved him and say my goodbyes.

I think I was in denial. She'd said exactly that and I'd heard something completely different. I'd heard what I'd wanted to hear.

You could hear me howling all up the stairs. I didn't care who told me to shut up or tried to comfort me. It was beyond painful. I wanted to run into the sea and never come back.

I couldn't believe he was gone.

All my *delegada* duties went out the window. I didn't collect payments, I didn't make decisions, I didn't keep order. I hid in my cell, sobbing, writing letters, trying to remember every moment of my time with Gene and feeling such a traitor that I wasn't there at the end. To not even be able to attend his funeral made me sick. He deserved better.

I was in a bad way. And not once during those five weeks did I consider my papers. If anything, I wanted to stay longer. For the hurt I'd caused my family I didn't deserve to be let out early.

I got in such a slump that I couldn't get out of bed. The guards were considerate, amazingly. They did the head count with me indoors. I wasn't eating. I wasn't even sleeping, really. All the experiences of the past two years that I'd repressed came out. I think I was breaking down. Melissa got worried and persuaded the doctor to prescribe some antidepressants without seeing me. I got some Diazepam and Valium and a couple of other things and I started throwing them back. I went for it. Got totally hooked on the very thing I'd seen tear more fragile lives apart. I enjoyed the numbness they gave me. It let me tune out the day-to-day noise and quietened my self-loathing for a short while.

Why didn't I do this earlier?

My prescription was for a week's supply. I finished them in three days, then went back to the doctor and said I'd lost the rest. He prescribed another dose but warned me if I 'lost' these he wouldn't be doing it again. Good to his word, when I returned a few days later he refused to see me.

Well, I thought, *I'll still be able to get my hands on them. I'll have to go on the black market.*

As delegate you get to know everyone's secrets, and what people didn't tell me openly I picked up in whispers in the salon. I knew exactly who to go to for antidepressants.

Then three months passed in something like a haze. My memories of each day are blurred, wiped out by pharmaceuticals. I didn't eat. My face was gaunt and I looked sick. If you were charitable, you'd say I was slim. If you had eyes, you'd know my body was shutting down. I'd lost the will to live.

At some point during this time, Andrea pulled out of the

housekeeper arrangement. It was flimsy to start with, but I think she felt nervous when faced with having to declare things on paper and in court that she knew to be false. The fact that I'd gone into a vortex of depression and drug dependency can't have helped fill her with confidence. It was one more thing to add to my misery.

It's conceivable I could have spent the next four years in the same fug, if I hadn't got talking in the salon one day. My client, a lovely and glamorous Peruvian called Lisbet, was chatting away to me, telling me her boyfriend had been jailed for fraud. It was quite a scandal, as he was a judge. He'd been found out giving lenient sentences to criminals for backhanders. I guess we were both feeling sorry for ourselves. I started to tell her I was desperate to have an address and a job on the outside, so I could apply for parole. I was brought to tears by the telling of my predicament.

'I might know someone who can help you with that,' she said. 'A lawyer called Carlos. He's a friend of my boyfriend. He visits me sometimes. He can help you get your papers done quickly – for a fee, of course.'

Of course.

Lisbet gave me his number and I made contact at the first opportunity. We arranged for him to come in the following week. Previously, lawyers had been able to walk in at any time, with private rooms allocated in which to meet their clients. In Ancón, though, it seems somewhat less learned matters than legal cases had been attended to in these rooms, and inmates were now obliged to meet their representatives next to the rotunda, where all the INPEs gathered, in rooms with partitions, so there couldn't be any hanky-panky.

During the next few days I realised I was energised for the first time in ages. In fact, I resented not being able to think clearly. That was a great sign. A sign I wanted to change. I don't want to sound simplistic about it, because some people really suffer with addiction, but this chance was just the push I needed to get back on track. Suddenly, I was no longer ignoring people because of the drugs. My head was back in the game. I wanted to get out and I would do anything to make it happen.

Or, as it turned out, *almost* anything.

*

The first thing I noticed about Carlos was his immaculate appearance. When I greeted him, he smelled amazing – fresh and rich – and he was attractive, if a little short. He was suave and obviously well educated, in his mid-forties, with an air of success about him. He had classic Latin looks and a great head of hair.

The meeting was amicable. He said he could help me. He had any number of addresses and contracts of work he could present to a court. This suited me. I made it very clear that I could pay him. I suppose I knew that these contracts and addresses were spurious, but I let myself be led by his spiel. It was all part of the procedure in the way things got done in Peru.

'What I'm doing for you,' he said, 'I have to check with my wife that it's possible.'

'Okay,' I said. 'Just do whatever you need to do.' I assumed she was some kind of legal person as well. Maybe she was part of the whole system. I just nodded and went along with it. He rattled off some fees and explained the procedure of notarisation, and how expensive it was, and that was the meeting wrapped up.

When he returned a few days later, his demeanour had changed. He was edgy and acting strangely possessive. The first thing he told me was that he'd split from his wife because she'd cheated on him. And that she wasn't really his wife anyway. He admitted he'd said it as a test to see how I'd react, if I'd show any signs of jealousy. Now, this was a guy I'd only just met. It was crazy. The stereotype of the hot Latin temperament was being reinforced all the time, even by those in respectable professions. The country seemed rife with power-plays of sexual jealousy at every turn.

I tried to keep things business-like but it was difficult with his eyes burning into me with wolfish intensity. There was a lot of paperwork to be done, in addition to that which my official lawyer, Alberto, was gathering, so I pushed on with gritted teeth and tried to get through everything in a professional manner. Maybe he would come to his senses and start behaving likewise.

*

Alberto had been quietly working in the background, filing requests to the various channels for work reports and behaviour reports etc. At our next meeting he was surprised to see me so coherent again. He was even more surprised to learn I had a possible way out for the address and job requirement. Likewise, I was impressed by how much he had achieved. All the report forms had gone out. It was just a question of hassling now to get them back. He agreed to chase all the main players. A few, like the psychologist, I said I'd take care of.

'I'm seeing him today anyway.'

A few hours later I was in the psychologist's office, chatting about this and that when he said, 'I understand you want to leave us.'

'Oh yes, you got the request then?'

'I did,' he said, 'but I don't understand. You told me you are not eligible for benefits. Were you lying?'

There was an unusually hard tone in his voice.

'No, I wasn't lying. I thought that was true when I said it. It still might be.'

'So why are you bothering?'

'Because of reading about the two Thai prisoners – whose statements you gave me to translate, remember? If there's a one per cent chance I can get out of here early, then I'm going to take it.'

His face fell. 'You really want to leave that much?'

'Yes of course. Why wouldn't I? Why would anyone *want* to stay here?'

I couldn't get where he was coming from. Then, as he moved closer to me, I got the message. *He doesn't want me to go.*

It was a chilling thought. I needed perfect scores from everyone to stand a chance of impressing the judge. This guy had the power to derail my dream mid-flow. What on earth did he want?

'I think I will need to see you a few more times before I write my report,' he said, brushing my hair with the back of his hand. 'I need to check you are healthy enough for the outside world.'

I couldn't get out of that office quick enough. This predatory asshole had me dangling on a string. I wondered if I could get Alberto to have a word with the director, to say what was going on. Or since I was meeting Carlos the following day, maybe he could sort it out for me. He looked like the kind who wouldn't take no for an answer.

Never a truer word...

Carlos's next visit was on visitors' day, which meant we weren't in the partitioned zone. He obviously wanted to put things on a more informal footing. I don't know what kind of a relationship he expected to come out of this, but it was as if me applying for benefits through him was like some kind of code for me saying I wanted to be his mistress, or even his wife. I tried to talk about the contracts, but he stalled it, and instead started showing me photos of houses.

'Look,' he said, 'this one is on the beach.'

'It's beautiful.'

'I'm so glad you like it. I think we could be very happy together there.'

Here we go again . . .

'You can live here,' he said, 'with me. I'll leave my apartment in the city and we can have a beautiful life there together.'

The place was stunning – a tropical paradise – which he must have known would look highly appealing to me in my situation. But I'd never felt so uncomfortable. I couldn't believe what was happening. I wanted to get all the paperwork signed off, but how could I manage that with Carlos acting the way he was? He even wanted to kiss me. He told me he'd fallen in love with me. I was like a captive bird in a not-so gilded cage.

Yes, he was attractive and well-off and groomed, but still . . . I didn't know what to do. My whole case would stall without an address and work contract, but the guy was clearly unhinged. He was behaving like a cartoon character. What if I did get released and he then immediately expected me to stay with him as his lover? That's not how I saw my life playing out.

*

Melissa was her usual sympathetic self where my admirer troubles were concerned. Lisbet was more practical.

'Carlos is a good man. Very rich, very powerful. You would be very happy.'

'No, I wouldn't! I'm not throwing myself into a relationship with a man more than twice my age to get an address.'

'Well, be careful how you tell him,' she warned. 'He is used to getting his own way.'

I had to think quickly because I was called downstairs the next day and there, looking formal, was Carlos. He was professional at first but I could tell he wanted an answer from me straightaway. I tried to fudge it. The more I did, the more he declared his love for me. He had everything worked out. But what he saw as romantic, I saw as controlling. I could see a future where I was his prized possession, locked up in this beautiful house and treated like a trinket, not an equal. I'd be exchanging one prison for another. By his fifth visit of the week I couldn't bite my tongue any more.

'Look, Carlos, you're a nice guy but I just want an address and contract from you. I don't want a boyfriend. I need to be on my own for a while.'

The look on his face. You'd think I'd shot his mother.

'You have another man?'

'No, no, I just want to be by myself.'

'You *do* have a boyfriend. I already know. You are scum. Filth. You go with everyone who visits you! I know all about this Caesar. I know how many times he visited you. I know everything that goes on in this jail.'

I thought his head was going to explode. He started ranting and raging. He'd obviously got the stories about Caesar and Diogo from the guards. I didn't know what to do. Everyone could hear him. It was so embarrassing.

'I can stop your papers ever seeing a judge,' he said. 'I can keep you locked up in here for twenty years, thirty years. That's the power I have.'

He had to be physically escorted from the room. I could still hear him shouting when he got outside. One minute he was going to ruin me, the next he was declaring undying love. The guy needed help.

And now, sadly, so did I.

CHAPTER TWENTY-SEVEN

SHARK-INFESTED WATERS

There was only one other person I could appeal to for help in getting an address and proof of work. Father Sean had recently returned from the US. I called him and asked him to come in. When he did, I poured out an edited version of what had gone on.

'So,' Sean said, 'is it just the case that you need an address for a form?'

'It is, Father. And a job offer.'

'Well, I can do that for you. Get me the papers and I'll sign them. But I know the system here. I don't want you getting your hopes up. It's really unlikely this will succeed. You know that drug traffickers can't get benefits.'

He went on for some time about how slim my chances were and, to be honest, it made me feel a little cross. He was supposed to be a man of faith, and yet he was being extremely negative. I sat there nodding my head, saying I knew it was unlikely, but I had to try it.

When he left, I had a weird feeling that his negativity might impact my claim. Still, I'd told the prison admin guy doing all my paperwork to take Carlos's name and contract out of the file and to issue Father Sean with new papers to sign as my guarantor.

I didn't hear anything for a while, then, one day, Alberto arrived unannounced. He'd sent all the paperwork he had so far to the courts, where it had been signed for by the main office.

'That's great, Alberto.'

'Wait,' he said. 'It's not so great, actually. When I just called Lupe, the court administrator, for an estimated date for your hearing, he didn't have the file.'

'What do you mean?'

'I mean it left the main office but never made it to his desk. It's gone missing.'

'Lost or taken?'

He wrung his hands. 'In this system, Michaella, it's the same thing.'

We were back at square one. And I knew why. That toad Carlos had obviously been as good as his word. He was in everyone's pockets.

But my family were paying Alberto handsomely for his services, so he should have had a better angle on security. I was heartbroken. What made it worse was remembering the last call I'd made on my old Chinese mobile. It had been to my mother, telling her I was seeing a judge soon. How was I going to explain this enormous setback? She'd had enough heartbreak recently. She couldn't understand how corruption or, at best, utter ineptitude, was the normal way of things in this country.

Alberto swore he'd get going immediately on the process again. Even though he had photocopies of some of my paperwork, things like my work dockets and the twelve reports needed to be original copies on prison paper. Which meant going back to everyone cap in hand once again. And paying for the whole process again.

*

My tenure as delegate had come to an end by this time. The new woman, Anna-Marie, knew about the phone, so I gave it to her on condition she never revealed where it came from. I couldn't risk being caught with it so close to my chance of a court hearing. She liked me and was desperate for me to join her delegate committee, but I couldn't. I had too much else to do – not that I could tell her that.

I was desperate for a lucky break and finally that happened. I'd seen this guy in and around the block a few times and one day I was introduced. His name was Fernando and he worked at the courts. At least, that was his day job. What he really did, and why he was in the prison so often, was to hire himself out to people who didn't like waiting for paperwork. He basically took a healthy fee then greased the appropriate wheels to expedite his client's case. Within a second of me hearing this, Fernando had himself a new client.

It was the best thousand soles I ever spent. The man was a miracle worker. Within a month he had fresh reports from the INPEs, the director, the OTC and the psychologist. Alberto and Fernando were confident I had a very good case. We just needed to ensure our brand-new file didn't disappear.

Alberto assured me Lupe had the new file under lock and key at the court. Fernando assured me the same thing. I even rang Lupe personally to hear it from the horse's mouth. They all said the same thing.

'It's fine. We're on track. But there's a problem with one of the reports.'

'I bet I know who that is,' I said. 'It's the psychologist, isn't it?'

I was right. Carlos hadn't been the last of the sexual predators to cause me grief. The psychologist seemed to be made of the same stuff. When asked to submit a new report, it had changed in tone massively from his original. After outlining that it was against the law to even apply for benefits, he'd then branded me as psychotic, saying I was a danger to society and shouldn't be released! And Ancón's in-house lawyer had put his stamp of approval to it as the legal representative of the prison – knowing that his original report had been completely different.

The psychologist must have either intimidated him or paid him off . . . but then I thought about it and realised that the most likely explanation was one of bare-faced misogyny – labelling any woman who spurned the advances of a professional, powerful man as crazy. His ego had been dented and he'd had to take revenge. It would have been easy to convince his friend, the prison lawyer, in a man-to-man chat how they could get one back on this troublesome woman who had denied him his pleasure. They made me sick. I was taking two steps forwards and five back.

In a twist I didn't anticipate, one of the legal secretaries at the court said she could get a more flattering document from other sources – for the right fee.

'But the report needs to come from this psychologist,' I pointed out.

'Oh, it will be his words,' she replied, with a knowing look. It seemed too good to be true. But what if it was like the airport fiasco? What if I was being set up by a greater power to prove the legal system didn't allow bribery to influence policy? What if I was being cast as a patsy once again?

I had to put my trust in people I'd never even met – associates of associates of the people paid to represent me. My sense of vulnerability was acute. I was at the mercy of hot tempers, wounded egos, flimsy arrangements and the power of hard cash.

But as long as my poor family kept the latter coming, deals could be made and bargains struck. Once I had assurance about the replacement report, there was another conversation to be had about the court date. Normally, appeals cases waited many months for a hearing date – a year or more sometimes. I didn't think I could stand it.

After another few weeks went by, I rang Lupe again.

'At the moment we're looking at November,' he said. Months away. Then there was a pause: 'But there is a way of making that happen quicker.'

Effectively, for a fee (of course), you could take someone else's date. It wasn't bribery – it wasn't even illegal. It was rotten for the person concerned but, in this country, the game was survival of the richest. The wheels of bureaucracy needed regular greasing and only a fool didn't play the system if they could. So, yet more money changed hands. And I went back to waiting.

I was a nervous wreck – and not just because that piece of work Carlos was out there doing everything he could to ruin my benefits. If anything, the danger inside the prison was even greater. Monica, Carmen, Danielle – if any of them caught wind of my impending parole they'd scupper it, just like they'd done for Kaouthar so many times. They were envious of anyone who had something they didn't. And they were especially envious of me and Melissa. They knew that once we were released we would most likely be returning to a decent life – practically an impossibility for working-class women in Peru.

Time dragged on. I couldn't eat, I couldn't sleep. I was sick with nerves. Every time a guard called me, or I had a visitor, or Alberto rang, I expected the worst. Something was bound to go wrong. I didn't know what, I didn't know how, I didn't know when. It just always did.

*

The Peruvians know their penal system is awash with corruption but they do make some attempts to limit it. For example, every two years the entire management team of every prison is replaced to ensure no long-lasting cosy relationships can get embedded. When the prisons changed staff, so did the courts. This can either work for or against you.

One day, I was summoned to the lawyers' visiting area. When I arrived, Alberto was waiting. He didn't look sad. On the other hand he didn't look happy either. I think his resting face was one of resignation. He had news.

The judge that he and Lupe had been confident would try our case favourably – the guy who was eating crackers with his feet on the desk, back when I was originally sentenced – had been replaced by a woman with the most severe reputation in all the judiciary. Basically, the Queen Bitch of prison law.

'Alberto, what are you saying?'

'I'm saying she hates drug smugglers, she hates people trying to get out of paying their dues, she hates being taken for a fool.'

I knew my foremost task was to convince her I was a rehabilitated individual. I could tell her about my flawless work record. I'd never been put in *calabozo*. I was a young person who had made a stupid, stupid mistake. I was from a good Catholic family. I knew priests and nuns who did charity work in Peru. It was all true, and I'd use everything I could to convince her I should be free.

'There's also good news,' said Alberto. 'Your court date will be sometime in March. We just have to win by having a strong case,' he said. 'You've done your time, and the law is on your side.'

'The old law,' I said.

'Yes, exactly. But we're hoping they will remember that.'

In preparation he gave me a list of forty questions he'd heard judges ask in similar cases. They were fairly straightforward but having advance notice meant I could brush up on my Spanish replies. It's amazing how your language skills vanish when you're on the spot.

After 1 March came and went without a date, I bombarded the judge's secretary with calls until finally she had an answer: Tuesday, 29 March 2016. Never had a date held more significance for me. I was going up against the impenetrable forces of law in a country where my status was the lowest it could be – that of a convicted drug smuggler. I had a female judge with a fearsome reputation who probably loathed me even before she'd met me.

I was swimming in shark-infested waters. When would I ever reach safe shores again?

CHAPTER TWENTY-EIGHT

COURT IN SESSION

I set to work learning as many Spanish legal terms as possible, so I'd have a better idea of what was being discussed. My family were over the moon to hear I finally had a date for my court hearing, and they would fly out to be with me, which I didn't think was a great idea. The earliest they could arrive was 30 March, so they would actually be in the air when my verdict came back. What if I wasn't released? I couldn't bear to think of my mother's disappointment if I didn't succeed.

Everything was gearing up for the big day, but I couldn't give away any indication of what was happening to my fellow inmates. I just couldn't take that risk. I'd heard enough in the salon to know that I didn't even need to have enemies to be thwarted at the final turn; a petty squabble over the microwave could screw my chances if any of the more hot-tempered women got wind of my opportunity.

The court too was getting prepared. Alberto told me, for transparency's sake, the prosecutor was chosen at random from a pool of available qualified people just days before a hearing. It was the only way they could guard against them being bribed or intimidated.

The prosecutor would have read my file and would have been asking people about my character. I hoped to God she didn't have a hotline to the psychologist. She was also there to answer questions the judge might have, as to whether I could be trusted with early release.

There was another option that Alberto had discussed with me shortly after I'd initially taken him on as my brief – if you were granted benefits, there was an option to get what they called a 'transfer', which was more commonly known in Europe and the UK as being extradited. You were put straight on a flight back to your own country and barred for life from ever entering Peru again. That was it – *adios*.

My gut feeling was that this would not be the best decision for me. I wanted time to decompress – although the recommended two years was quite a bit longer than I'd like. But I just couldn't bear the thought of flying into the tabloid media scrum that I know would await me if I returned to Belfast immediately. I knew a few people on the outside now – good souls like Father Sean, Maureen the nun and Andrea. I wanted some time to adjust to life outside again and I knew they would help me.

*

I barely slept on the night of the 28th. I knew I had to put my best foot forward, and also make a good impression on the judge. I couldn't go to court looking like a backpacker or a party girl. I had a smart pair of white jeans and a couple of nice tops put aside for the occasion. And now that moment had arrived.

On the morning of the hearing we were called for head count as usual. Normally I'd shuffle down in night clothes or pyjamas like everyone else. This morning I looked not exactly a million dollars, but passable enough to work in an office.

All it would take was one scuffle over breakfast and I'd be put in *calabozo* with my shot at parole up in smoke. By the time the first person asked me why I was dressed up, I had my story straight. I said, 'I'm going to the dentist again.' I got a few strange looks, but I was out of there before most of the nosy and noisy ones were fully functioning.

It was a twenty-minute walk to the front office where I had to wait for transport for the two-hour trip. My case was due to be heard at 10 a.m. At nine the battered mini-van pulled up. I was the only passenger, so I jumped in and hoped the driver would floor it. Instead we cruised casually around the prison complex and picked up a bunch of men with their guards. My heart sank. They all looked terrifying. One of them, a black Dutch guy, originally in Sarita Colonia for trafficking, was keen to tell everyone his story, of how he had bribed a guard to smuggle his girlfriend into his cell round a side door so no one knew she was visiting. It didn't surprise me; I was fully aware that for a few soles you could pay the guards to turn a blind eye.

But there was more. He went on in horrifying detail – their patio area in Sarita had been renovated, and he'd volunteered to help build a new concrete wall in the garden. He'd also done some concreting in his cell: he'd smashed his girlfriend's brains out on the bedpost in a fit of jealousy and buried her body under his bed then cemented it over.

Her family was frantic because she'd disappeared and there was no one to look after her children. There was also no record of her having visited him in jail, as she'd been smuggled in. Her family knew she'd been visiting him, but they had a terrible struggle with the prison, because her name didn't appear anywhere on the visitors' log. But in time, the smell gave him away. Eventually he was convicted of her murder and moved to Ancón 2 men's *maxima* wing.

God knows what the others were in for, because they all found this story hilarious. His delivery was as deadpan as describing a trip to the shops. For nearly three hours I was wedged thigh to thigh in 45ºC heat with these characters.

When we disembarked, I was crestfallen. We were at Penal Sarita Colonia – the court where I'd been sentenced. The court must have been running late because I'd clearly missed my 10 a.m. slot but nothing was said. After a while in a waiting room with the psychos, I was taken into the court and it was the exact one where I'd been sent down by the judge eating crackers. Except this time it had a fiercer lady judge presiding.

I felt hideous as I walked in and all eyes were on me – I was sweaty and unkempt and my lovely white jeans were dirty from the van. I felt nervous because I wasn't looking as good as I wanted to.

I entered from the back of the room and was led into a small cage to the side, which contained a bench and nothing else. In the centre of the room, only about three feet from me, was the judge's large table. Lupe, the court administrator, was sat at the end. The prosecutor had a small desk to the side of my bars. If I tried, I could probably reach it. There was also space for my lawyer and a translator.

Father Sean Walsh was there too. He'd stuck to his word and stepped up as my guarantor, with an address and offer of work. How that would play out, I still wasn't sure, but a document with his name signed on it was secure in the file.

The judge looked as formidable as her reputation suggested. Like Lupe, she gave no clue that she knew I existed prior to that moment. She thumbed through my file without emotion and read out the salient points.

After some administrative announcements, the court secretary stood up to read out the process of what was going to happen. The translator began to translate into English, but I announced, as politely as I could, in perfect Spanish, that I understood what she was saying. I could see astonished looks passing between court officials, and even the judge registered mild surprise. I didn't know how many foreign nationals bothered to learn the language to the extent I had, but I'd certainly got off to a good start.

The judge said she had read my reports, which were good and seemed in order. But she was there only as a figurehead almost. It was the prosecutor who did most of the talking. And she had plenty to say. It wasn't the judge Alberto should have warned me about – it was the prosecutor!

Her opening gambit was harsh. She cited the 2013 amendment to Rule 273 which didn't allow for foreigners convicted of drug offences to apply for benefits, so she wasn't even going to look in the file or read out from it.

'You need to convince us now, yourself, in a court of law, that you are fit for release,' she declared.

She looked me in the eye, and I could tell she was really serious. There was a room full of people but I dedicated my attention to her.

She began her series of questions, about twenty-five in total, all aimed at getting to the truth of my crime and examining why I felt worthy of an early release. To my relief, all but a couple came from Alberto's list. What had I done productively with my time in prison? What had I learned about Peruvian values? What had I learned about psychology? People? Business? Rehabilitation, etc., etc.

Until the whole rigmarole began, I hadn't realised just how well equipped I was. I'd been a delegate, I'd run the salon, I had a spotless disciplinary record, my work docket was exemplary, I'd learned the language, taken courses, studied psychology when I had the chance. I couldn't have done much more. I made my declaration about all this in Spanish. I put my heart and soul into it.

The judge then cut in suddenly to ask about my family – something I hadn't mentioned yet because I was worried I'd break down. I knew they were on the first leg of their journey by now, on their way to see me. I couldn't fail them, but the pressure was immense.

If I appeared on *Mastermind* this could be my specialist subject. I could list all the ways my behaviour had hurt my mother and siblings and cousins and friends and not come up for air for hours. I said how they'd stood by me through everything. They knew I wasn't a bad person, and I was so lucky to have them.

'I'm a child of ten,' I said. 'The youngest daughter. The time I've spent in prison made me realise how important my family are to me. No mother wants to see their youngest child in prison in a foreign country.'

I spoke for about ten minutes without pause. The tears arrived around the five-minute mark. When I finished, I could barely see straight for crying. I could, however, make out the prosecutor's face, unmoved and cold.

'As far as I'm concerned,' announced the judge, 'the defendant has served enough time in jail for her crime. I consider her suitable for early release.'

Alberto's face didn't alter a fraction. He'd been around the block a few times. He would celebrate once the prosecutor concurred. As if to relish the moment, she immediately asked the question: 'How do we know this woman is not a repeat offender?' She obviously really enjoyed her job.

I stared at her, mouth hanging open. She hadn't even bothered to open my file. What did she know about my life or my crime or my rehabilitation?

'Why do you think you're ready to be reunited with society?' she continued.

'My family deserves so much better than me,' I said, 'but my mum cannot relax until I'm home.'

'What would it mean to you and your family if you were to leave here today?' she asked.

'One word,' I said. 'Everything.'

The whole procedure lasted about an hour and a half. It would have been even longer if I hadn't learned Spanish. And it's true to say the effort I'd made in that regard had made a fantastic impression. It was obvious I hadn't squandered my time. I'd made every effort to turn myself around. I needed a second chance.

Then it was suddenly over. The important people started talking while I sat in a daze. All that talk of my family had pushed me over the edge. All I could think of was my Uncle Gene and how I'd abandoned him and everyone else. I was so wrapped up in torment I didn't really listen as the judge started talking about alcohol bans, behavioural guidelines and geographical restrictions. When I did return to Planet Earth, I had no idea what they were talking about.

That's when I caught a glimpse of Alberto. He had the biggest grin.

'What?' I mouthed.

He rolled his eyes, pointed to the judge and whispered, 'Listen.'

'Michaella McCollum,' the judge said, 'I see no reason why you cannot receive early release. I'm satisfied that you have served your time to the best of your abilities, and have done so with respect for our customs and our laws. You have spent your time wisely, particularly learning the language, and most importantly you have shown remorse and regret for the mistakes of your past. I see you as not being a threat to the Peruvian people and I recommend your early release.'

Then she looked at her colleague.

'Prosecutor?'

She opened my file for the first time, but didn't really look at it. 'Initially I saw no value in even trying this case because the rules are clear: you are not entitled to benefits,' she said. 'Having heard your story, having listened to your testimony, I now believe it would serve no purpose for you to remain behind bars any longer. I withdraw any and all objections.'

She looked me directly in the eyes and for the first time that day she smiled.

'Good luck, Michaella,' she said. 'And please look after yourself.'

You know what, I thought. *I will. This is a new start. A new beginning. More importantly it's the end of the old.* From now on I was going to look after myself. I wasn't getting in any more trouble. I wasn't going to do anything just because some handsome man asked me to.

And most importantly, I wasn't going to do it alone.

As I waited for the van to take me back to Ancón, I thought of my family hurtling 30,000 feet above my head. My thoughts were flying as fast as the plane. I couldn't believe what had just happened. My new life started now.

CHAPTER TWENTY-NINE

EVERYTHING ON THE MENU

'**A**iyeeeeeeee!'

Samantha's cry of joy rang in my ear as I stood at the guarded payphone in the corridor of the court. While Mum, Stephanie and Glenn were in the air somewhere over the Atlantic, my family back home were waiting in a state of anticipation for the decision, praying that my hearing had gone well. I hadn't wanted to think what this call would have been like if the outcome was bad. Thankfully, that wasn't the case, and the McCollum clan were over the moon. I could hear cheering in the background as Samantha handed the phone to my other siblings – who all had questions.

Was I free immediately? If not, how many days before I got out? Was Melissa being released at the same time? Did I know where I was going to live? I couldn't answer them all as I wasn't sure myself. Legal bureaucracy needed to kick in. Documents had to be signed and verified, and taken by hand from the court to the prison, but for now, all I wanted to do was share this happy, magical moment.

I knew I had to be really careful, and even a bit sneaky, to ensure my final exit from Ancón 2. Being awarded my release was amazing, but it was still the penultimate hurdle; I had yet to return to the jail and await my release papers. I'd been told in the summing up of my case – when I was read my conditions of release – that it was likely I would be free on Thursday. That was in two days' time – two days where I would be vulnerable to the malevolent tricks of jealous inmates. Drugs could be planted in my cell. Someone could accuse me of something and start a fight. I would be a prime target for bringing down at the final furlong. Until I was walking out of the door of Ancón with my possessions in a bag, I was still an insider.

I told different people different stories: the INPEs escorting me back in the van knew I'd got my benefits, as they'd been at the court, but I had to stop the contagion of joy reaching the ears of those they'd be handing over to once I was back at the jail. My impending release would be hot news in Peruvian and English-speaking media, and I was terrified of bringing an unwanted invasion into both my life and the lives of my family back home. The closer we got to Ancón, the more fretful I became. I told the female guard, who was supervising the van, to please not tell a soul I'd been granted my benefits, and she promised she wouldn't. The INPEs she was handing me over to, back at the prison, also knew I'd been at court, but I told them the hearing had been postponed. If they suspected anything, they didn't say. It was the best poker face I'd ever played, as in reality I was bursting with excitement.

Waiting at the gate of *maxima* were three familiar faces – all beaming. Was this a coincidence? They seemed inordinately pleased to see me. I was barely through the door when Melissa, Miguelina and Sharda threw their arms around me and ushered me into my cell. Once we were alone, we jumped and yelped in celebration of my triumph.

'How did you know?' I quizzed them. It wasn't possible for anyone to have told them face to face.

'I rang Samantha,' said Melissa, evidently pleased with her resourcefulness.

'She was very noisy on the phone,' said Miguelina, 'so I knew it was good news. I knew you weren't at the dentist.'

Oh no! I didn't want to ruin their moment, but it was essential they kept everything completely watertight. Melissa was canny, but she could be so trusting and impulsive. If it had been Danielle who'd seen her whooping on the phone, my imminent freedom could have unravelled before I was even back in the building.

'We've got to keep it down,' I said, with more than a little sense of panic in my voice. 'You know what the others are like. This has to be absolutely secret. Not even the INPEs know. Really. I'm serious about this.'

'Don't worry, don't worry,' they said in unison. I had to hope that my guardian angel was looking out for me and nothing would go wrong. The stakes were as high as the risks. It was like holding a precious jewel that could be stolen from me at any moment. I wouldn't be able to relax until I was sitting in a restaurant with my family ordering drinks and a juicy steak.

*

It was only a few minutes before others dropped by the cell, asking how I got on at the dentist. I brushed it off.

'Oh, it was OK. I'm just looking forward to seeing my family tomorrow.'

I swiftly changed the subject to them because they were landing shortly and I could direct my energies to that. I no longer had a phone, but Samantha would be texting the good news to my mum. They'd know I was being released the second they picked up a signal after landing.

I wanted to project myself into the near future, one where I'd no longer have to go through this tortuous time on a knife edge, lying to guards and dangerous cellmates. I just wanted to leap into next week. The momentum to get out was driving me forward but I was still incarcerated. I was desperate to catch up with what my imagination was dangling in front of me.

The only thing I could do was wait – for access to the phones, to speak to my mum – and for my paperwork, which when handed over to the prison director and signed by her meant I was free. I'd already been told they needed twelve hours to prepare it, so I'd missed the deadline for tomorrow morning. But tomorrow was Wednesday – female visitors' day, and I was about to have the best reunion of my life.

The usual operations and squabbles of Ancón 2 went on around me as I pondered what to do with all the stuff I'd amassed over the past two years, such as books, and the clothing parcels my family had brought on visits. I'd give them away to those I thought needed them the most. The sweet Thai girl who I paid to be a cleaner didn't even have underwear. All my M&S specials were hers. I wanted to write letters to other prisoners whose stories had touched me, or who had shown me small kindnesses.

I managed to have some quiet conversations with Melissa, the person with whom I'd been through so much. She had applied for benefits some time ago, but my grant of release was obviously a massive boost for her. Her beaming smiles weren't due only to her sharing my joy – we'd been treated as the same case from Day 1, so she definitely had the whiff of freedom in her nostrils.

'If I get out as well, I'm going for the transfer, no question. I'm not staying one day longer than I have to in this lousy place,' she whispered.

A 'transfer' meant immediate expulsion to the UK. I was effectively on parole, the conditions meaning that I serve the rest of my sentence outside of prison but still in Peru. I had originally been told you had to remain in the country for two years, but serving my full sentence would mean that I wasn't eligible to leave the country until August 2020. But *unofficially* . . . well, I knew that every part of the legal system in Peru had its price. As sure as I got my benefits, I was equally confident that I would be home within a year.

'I'm wondering if I've done the right thing,' I said. 'But I don't mind living here for a while, on the outside. The weather is amazing, and there's beaches very near Lima.'

I genuinely wanted to spend time in the country. I'd learned

enough of the language not just to get by, but to work. I'd changed
– grown up a lot – and learned to be more resourceful. I started to
think about the opportunities there might be for me. I missed my
family terribly, but I was in no hurry to return to the hounding I'd
get from the media. Or the Dungannon weather.

Melissa's face was one of shock and disbelief.

'Fuck that! I wanna get home. I don't care if it's cold. It's Scotland.
I'm used to that. I'm done. Anyway, I don't have the relationships you
have, with all the priests and nuns and that.'

That got me thinking about Father Sean. We'd spoken just after
the judge had left. He had never expected the decision to go my way.
He had acted as guarantor for me but he was now faced with the
realisation that he had to give me a job – and an address.

'Michaella, I – I can't put you up at my place, you know that, don't
you? It's just not going to work,' he stuttered. I could see he was in
shock. He'd signed those papers as a huge favour, but he was now
worried he was going to have to make good on his official promise.
Although, who would be checking? As long as I signed my name at the
INPE office every couple of weeks, stayed out of trouble and told them
I was working, there was nothing to be gained by them following me.

'Don't worry, Father, it'll be fine. My family are renting an
apartment and we'll probably keep it on.' The look on his face was
sheer relief.

'I am going to line something up for you to do, though,' he said.
'It won't be a full-time job but it'll be something – a few hours every
week working on the church newsletter and marketing.'

'Really? OK, that's great, thanks.' It was a far cry from the party
world I'd known before, but it was time to change direction, to prove
I could adapt to a new life. There wasn't much trouble I could get
into working for a Catholic mission, after all.

I had to keep my voice down, as too much excitement would raise
suspicions but my fingers were shaking as I picked up the phone to
speak to my mum, knowing she would have landed by now and be at
the apartment waiting for my call. In complete contrast to the call I'd

made nearly two and a half years earlier, she answered. But this time she was in Peru herself. And the shock was a nice surprise.

'Thank God, Michaella! We can't believe it's true. It's amazing,' she wept.

'Oh Mum, I'm getting out, I'm getting out. I can't wait to see yous.'

'Now, love, look, the thing is . . . we're not coming there tomorrow. We can't. We just can't do that journey again.'

'Oh no!' I cried. 'I want to see yous as soon as possible!'

'We can't go through all that again, with the searches and those guards stealing stuff, and it's such a long way.'

'But you're here, in this country, and I want to be with yous,' I pleaded.

'But you're getting out the day after. Samantha said Thursday. We just can't, love. You'll see, the time will go really quickly.'

'I suppose so,' I said, deflated. I so wanted that reunion embrace, but I realised I was being selfish, wrapped up in my own triumph. I'd neglected to consider what they had to go through every time they visited. It was invasive and harrowing.

'It's fine . . .' I said. 'But you will come and meet me when I get out, won't you?' I asked cautiously. The thought of making my way down the road carrying my belongings alone was too tragic.

'Of course, of course! We want to see our girl without everyone looking at us, or going through those prison gates. We'll have a fine time, don't worry.'

*

'*Dónde están tu familia?*'

Where are your family? I was asked this more than twenty times the next day, when an absence of the McCollum family raised eyebrows among the old gang.

'They're coming later, later,' I said to each inquisitor, giving them white lies about upset tummies and late flights.

'Well, you look quite happy about it,' said Carmen, suspiciously.

'Oh, you know: *a mala hora, buena cara.*' I used a phrase that worked for a multitude of difficult situations. Literally 'bad hour, good face', the Spanish version of keeping a 'stiff upper lip' but with more smiles. I thought for a second how true it would be if the judge hadn't granted me my benefits; if Sean Walsh hadn't stood as my guarantor; if the court secretary hadn't done her feminist intervention in the psychologist's report. So many elements had aligned to make this very much my *good* hour. As if to 'cheer me up', Miguelina made a lovely lunch for me, Sharda and Melissa – which was in fact a goodbye meal for us all to share.

I stayed in my room the rest of the day, keeping quiet and allocating my stuff to various recipients. The last night, Melissa and I shared a bed like best pals, having a cuddle. We laughed and fantasised about all the things we wanted to do on the outside. We talked about me visiting Scotland, and staying in touch, but I knew in my heart of hearts that was unlikely, and that we'd go our separate ways.

It had been such a love–hate relationship, me and her, but doing prison time together bonds you in extremis. I wouldn't have wanted to go through everything I'd experienced without her. We'd learned towards the end of our time together not to let other people's problems affect our relationship. We even laughed about the horrendous things that had happened to us – me screaming at her on the bus in Cusco; us finding the guns in the house in Mallorca; the dramas with Caesar and Diogo. I lay awake, absorbing the whole situation, knowing it was the last night I was going to be there. And the last time I'd be sharing a room with Melissa.

*

On the morning of 31 March 2016, I got my hair done, so I'd look my best for when I met my family. I'd checked with the guard on my way into the salon, who told me she'd received the letter that morning to say I was leaving. One more sigh of relief – one more mountain climbed. The gates were opening for me at 11 a.m., supposedly, but in a Peruvian prison, time was a mutable thing.

After some serious grooming, I sat in my room, my small bag containing only the essentials at the ready, and the stuff I was giving to others being looked after by Melissa until I'd safely left. As eleven o'clock came and went, my stomach was doing somersaults. I was the only one being let out that day, so we weren't waiting for other prisoners.

I didn't have conversations with anyone; I couldn't fill my head with any irrelevancies. I'd never been more totally focused on one thing with this much energy since I was at the check-in desk at Jorge Chavez, with six kilograms of cocaine in my suitcase.

I kept asking the guard, 'Am I going? Am I going?' I was a nervous wreck.

Finally, it came: 'McCollum, McCollum, *vamos, vamos!*' The words rang out on our corridor. When everyone realised what was going on, there was an uproar. People really didn't know. My friends had kept my secret. An avalanche of women came to hug me and wish me all the best. Melissa was crying. I stood in front of her with my bag and my mattress ready to hand back in to the office.

'Oh my God, you're going to be all alone!' I said to her, before I had time to think that probably wasn't the best parting shot.

'It's fine. I'll be fine. I'll be right behind you,' she said through her tears. She was putting on a brave face, but I could see it was dawning on her that the separation was final. We'd been called 'The Peru Two' by the media, but we were now back to operating independently of each other. I felt awful leaving her, but she'd always seemed more casual about the whole situation than me. She took things in her stride, whereas I was relentless. It was only recently that she'd started to really push for her benefits. She too had been a good prisoner – had attended all her classes – so I hoped she too would be leaving very shortly.

In a flurry of tears and waving arms I was escorted out of *maxima* and down past the rotunda, through yet more corridors, and then into a holding office – where I sat for hours and hours, waiting for the prison director to sign my form. By 3:30 p.m. I was hysterical. I'd been there for three hours. I started to have serious doubts. Maybe it was all an elaborate hoax. I was thinking, how could I have fallen for this wind-up? Maybe I wasn't being released at all. The next time a guard entered the room, I launched myself at him, begging to know what was going on.

'I don't know,' he said casually, as if I'd asked him the time. 'The prison director is leaving now. Maybe you can't go today. Maybe tomorrow.'

His relaxed tone was making me apoplectic. Doing the walk of shame back to *maxima* would be worse than sleeping on the floor all night – and also leave me exposed, as everyone now knew I was being released. I was dry-mouthed with panic and being kept in a state of utter desperation until the very last moment by this system run on corruption and chaos.

'You must go to her. Now. Please. I need her to sign my form. Please!'

The guard stood there. And then, in a moment of automatic realisation, I realised the one thing that would make the difference. I reached into my bag and produced fifty soles. Right to the last, it was all about the money.

'Please. Please, my family are waiting for me outside. They've been waiting for me since eleven.'

Eventually he came back with it signed, and then handed it to an admin guy, who had to copy the document word for word – not by computer but on an old typewriter! I couldn't believe what I was seeing. And the frustrations kept on coming. The admin person had graduated from the one-finger typing school; the painful slowness with which he did everything would have been laughable if it wasn't my life that was affected.

I sat and watched as he scrutinised the document in the silent room, an overhead fan rotating above him, an index finger intermittently pressing a key. *Whirr, tap, whirr, tap, whirr, tap.* I was crying with frustration by this point.

I went and stood in front of him. 'Please, can I type this?' I offered.

'I'm a really good typist. I used to work in an office. Please! I need to go!'

He glanced at me with no emotion whatsoever registering on his face. Just gestured to me to sit back down. Until my final seconds in that building I was being shown that my needs, wishes and situation were of little importance. I may now have been on parole, but I was still in the system. The wheels would turn in their own sweet time. The main thing was, I was facing the right way; I wouldn't have to turn back and march towards the rotunda.

Finally, after agonisingly long minutes of the administrator re-reading what he had typed, the document was stapled and placed in an envelope. It was time. Now, at long last, I was being led towards the exit. I had no idea what part of the prison we were in, but we finally reached a huge electronic door.

'*Esta bien, ciao*,' said the guard. And he then gently pushed me through the door that opened onto a massive garden at the top of a long path sloping downwards to some gates. It was a side exit I hadn't been to before. I was free, but I was looking back for directions.

'Down there, keep going, keep going.'

The feeling of sunlight on my face was glorious, but I'd enjoy it only when I could see my family. Thankfully, there was no media running towards me. There was nothing and no one. I walked down the hill for about ten minutes and then, finally, I saw Mum and Glenn waving at me. This was it! I ran the rest of the way, my blow-dried hair swishing behind me. I felt like a creature that had been released from its cage.

We hugged for about twenty minutes. My mum was touching my hair, looking at me, then pulling me into her warmth and absorbing my presence, as I was absorbing hers. She hadn't seen me since I'd become blonde, and she kept stroking my hair, staring at me, saying how beautiful I looked. The tears were flowing hot and fast.

Glenn was standing there, looking tall and reassuring.

'Is it just yous?' I asked. 'Where's Stephanie?'

'She's at the apartment. She didn't want to risk coming here in case there was a load of press about. Now, let's get in this taxi,' said

Glenn. 'We've had to pay him twenty soles an hour for every hour we've been waiting.'

'Oh no!' I said. 'I'm so sorry,' and I proceeded to tell them about the painful delays I'd endured.

'Nothing surprises me in this country,' said Glenn. 'But we've got a nice apartment ready for you.'

'Let's go to a restaurant!' I cried out. It was the simplest thing that I'd completely taken for granted until I'd been locked up, but now, it seemed like the ultimate luxury.

We bundled into the taxi and headed into Lima. The apartment was in a really tall building on a long main road that was busy with cars and shops and noise. Oh my God, the noise! I hadn't heard or seen moving cars in over two years, and the colours and clamour of people going about their lives was almost deafening. I held my hands over my ears and laughed hysterically.

We found a restaurant with a barbecue grill, where Stephanie joined us, and of course there were more reunion hugs. I was beaming with my new sense of freedom. I just kept saying 'Oh my God, oh my God,' as I scanned the delicious things on offer – from steaks to freshly grilled fish caught that day to all manner of cakes and desserts. To sit down and order from a menu was the best thing ever.

'They've even got Dauphinoise potatoes!' I exclaimed.

I couldn't decide what I wanted, so I ordered pretty much everything on the menu. I'd never eat it all, but it was my celebration and I wanted a blow-out this once in style. I'd been eating packet noodles and microwave meals for nearly three years. The staff couldn't believe the fluent Spanish that was coming out of the mouth of this obviously Northern European girl. I told them I'd been studying it for many years. It was a line I'd repeat often over the coming months.

We ordered cava and the bubbles went straight to my head. I felt giddy and alive again. I'd been contained in this tiny world where my life was at a standstill and discontent permeated everything. Now the world felt wide and glorious.

When we got back to the apartment, on the twelfth floor, we

were all exhausted but we FaceTimed the folks back home – many of whom were shocked to see me with blonde hair. At first they couldn't believe it was me. They must've thought I'd gone crazy, as I was saying how amazing it was to be somewhere that had things like doors, and cups. The emotion and high tension of the day had wiped me out. But my mum had an unusual request.

'Michaella, will you share my bed tonight, sweetheart? I just want to hold my baby girl.'

'Oh, poor Mum, I'm really sorry, but I just can't do anything but be alone tonight. I haven't slept alone in nearly three years. I need total quiet. You know, no snoring!'

She laughed and I hugged her, and although she was disappointed, she understood my needs. She'd thought I wouldn't want to sleep alone. As I closed the door to my bedroom, then slid under the clean duvet, on a cockroach-free bed, I vowed never again to take life's simple everyday pleasures for granted.

*

I awoke just before six, as usual, for roll call, and then savoured the wonderful feeling of lying in a real bed, realising I'd never again have to stand in a line at daybreak and answer my name in a maximum-security jail. I wondered how Melissa was getting on, and how long it would be before she too could reclaim her life. I'd promised to visit her as soon as I'd settled.

Later, when I got up to make coffee, Stephanie was waiting to speak to me in the sitting room. What she had to tell me set the subject of discussion for the rest of the week.

'Michaella, you know the media are going to be wanting to talk to you, don't you?'

'I know, but I'm not talking to any of them. I just want to keep my head down.'

'Well, the thing is, you know I've got a friend who's a producer at RTÉ . . .'

I knew what was coming.

'Yes, but—'

'They want to do an exclusive with you.' There it was.

'Well, they'll be waiting a long time. I'm supposed to stay in Peru until 2020.'

'No. They're already here. In Peru. They've flown out specially. They want the first televised interview.'

It was worse than I thought. 'You're kidding me? No way! I'm not doing that!' Give me their number and I'll tell them myself.'

'I told them they could talk to you today,' Stephanie admitted.

'*You did what*? Why? I just want to relax and get my life back together. I don't want to speak to TV people. Why have you done this?'

'It's for the best, Michaella. You'll be able to tell your story properly, and apologise. Then they'll leave you alone.'

'You must've set this up before I was even released. I'm not happy about it. I'm not ready. I'm not talking to anyone. Not today, not tomorrow, or the next day.'

I shut myself in my room. I was distraught. It was not what I'd envisaged for my first days of freedom. Mum wasn't keen on the attention either. I was really pissed off that my sister had done this without running it by me first. Since this whole saga had begun, our family had stayed away from the press. We'd kept things low-key. We knew the media couldn't be trusted. And even if they did let me speak and tell my side of the story, social media had exploded in the couple of years since I'd been in jail. My story was going to prompt all sorts of comments, and allow intrusive, and possibly abusive, people to start wading in. I'd seen enough from the 'throw away the key' brigade who liked to sound off anonymously on news websites.

But independently of Stephanie's encouragement, word was already on the street. Someone had leaked the news that I'd been released, and the UK and Irish media were already reporting it. Although I said no to interviews for the next twenty-four hours, RTÉ stayed put, and, to my horror, other reporters had discovered the location of our apartment block.

The following night, we were all really hungry and risked leaving the block to go to a restaurant. The second we set foot on the street we were chased down the road by three journalists from an Irish newspaper. Mum, with her arthritis, was running with us, as we hailed a taxi to get us away.

And then, in echoes of my thwarted escape from Michael years earlier, the cabbie didn't drive on. Just kept saying he didn't want any trouble, as the three persistent guys were shouting my name, trying to film us and banging on the car. It was awful, and extremely stressful. It was only my half-decent Spanish that persuaded the driver to put his foot down.

For the rest of the evening, Stephanie kept on and on until I eventually relented and agreed to speak to RTÉ. I wasn't happy about it at all – but at least I had time to compose myself and get some new clothes. On 3 April they sent a car for me and brought me to a big house converted into a TV studio. The interview was quite long and not something I enjoyed. But the interviewer was respectful, and it was done. Apparently, half a million viewers tuned in.

The next day, I was looking forward to meeting up with Andrea for the first time on the outside. We arranged to meet at a Starbucks in the commercial part of town. I went along with my mum and we were seated on one of the sofas opposite a guy on his phone, who kept looking at me. Andrea turned up with her adorable little daughter, Ilana, who was now seven months old.

We hadn't even finished our coffees when a media scrum broke out. It turned out that the guy opposite had been taking pictures of me and mum on his phone, and must have tipped off his media contacts. Suddenly, the press were outside causing a fuss, and the guy with the phone was part of it. I just wanted to leave – but how? Andrea had arrived by car, and had her own driver, so we ran the gauntlet yet again, this time with a baby, but we were followed. All at once, we were in this really crazy car chase with Peruvian journalists and photographers desperate to get photos by any reckless means. They were driving really dangerously, forcing us to go faster and faster, even though they knew we had an infant in the car. We eventually lost them, but we were all really shaken by it. Andrea said she was going to press charges.

I still couldn't understand why I was such a big issue. Of the many hundreds of people arrested in South America each year, why was I being singled out for this ridiculous level of attention? Andrea explained with one word: money. Pictures of me were selling to the press for top dollar. Not many news stories from Peru are interesting to British and Irish newspapers, so they were going after everything they could. It was feeding time for them.

*

My family left after another few days. Although at first it was strange being by myself in the apartment, I started to relax properly for the first time in ages – years, in fact. I told myself this was my new home for a while – at least for six months. Although Lima was beautiful in parts, I had no intention of staying for another four years. I was still in touch with my lawyer, Alberto, and, once I got settled, I'd apply for expulsion. For now, I was bound by my terms and conditions, which was like having a part-time job in itself.

I had to go to offices, sign documents, have therapy, and report on jobs I was applying for. I saw Andrea and baby Ilana quite a lot at the apartment she shared with her husband, the TV news presenter. We made food together and did girly things.

They tried to help get me work, but as a foreigner I needed to show a passport, and mine had been seized by the authorities when I was arrested. It was one of the terms of my release that I worked, yet I couldn't get a work permit because I was on parole. It was a classic catch-22.

The only thing available to me through a friend of Andrea was restaurant work. I went to an interview, but the wages were so low that my earnings for a ten-hour shift wouldn't have covered much more than my transport costs to get there and a few cups of coffee.

I did the design and marketing work for Father Sean's church magazine, all the while liaising with Irish, American and Peruvian missionaries, although it didn't pay much more than expenses. Sean was very caring and fatherly, but rather stricter than I was used to, and very observant of his faith. He was a bishop, after all! He was keen to engage me in closer work with the church and asked me to attend mass. I felt like he was steering me to become this model Catholic girl, which really wasn't me.

Working for him gave me some structure I wouldn't have had otherwise, though, and offered some unusual opportunities. He set me up to teach English a few hours a week to local priests – men in their fifties and sixties who'd had families but had come to their faith later in life. I really enjoyed the teaching, and was also able to improve my Spanish at the same time. My surroundings and clients couldn't have been more different from my previous employment in Ibiza!

Since being incarcerated, I was determined to turn my life around and make my future a success. I left prison a very different person to the one who'd gone in. For some women, however, the circumstances of their lives meant their release exposed them to a cycle of criminality all over again. The vast majority of people convicted for drug offences in Peru have no access to legitimate ways of earning once they've served their sentences. As soon as they get out, they are targets once more for the manipulative and dangerous characters who populate the criminal economies. And some women simply prefer the excitement of being with bad boys – the richer the better. I was determined to stay away from them!

CHAPTER THIRTY

THE RED LIGHT

One exception to the women who attracted troublesome men was Jackie, the Asian girl who had passed on her salon operation to me in Ancón. We met up and continued our friendship. Since getting out, she had established herself in the beauty business, and was now managing a high-end beauty salon in Lima. She wanted to use me as a model for eyelash extensions, which was fine by me! I loved spending time there.

Jackie wasn't the only ex-inmate I saw on the outside. There was another girl I'd got to know in *maxima*, called Steffi. Now, me and Steffi had a fair bit in common. She was in her early twenties, into fashion and fitness and having fun. We started meeting up and going to a gym together near to where she was living. I got the bug for exercise. Steffi was slim when I first met her, but since leaving prison she'd lost a lot of weight and was now a size 4. She had a load of nice clothes she could no longer wear, which at size 8 were perfect for me.

I also met up with Kaouthar, who had been released from Ancón a couple of months before me. We'd go to the gym in the morning, and at night we'd go out on the town. Lima has tons of great restaurants, and we liked eating out, enjoying ourselves and drinking cocktails, which in Peru are really cheap – and delicious! The locals would stroll around chatting until the early hours, but you would never see the brawling drunken behaviour familiar to British high streets at that time of night. We had some good times.

The weeks passed. One day I was at the gym with Steffi, worrying about money, when she suggested I move in with her, rent free. I jumped at the opportunity. The twelfth-floor apartment I'd been in since leaving Ancón was being paid for by my family. I wasn't earning enough to stump up for it myself, and it would help them out massively if I could take that burden off them.

'Are you sure I won't be in the way?' I asked.

'Not at all.'

Father Sean wasn't keen on me moving in with an ex-prisoner. He advised me not to go out after dark, to stay away from nightclubs, and questioned me about Steffi. It wasn't just her he was concerned about; it was her friends, he said – not that he knew them. He was terrified of me getting sucked back in with the wrong crowd. However, he was due back in America to see his family for a couple of months, and his protective eye was soon taken off me.

He wasn't the only church person I associated with. I continued to see the lovely nun, Maureen. Maureen is an exceptional individual. She lives in the most densely populated part of Lima – San Juan de Lurigancho – which is really poor and pretty dangerous. The first time I went to visit her, my mind was blown. You would describe it as a shanty town. Dirty, industrial and crime-ridden, it was horrendous – certainly a place the tourists don't visit.

Maureen warned me never to get my phone out on the street, or show I had any money. She expected me to get the bus, like she did. But there was no way that was going to happen. People crowded into vehicles designed for far fewer passengers, and drivers were rarely able to close the doors. I had to be realistic – a sixty-something nun was less of a target than I would be, pressed up against all sorts of random people. I chose to get a taxi every time I visited. And I'd always stay at Maureen's, so I was travelling in daytime.

She took me to her church and we talked. I asked her why she lived there, when she could have been somewhere nicer. A lot of her fellow nuns lived in more pleasant places.

'I'm not better than these people,' she answered. 'I want to be among them. And to understand them, I need to live like them.' Her selflessness and love showed the very best of the church. She had been doing this for nearly forty years. She took me to a shack where a family lived with just sand on the floor. The kids were mesmerised by my clothes. They didn't even have shoes.

I thought back to when I'd first arrived in Lima and seen people just like them, wearing rags engrained with dirt. I'd been shocked, and had fled whenever people like this approached me. And now here I was standing in their home, playing with their children. Every day I was being humbled by the circumstances people endured, and I was grateful for the experience to witness the lives of others.

The next time I went there, I took some clothes and other bits and pieces for the family I'd met. I'd bought some sweet little ballerina shoes for the girl. Maureen wasn't keen on me taking them gifts, saying they'd just sell them. I wanted to take that risk – and I was overjoyed to see the little girl still wearing the shoes when I visited a couple of months later.

Someone else I visited was Melissa. Yes, I actually returned to Ancón 2 to see her, because I'd promised I'd do that. It took hours to get in and was an awful experience. I knew my family had been subjected to invasive searches and kept waiting ages to see me, but I hadn't realised quite how bad things were for visitors. For the first time, it really sank in what my family had had to endure. No wonder they didn't want to come the day before I got out!

Of course, it was strange going back. My mind started playing tricks on me – as if they might change their minds about my release, and a guard would handcuff me and take me back to my old cell. After all, if I hadn't been able to negotiate the whole issue of benefits – which I'd discovered by pure chance while translating for the psychologist – I could still be there.

Melissa's application was going well and she reckoned she'd be getting her expulsion approved within weeks. I told her about the crazy press chases and the work I was doing with Father Sean. She thought I was mad spending time in Peru – something we'd never have dreamed of in 2013. She was counting the days until she could return to Scotland.

Living with Steffi was okay – I had my own room and loads of space – but I was spending more time with Andrea – who had been so amazingly helpful. Her life was more grounded and 'normal' than anyone else I knew in the country. She introduced me to her neighbour, a lovely guy called John. We got on really well. He had a motorbike, and we'd roar up and down the highway, visiting the beautiful coastal places I wouldn't have seen otherwise.

John and Andrea had some discussions, and when I was visiting one day, they offered me a temporary room at John's place. I couldn't believe my luck.

After being out of prison for three months, it felt like the time was right to begin getting my paperwork sorted for leaving Peru. My family had successfully sued a tabloid newspaper back home for publishing some of my private photos. With the modest four-figure sum I got from that, I was able to engage Alberto once more to speed up the process. Although I went to the gym with Steffi, and also met up socially with Kaouthar, I was putting all my energies into getting back to Ireland and thinking about my education. Father Sean would be proud.

Melissa had been granted her expulsion order in June, and had already left the country. Her exit was more of a clean break than mine, but, as she said herself, she didn't have links to the network of Catholic missionaries based in Lima that I did, and she had no desire to see the city.

I started to socialise more with John and his friends, experiencing everyday life in Lima. My time at his place coincided with his birthday, and on that night we celebrated with his friends at a fantastic salsa club with an almost 100 per cent Peruvian clientele.

The music was brilliant, the vibes were good, and the atmosphere and energy were so infectious that it was impossible to feel anything but happy. Obviously I stood out from the locals, but I was made very welcome.

After a couple of weeks of bureaucratic back and forth with the immigration department, and many soles handed over to speed things up, it was time for me to go to the court for an interview with an official. I was very relieved to find out the meeting wasn't going to be back at the awful penal court where I'd been granted my benefits. It was at a lavish, colonial-era building that looked like a palace. Andrea kept telling me not to get my hopes up as we approached this imposing building together.

The meeting was brief. The presiding judge was the same woman who'd granted me my benefits! She asked me my reasons for wanting to go back to the UK, and I once more talked about my family. I told her how difficult it was for me to get work in Lima, and I was emphatic in telling her I'd learned my lesson and would never commit another crime again.

For such an important decision, it was made very quickly. And it went in my favour. Yes, I could return to Ireland. But I'd need to apply to the Irish Embassy to get the document that would allow me to leave the country, as I had no passport. Thankfully, they now had an office in Peru again. This would only be issued the day before I left, so getting the timings lined up with buying a flight home was yet another logistical challenge. Alberto was on hand to liaise with the embassy, but I was reliant once more on my family to pay for my flight, which ended up being really expensive, as my mum refused to buy it online, going to an old-fashioned travel agent instead! It would fly me into London first, then I'd have a four-hour wait for my connection to Dublin.

This was it. I was on my way home. I had amassed a lot of stuff: three years' worth of letters from my family and loads of mementos from prison, plus clothes that I didn't want to leave behind. I made a final visit to Maureen, and we promised we'd stay in touch – and I meant it. Her kindness had given me so much support when I was at my lowest point. She was a true angel.

I didn't tell John I was leaving until the very last minute, as I knew he'd be devastated. We had become really close friends. No one thought I was going to leave so soon. On my last day I went to Jackie's salon and her boss did some photos of me for their windows. Andrea made food and we had a lovely evening. She even helped me pack.

When the day of departure arrived, 12 August 2016, Jackie and Alberto came with me to the airport. It was fantastic to have their support, but it was Alberto's presence that helped to avert a potentially devastating hitch at the very last moment. As I was clearing security, walking alongside the two-way mirrored sections that you see at customs, an official stepped out and I was pulled into a room.

'Miss McCollum,' he said. 'You can't leave. A red light has come up.'

I couldn't believe it.

'What red light? Show me this red light!' I demanded.

'We don't have to show you the red light,' said the official. 'But you can't leave.'

'My departure gate is open. If I miss my flight, you'll have to reimburse me,' I said.

'That's not our problem,' they replied. I couldn't believe there was an issue at this late stage. My papers were all in order. Alberto had checked them. My bags had been scanned.

'Well, if there has been a red light, there's obviously something wrong with my paperwork,' I said. 'Let me call my lawyer. He is in the airport right now.'

They certainly hadn't expected me to say that. I took a long cool look at the situation – just like on my final morning in Ancón, officialdom was taking its own sweet time with my future in the balance. But this wasn't about being slow. I had 200 soles in my purse that I know they'd seen, as they'd searched my handbag when I came in. They were conferring with each other on the sly as I sat there.

They came back over to me with cheesy grins.

'There's no need for your lawyer,' they said finally. 'Perhaps if you pay us something, just to get some food, we'll let you go.'

Their bare-faced cheek was astonishing, but I was determined to stand my ground. Right to the last, those in uniform were on the make.

'I'm not paying you to get food!' I said. Then I resorted to some tactics of my own. 'Fine, keep me here, then. I don't even want to go. I'm only going because a judge has ordered my extradition.' I sat back in my chair and got my phone out. 'I'm calling my lawyer now . . .'

That did it. My ploy worked and they let me go. They hadn't banked on me having a lawyer, let alone one on call in the same building where they were trying to shake me down. Fuck them and their so-called red light! I was out of there. And out of Peru.

CHAPTER THIRTY-ONE

YOU ARE THAT GIRL

Aside from the corruption, and what had happened to me there, I never disliked Peru. The people were lovely and seemed to really appreciate the things that we take so much for granted in richer countries. I would have liked to stay longer, but I was focused on pursuing my education. I was still young. I wanted to take A Levels and possibly do a degree. And in order to make that happen, I had to return home. I also needed to earn money.

As my plane took off, I was a riot of emotions. I was happy to be getting some stability back in my life, yet I was sad to be leaving the energy of Peru. But the overwhelming feeling was one of freedom. I'd done it – I'd fought for my benefits, I'd worked hard, I'd navigated the legal system of a country I'd never even thought of three years earlier, and no one on God's earth was able to take me back to jail.

Maybe it was naive of me to have the notion that I could enter the UK without any fuss. When we landed in London, everything was fine. There were no journalists running after me as I changed flights. But there was a four-hour wait for my flight to Dublin. The phone I'd been using didn't work in the UK, although I'd been able to tell my mum I was boarding the plane in Lima, and I told her my arrival time.

By the time I got to Dublin, I was exhausted and full of trepidation, but my London arrival had gone okay, so I figured that maybe the tabloid press was tired of hounding me. I was wrong. As I emerged into Arrivals at Dublin airport, and turned the corner from customs, about twenty reporters were lined up waiting. I couldn't turn back. I was so angry. Microphones, news cameras and cellphones were immediately shoved in my face. I just kept walking, but I didn't even know where I was going. I couldn't see my family and I started to feel really anxious.

When I ran out of the airport and found myself outside, they surrounded me, firing questions at me. It was horrible, but I'd been through worse in Peru. I stayed completely silent, fled back inside, and ended up diving into the ladies' loos.

I was thinking, what the hell am I going to do? And where were my family? I needed to find a phone. A woman came into the loos with her toddler, and I approached her. When you don't have access to basic things like a phone, and you're in a tight spot, you feel so awful begging from a stranger, but I had no choice. The woman agreed before she'd even looked at me properly, as all her attention was on her small son.

'Oh, are you that girl?' she asked the second she saw my face. 'The girl from Peru? You *are* that girl, aren't you?'

I was shocked she recognised me. Trying to ignore her questions about my identity, I called my mum in a panic. There'd been some kind of a mix-up and they'd got the arrival time wrong. I was ranting. I hated that moment – and the fact that the very first person I spoke to in my home country knew who I was, and my story. Mum said she would be there in five minutes. She turned up with my niece, we ran the gauntlet of the media, and were soon on our way back home at around 10 p.m.

When we reached my mum's place, the first thing I saw was a crowd of reporters waiting outside the house. One of my brothers was there and he immediately put a jacket over my head and ushered me inside. A lot of the family were there, not only for my homecoming, but also because the next day was the christening of my sister Samantha's baby, who had been born six months earlier. She had wanted to hold off the christening until I was back home. And now I was, I was going to be a godmother. We had an emotional reunion that night – and then a party in the McCollum family home.

The next day, Samantha was freaking out because the reporters were still outside our house, and we had to leave to attend the christening. Of course, she didn't want to risk them snapping away and her baby's picture being in the newspapers and online. That's not how it should be when your family are marking a private occasion. The invasion of privacy is immense in these situations, and seemed totally out of proportion for a mistake I'd made three years ago in a country on the other side of the planet.

The situation was tense and stressful. I had to hide from them, wearing a hoodie and scuttling about. In the end, my brother-in-law did a massive detour in his car to lose them, and we got to the church and had a beautiful day, rounding off with a party and a barbecue back at Samantha's place, without further invasion of our privacy. But only because of my brother-in-law's driving skills.

*

Things calmed down enough for me to enrol on an access course in psychology and sociology at a college in Belfast, which would enable me to get into uni. I'd timed my return just right for the autumn intake. I was feeling positive about returning to learning; I hadn't foreseen there'd be problems at the first hurdle. In applying for higher education, you are asked on your application form if you have a criminal record. I took advice on this from a lawyer – and he reckoned that because my crime was committed in Peru, and not Northern Ireland, then I didn't have to declare it. It was out of their jurisdiction.

I ticked the box saying 'no', but of course my name reverberated around their offices like a wall of sound, and they were on the phone without delay, telling me I had to declare it. This started a whole other bunch of bureaucracy, which meant I started the term quite late – towards the end of October, a month after everyone else. Which of course marked me out as different.

I felt like I was branded 'trouble' before I'd even taken a seat in the classroom. Everyone stared at me on my first day and continued muttering through that term. I knew what the topic of their whispers was – *it's that girl*. I got really paranoid and felt quite isolated. I started to get really fanatical about the gym, going every morning and evening. What I looked like was the only thing I felt I had any control over. I was super-fit, but I stopped wanting to go out.

My old friends, unsurprisingly, couldn't relate to what I'd been through, and although we were the same ages, they seemed so naive about the world. They hadn't seen the kind of things I'd seen in the past three years. They'd not had to beg for water, or go to the toilet in front of all their housemates, or been groped by rapists and murderers. I started to lose patience with their carping over stupid things. They didn't know how lucky they were. At the same time, my incarceration in Peru was like a taboo subject in the family home. Their attitude to what I'd done was: 'We're not going to talk about that.' So they didn't.

But I was still reliving it every day. I was edgy and couldn't relax.

Every week there was something new in the press, which really got me down – not even about specific things, just wild speculation. In shops and bars, everyone knew who I was. It felt like there was no hiding place. I put my head down and tried to focus on work. I landed quite a few jobs outside of college hours, but when they found out who I was they dropped me like a hot potato. I found work with upmarket brands at Christmas, like Hermès and Dior, but I would last two shifts and the second they found out I was *that girl*, I was told I was being let go. I was knocked back everywhere I turned. The media portrayal of me was totally unforgiving – and wrong. I just knew there would never be this kind of scrutiny if a guy had made the same mistake as I did. But maybe that's because the guys are the ones controlling it all. There was no hiding place for a young girl who had been a 'drug mule'; she had to be painted as a social pariah over and over. It was brutal.

Because of what I'd done, my family were in debt. I was desperate for a way to pay them back. I'd been trying so hard to get a job but it just wasn't possible. I'd always worked, even when I was a young teenager, so it was incredibly demoralising to suddenly find myself 'unemployable'. Even a door-to-door selling job came with unexpected scrutiny. They thought I was presentable enough, but at the interview the guy got all serious and leant across the table to ask me, 'You are finished with drugs, aren't you? We have to be sure you're not involved in that any more.'

I couldn't believe it. Did they think I was going to try and push some coke on the side, along with the cosmetics they wanted me to cart around door to door? I said firmly, 'No', but I wanted to say, 'Do you think I'd be coming to you for a £7.50 an hour job if I was dealing drugs? In the end, it was the online economy that came good for me. I did a quick online marketing course and finally found work marketing and advertising for all sorts of companies without the risk that – *shock horror* – someone might recognise me and complain.

*

Come February 2017, there was still stuff about me in the press every two or three weeks. My image was out there so often that a media management company approached me looking to take me on as a client.

The offer was put forward that I write a book to tell my side of the story. This would never have occurred to me, but I was excited by the idea. Every time I tried to get back into mainstream working society, I'd been thwarted. So why not tell my story? I agreed to this just before I finished my first year at college.

I started going back and forth to London that summer of 2017, visiting family, going out and having meetings about the book. I had a lovely summer. I was feeling free for the first time in ages. And then, just as I'd started back at college for my second year, I found out I was pregnant. They say life is what happens to you when you're making other plans, but this was totally unexpected. While I was in London I'd met someone. We'd been seeing each other for a couple of months, but we'd hardly got to know each other before my body was letting me know something was changing. Not only was I pregnant – I was having twins! For nine months there'd be three hearts in one body! My life would be changed for ever.

I'd always expected that I'd have everything perfectly in place in my life before I had kids. I'd be married, or at least madly in love, and have a lovely house and a career. But life isn't like that, is it? I found it hard to open up about something so private. I told my sisters, but not my brothers, until five months later when my pregnancy could no longer be concealed!

I chose not to stay in London. I reasoned I'd be quite isolated. I wanted to be near my mum, who'd had ten children and would be the safest pair of helpful hands I could hope for. London was insanely expensive, too, and I wanted to be on familiar ground. Of course, the media caught on to the fact I was pregnant, although no one knew I was having twins, or boys, except those very closest to me.

I was due to give birth in May 2018, when I was supposed to be taking my exams. I had thought about going on to study law at university, but when I found out I was going to be a mother of twins, I knew that would be impossible. But I also had the option of studying an international business degree in Spanish, which seemed more doable, although I'd need A Level Spanish before I started that.

My labour was planned, but my babies really didn't want to come out on their due date. In the end, I had to be induced and have an epidural, which made me sick. I hadn't known what to expect – does anybody? – but Mum was with me in the room, although she was very stressed, which was making things even worse. There were six or seven other family members outside. It was horrible, very painful, of course, but very emotional.

My beautiful boys came into the world at 22:58 and 23:02 on 8 May 2018. If I'd had an ideal picture in my mind of what my two babies would look like, they exceeded it a hundred times. They were so perfect, and so pretty. You think you know what love is, and then you give birth and that surpasses everything you've ever felt before. They would be my treasures always.

I breastfed them right away. I was feeding one while the other was crying in his crib and I didn't know what to do. Then I was crying because I was so overwhelmed that these little people were mine and would need me for years to come. This feeling stayed with me for months. The whole phenomenon of having created them was mind-blowing.

When it came to choosing their names, the Spanish influence was right there. I'd always loved Rafael Nadal, the tennis player, and his name – *Rafael* – it was so romantic! And then I heard Rio, and I really loved that name too. I thought how well they went together, and I knew before they were born these would be their names – although I'd spell Raphael with the classical 'ph'.

Wrapped up in my whole new world, with my baby brain, six weeks after giving birth, I had to sit my second-year exams. They'd let me delay them until July. I'd prepped for them before, but after giving birth I'd forgotten almost everything. I had to take my mum with me to Belfast to sit outside and look after the boys while I was inside, writing about psychology and sociology. It was crazy! I had to keep coming out of the exam room to feed them. Failure was not an option, though. If I flunked it, I'd have been stuffed. I had to pass, to get myself onto the business course, but my concentration levels were shot.

Once again, my guardian angel was looking out for me. I passed both psychology and sociology. And a year later, I've also passed my Spanish A Level.

I'm now weighing up my options. My beautiful boys get livelier and more inquisitive every day. I feel excited about our futures together. Ultimately, I'd love to live abroad – and bring up my boys abroad – away from all the nonsense that still blights people's lives over here in Northern Ireland. I love Spain and Spanish culture so much, and I now prefer speaking Spanish to speaking English. The Spanish lifestyle seems much more relaxed and generous. Things like family and eating together is still important to people. The streets are generally much safer; you don't see the brawling and stabbing that's become commonplace in the UK, and people seem happier in their skins. Maybe it's the sun – which I also pine for! When I was in Peru, I'd dream of a rainy day, then when I came back to Ireland, I was like, 'Where's the sun?' South American heat was extreme but Spain might just be perfect.

I want my boys to grow up somewhere that's not politically divided. I get the feeling those old aggressions I witnessed in my childhood are never going to die down. Sometimes I think I want to move to a deserted island where there can be no trouble. I want Raphael and Rio to grow up somewhere without bitterness, where schools aren't segregated along religious lines. I'm prepping for that now, hoping to do my degree in time for the kids to start school. I'm getting them used to hearing Spanish already – when they watch cartoons I make sure they're in the language. I visit the country quite a lot and I'm hoping I'll be able to practise business there.

When I think of all I've been through, even though it was the worst possible thing at the time, it was the making of me. I'm so happy with what I've achieved from where I was five years ago, and that I learned the language to a level that enabled me to negotiate the Peruvian legal system.

I was so lucky with the Irish network out there. With the exception of a couple of sneaky journalists, all my fellow countrymen and -women I met while I was in jail were absolutely marvellous. Their intentions were so good and the work they do with their charity missions is amazing. People like Father Sean Walsh and Father Maurice Foley, who sadly died a couple of months after I returned home, went out of their way to help me. I'm still in touch with Maureen, my lovely nun. She's even been over to Dungannon to stay with us. I'll never forget the day she turned up with those freshly baked buns for me and Melissa when we were desperate for good food.

I'm so grateful for the way things have turned out and I really, really believe everything happens for a reason. If I hadn't agreed to do this book, I wouldn't have been in London; if I hadn't been in London I wouldn't have met my baby's father and had these two amazing, loveable, crazy boys. Everything is exactly as it should be.

Hey Mummy, I got your letter yesterday. Today is Sunday 15th September. Again visting day for women only. I Feel good 2day I think its because I prayed to my Angels last night + today and did Some positive thinking. Im So happy that atm our letters are getting trasfered by email it makes the process So much quicker, it would take months if we did this by post. I was so happy yesterday To recieve your letters plus getting photos. Mel + the other prisioners could See a change in my brood. its crazy how Some letters from family can make me So happy! Iv alread reread the letters atleast 10 time Since I recieved them! I noticed you were wearing the ring I bought you at the wedding that made me Smile :- I clearly remember the phonecall it was about 4/5pm peru time. I was like mummy its me its Michaella, your respones was "oh Michaella" I could hear your voice break and you started to cry :- and So did I offcoase you started telling everyone its Michaella and I was trying to tell you what happend but you were Just so happy to know I was safe and alive. That Phone-call was the hardest thing iv every had to do. iv replayed that conversating over my head 100 hundreds of times. it will stay with me forever! I have confinced myself now that im getting the 6.8 sentance and will be out 2½ years. I know thats Still a long time but we can deal with that. And its the best outcome of the Situation. Astrid sayed in her letter "God wont give you more than you can handle" So I totally believe that and Im glad She said that. Cant believe Sami + Aaron didnt go on there holiday :- they should of could maybe been a break for them. I will Stay strong ill pray to my Angel's everyday they will get us threw this. I know you would be here if you didn't have David. Im Surprized you didn't say "if I didn't have my baby boy (baily)" haha please sleep in your bed. it will not be good for your back and I don't want you to have sleepless nights. I know that will be hard with me here. Im So lucky to have such a supporting femily and too have you mummy you have done such a good job raising us all on your own. And I never had or even Now wish I had a true dad in my life you have been everything I ever needed and more and its just made me love you even more and think you are with out a doubt on amazing women. Im so proud I have you ~~as that one mummy~~ I just miss you alot Mum. I miss when I went home and you always always met me at the door or gate with usually bailey in your arms. I miss your stories even when they were about the 2 animals, I miss coming into your room at night and making bailey jealous by hugging & kissing you, I miss sitting on your knee, I miss cuddeling + kissing you. I miss ~~the~~ your smell, I miss seeing you smile. I just miss everything about ~~it~~ U. I miss you mummy so bloody much You mean absalutly everything to me. Your the first person iv ever loved ~~and~~ Sounds stupid but its true. Its when I think of you my hearts sore. ~~Its~~ Im heartbroken :- And whats effecting me most in here, is not all the obvious stuff but the pain its causing you and everyone. Do you remember the time me Sami + you were on the bus to Belfast I handed you a piece of you ~~for~~ chocolate. whole nut. You asked were I got it and I sayed on the side of the seat, Your face! Haha I weirdly thought of that this morning. I didnt really find it there btw I remember when I was ~~young~~ young and I use to be so jelious of Danielle "in the eyes of a 7 year old trying to steal her mummy" But I feel im stronger now than befor and coping with things better. So dont worry about me im OK! Everything happen's for a reason. And God wanted me to experiance this maybe im going to face things latter in life and he wanted me to be super strong. I don't know but there is a method ~~instead~~ to everymadness. this all happend to us all for a reason. I hope ryan's baby takes your mind of this. Send my love to uncel Genie. tell him Im thinking about him alot, he was the closest thing I had to a important male ~~add~~ in my life. I hope he is doing ok'. ~~I Remember~~ marry o' the bitch never use to let me suck a dummy, he use to put iN his shirt pocket and give it to me when she wasn't looking! Aww! I love + miss you loads Num

Love from your baby girl
Kayla

ACKNOWLEDGEMENTS

I never really thought the day would come that I would be sat here writing this. None of this would have been possible without an incredible team of people who believed in me and believed in my story. My agent Kay, for coming into my life and presenting me with such an amazing opportunity, and for being there through all the hard work and ups and downs. This book really wouldn't be possible without you. I'm forever grateful, thank you.

My amazing publishing team at John Blake – my editor Ciara Lloyd, the incredible Kerri Sharp and my publicist Lizzie Dorney-Kingdom – Jeff Hudson and my literary agent, David Riding. Again, it wouldn't be possible without you all. Thank you for taking this chance on me, believing in me and allowing me to have this opportunity.

I have no idea where to start by thanking the most important person, my mother. Without her, I wouldn't be here to write this book. You were my strength throughout my whole prison sentence, you were my light at the end of the tunnel. You are such an incredible, strong woman and I'm so grateful to have you in my life. Your unconditional love is what saved me in my darkest times. I know I have said this many times but, from the bottom of my heart, I'm sorry for causing you all this pain. Thank you for always being there.

My family and friends have been amazing throughout my journey in Peru and returning back home. Thank you for your emotional support, for helping me through my financial difficulties during my time in Peru, and for loving me and standing by me. Thank you to everyone who flew out to see me in prison and enduring those horrible conditions. I can't imagine how hard that must have been for you all.

To all the priests in Dungannon parish who supported my family and I, and who sat through many emotional visits with my family.

A massive thank you to everyone who helped support my family emotionally and who helped donate money to my fund during this time. Some people I know and some strangers. Your kindness really is something else. For the people who took time out of their day to write me a letter or visit my family. It made me so happy to know that there was support out there for both me and my family.

For the people who came to visit me while I was in prison, who didn't judge me and just showed their support. I'm so thankful for all of you.

Maureen, what would I have done without you? You were a massive part of my Peru journey. I've never met anyone quite like you, so pure and good. Thank you for walking into my life. I'm blessed to have ever met you.

For all the missionaries I met in Peru, sister Clare, Cathal, Father Foley and Sean Walsh. I enjoyed my time with you all. You never judged me and continued to see me all through those years with nothing but love. I can't thank you enough!

Andrea, you know there will always be a special place in my heart for you. I don't know how I would have coped without you. Your guidance and support was amazing, both inside prison and outside. You are an incredible person and I'm so lucky to have met someone like you. Thank you for everything you did for me. I will never forget it.

To Melissa. Wow is all I can say. I often wondered how life would have been without you. If I didn't have you all those times I was falling. When I needed to cry, you were there. When I felt like I couldn't do it anymore, you picked me up. You were there for me through so much. It's a scary thought doing all of that without you. Thank you for being part of that journey and showing me what a real friendship is. Thanks to the Reid family for also showing me love and support through those difficult times. When I didn't have my family there, yous were the closet thing I had. Thank you so much for everything.

I met some incredible people in Ancón 2. Some people I will never forget. Thank you for being a friend to me, I wish you all nothing but happiness.